JOURNAL FOR THE STUDY OF THE OLD TESTAMENT
SUPPLEMENT SERIES
187

Editors
David J.A. Clines
Philip R. Davies

Executive Editor
John Jarick

Editorial Board
Robert P. Carroll, Richard J. Coggins, Alan Cooper, J. Cheryl Exum,
John Goldingay, Robert P. Gordon, Norman K. Gottwald,
Andrew D.H. Mayes, Carol Meyers, Patrick D. Miller

Sheffield Academic Press

The Books of Esther

Structure, Genre
and Textual Integrity

Charles V. Dorothy

Journal for the Study of the Old Testament
Supplement Series 187

To Metta Stanley Dorothy, Margit Westby Boganes,
and Camilla Terhune Dorothy, inspiring women all;
and to Charyle, Creston, Charina, Chad and Chrysti,
who have waited and understood in spite of all;
and to the memory of C. Verne Dorothy, my father,
William H. Brownlee, mentor, and Mark Kispert, friend,
who inspired one and all.

Copyright © 1997 Sheffield Academic Press

Published by Sheffield Academic Press Ltd
Mansion House
19 Kingfield Road
Sheffield S11 9AS
England

Printed on acid-free paper in Great Britain
by Bookcraft Ltd
Midsomer Norton, Bath

British Library Cataloguing in Publication Data

A catalogue record for this book is available
from the British Library

ISBN 1-85075-518-3

CONTENTS

ACKNOWLEDGMENTS

How does one properly acknowledge one's debt to those who have imparted so much to him, and at the same time taught him that he has so much to learn?

What I owe to parents and early teachers, all concerned with providing the best education possible, can hardly be quantified or expressed. I thank them all, regretting that so many guides along the way must remain nameless. At a more advanced level, special thanks go to Everett F. Harrison and William S. LaSor of Fuller Theological Seminary, who allowed me to begin Greek and Hebrew under unusual circumstances. Their generosity, coupled with the encouragement and advice of Jack Finegan, assured that my education would continue.

Along that continuing path, the faculties and staff of both the School of Theology at Claremont and the Claremont Graduate School deserve recognition for maintaining a caring human touch while attaining the highest standards of scholarship. At the doctoral level at Claremont Graduate School, where an earlier version of this study was presented as a dissertation in 1989, I am especially indebted to William H. Brownlee and Burton Mack for help and encouragement which does not receive mention within the footnotes. Above all, I recognize enduring indebtedness to, and thank, the dissertation committee, Chan-Hie Kim, Rolf Knierim, and the chairperson, James A. Sanders, all of whom exhibit high standards which never cease to challenge and inspire.

Special thanks must go to several scholars whose kindness contributed support, accuracy and correction in areas beyond my reach. John L. White supplied articles both published and unpublished on embedded letters, and generously gave of his time to critique the ideas on letters/decrees advanced herein. George W. Coats responded to telephone queries beyond what could be expected, and several of his insights are contained herein. At short notice, Stanley D. Walters shared some of his text-critical work which confirmed and enhanced my understanding of the emerging concept of textual integrity. Tim Hegg's contribution went beyond reference checking to thoughtful comments, stimulating discussion of many minor and major points, and timely encouragement. I am very grateful to all the above named scholars for their several contributions, but I take responsibility for any misapplication of their contributions and any other errors.

My debt to the loyal supporters of the Association for Christian Development, especially the congregations in Harrisburg, PA and Seattle, WA, can probably never be fully repaid. Among many who could be mentioned, I must single out Pastor Kenneth Westby and his exemplary wife Joan, without whose support and understanding this work might not have been completed, and Dick Aitkins, who not only unflaggingly encouraged, but also gave unstinting time in the printing area, and finally, Rosalie Friesen Funk, whose attention to detail and long hours of computer help were invaluable and probably unrepayable.

Deserving more than a mention are Richard D. Weis, former Director of the Ancient Biblical Manuscript Center, his successor Peter Pettit, and Chief Cataloger, Garth I. Moller; Ronald Hook of UCLA; and my student colleagues Steve Delamarter and Henry and Ellen Sun. Thanks must travel to Mrs Kirk and Mrs McCausland of the University of Washington Library for valuable help in obtaining sources, to John and Merrily Bennett of Vancouver, BC, to Vern Stranberg of Spokane, to Clyde and Ruth Brown, and Gary Arvidson of Los Angeles, Rod and Dawn Beemer of Salina, Phil Arnold of Houston, Andrew Wysotski of Oshawa and both Wertz families in Harrisburg.

Extra thanks go to my remarkably supportive wife, Camilla, and to our children who may have had to be deprived more than I would imagine. If anyone's help and contribution has escaped notice here, may it be covered by this final expression of gratefulness to friends, colleagues and supporters. My hope is that the work is worthy of the help given, and that the answer to the opening question may partly be discovered in its very asking.

Publisher's Note

During the course of preparation of this book for publication, Sheffield Academic Press was saddened to learn of the death of Dr Dorothy in June 1996. We wish to thank typesetter Iain S. Beswick and copy editor Duncan Burns for their work in preparing the manuscript for publication.

ABBREVIATIONS

AB	Anchor Bible
AJSL	*American Journal of Semitic Languages and Literatures*
AJSRev	*Association of Jewish Studies Review*
AnBib	Analecta Biblica
ANET	J.B. Pritchard (ed.), *Ancient Near Eastern Texts*
Ant.	Flavius Josephus, *Jewish Antiquities*
APOT	R.H. Charles (ed.), *Apocrypha and Pseudepigrapha of the Old Testament*
ATR	*Anglican Theological Review*
BA	*Biblical Archaeologist*
BDB	F. Brown, S.R. Driver, and C.A. Briggs, *A Hebrew and English Lexicon of the Old Testament*
BGU	U. Wilcken *et al.* (eds.), *Aegyptische Urkunden aus den Koeniglichen* (later *Staatlichen*) *Museen zu Berlin, Griechische Urkunden*, 1895-1912.
BHK	R. Kittel (ed.), *Biblia Hebraica*
BHS	*Biblia Hebraica Stuttgartensia*
BibLeb	*Bibel und Leben*
BIOSCS	*Bulletin of the International Organisation for Septuagint and Cognate Studies*
BKAT	Biblischer Kommentar: Altes Testament
BR	*Biblical Research*
BZAW	Beihefte zur *ZAW*
CAH	Cambridge Ancient History
CBCNEB	Cambridge Bible Commentary on the New English Bible
CBQ	*Catholic Biblical Quarterly*
CBQMS	*Catholic Biblical Quarterly*, Monograph Series
CTA	A. Herdner, *Corpus des tablettes en cunéiformes alphabétiques*
EG	Greek versions of Esther
EH	Hebrew version of Esther
EncJud	*Encyclopaedia Judaica*
FOTL	The Forms of the Old Testament Literature
GKC	*Gesenius' Hebrew Grammar*, ed. E. Kautzsch, trans. A.E. Cowley
Hanhart	R. Hanhart, *Esther* (Septuaginta, 8/3)

HAR	*Hebrew Annual Review*
HAT	Handbuch zum Alten Testament
HBT	*Horizons in Biblical Theology*
HOTTP	Hebrew Old Testament Text Project (United Bible Societies)
HSM	Harvard Semitic Monographs
HTI	Historic Texts and Interpreters
HTR	*Harvard Theological Review*
HUCA	*Hebrew Union College Annual*
ICC	International Critical Commentary
IDB	G.A. Buttrick (ed.), *Interpreter's Dictionary of the Bible*
IDBSup	*IDB*, Supplementary Volume
IMWKT	*Internationale Monatschrift für Wissenschaft, Kunst und Technik*
Int	*Interpretation*
JAAR	*Journal of the American Academy of Religion*
JAOS	*Journal of the American Oriental Society*
JBL	*Journal of Biblical Literature*
JBS	Jerusalem Biblical Studies
JES	*Journal of Ecumenical Studies*
JETS	*Journal of the Evangelical Theological Society*
Jos	Josephus, *Antiquities*
JQR	*Jewish Quarterly Review*
JR	*Journal of Religion*
JSOT	*Journal for the Study of the Old Testament*
JSS	*Journal of Semitic Studies*
JSSR	*Journal for the Scientific Study of Religion*
KAI	H. Donner and W. Röllig, *Kanaanäische und Aramäische Inschriften*
KAT	Kommentar zum Alten Testament
L	The 'Lucianic' or A text of Esther
LCL	Loeb Classical Library
LXX	Septuagint (also abbreviated as o')
MT	Masoretic text
Murphy	R. Murphy, *Wisdom Literature* (FOTL, 13)
NCBC	New Century Bible Commentary
NLH	*New Literary History*
NTS	*New Testament Studies*
o'	Septuagint (also abbreviated as LXX)
OBO	Orbis Biblicus et Orientalis
OGIS	W. Dittenberger (ed.), *Orientis Graecae Inscriptiones Selectae*
OG	Old Greek
OL	Old Latin
PAAJR	*Proceedings of the American Academy of Jewish Research*
PMLA	*Proceedings of the Modern Language Association*
PSBL	*Proceedings of the Society of Biblical Literature*

PTMS	Pittsburgh Theological Monograph Series
Rahlfs	A. Rahlfs (ed.), *Septuaginta*
RB	*Revue Biblique*
RN	royal novella or *Königsnovelle*
RSV	Revised Standard Version
SBL	Society of Biblical Literature
SBLDS	SBL Dissertation Series
SBLSBS	SBL Sources for Biblical Study
SBLSP	SBL Seminar Papers
SBM	Stuttgarter biblische Monographien
Sem	*Semitica*
SJ	Studia Judaica
SOTSMS	Society for Old Testament Study Monograph Series
TDOT	G.J. Botterweck and H. Ringgren (eds.), *Theological Dictionary of the Old Testament*
TOTC	Tyndale Old Testament Commentaries
TZ	*Theologische Zeitschrift*
USQR	*Union Seminary Quarterly Review*
UT	C.H. Gordon, *Ugaritic Textbook*
VT	*Vetus Testamentum*
VTSup	*Vetus Testamentum*, Supplements
ZAW	*Zeitschrift für die alttestamentliche Wissenschaft*
//	connects parallel passages of o´ and L
-∣	up to (including) the last word of the verse

Chapter 1

INTRODUCTION

The Hebrew book of Esther (EH) dramatizes the life and death struggle for the survival of the Jewish people under Persian rule in precisely 3,044 words. In all of these words a secular air prevails and the divine name is not once found. Greek Esther (EG) on the other hand, although it chronicles the same life and death struggle, comprises something generically quite different from the Hebrew narrative. Standing in three variant textual forms (LXX, so-called A or L, and Josephus' version), EG sounds pious notes throughout: there are multiple divine names, long prayers, a prophetic type dream (serving as prolog to the whole book) and its interpretation (standing as epilog), two (or in one tradition, three) dramatic divine interventions. One cannot help being struck by the contrasting tone of the Greek and Hebrew stories, the greater length of all three Greek texts versus EH, and the notable divergences in content and order of events among all four texts.

One does read of 'four Greek texts of Esther',[1] and even a 'Greek text...known in five variant forms'.[2] These numbers mislead: the Old Latin (Bickermann's fourth 'Greek text') constitutes a possible witness to a Greek text (different from any now extant), but is not an actual Greek exemplar; to obtain five, Saunders presumably includes two other text traditions, Coptic/Sahidic and Ethiopic. Even though these latter two are also presumed to derive from Greek,[3] the same objection

1. E.J. Bickermann, 'Notes on the Greek Book of Esther', *PAAJR* 20 (1950), pp. 101-33. In addition to LXX, L and Josephus he counts the Old Latin as a fourth text, following a general consensus that it was translated from a Greek *Vorlage*.

2. E.W. Saunders, 'Esther (Apocryphal)', *IDB*, II, p. 152. It is not stated which texts make up the total of five.

3. See the sources cited in A.E. Brooke, N. McLean and H.S.J. Thackeray (eds.), *The Old Testament in Greek* (Cambridge: Cambridge University Press, 1940), III, pp. 1-42. Cf. C.A. Moore's detailed work, 'The Greek Text of Esther' (PhD diss., Johns Hopkins University, 1965), pp. 17ff.

applies: they are not Greek exemplars. While the four count includes Josephus and one derivative text, it leaves out the other two derivatives, Coptic and Ethiopic; conversely the five count includes all three derivative texts, but leaves out a Greek exemplar, Josephus. If Josephus' version (hereafter Jos) and the presumed derivative texts all count, then the total would be *six* 'Greek' texts in addition to EH, Targum Rishon and Targum Sheni. Each of these texts deserves investigation, but this study will limit the terms 'Greek text' and 'EG' to the three actual Greek language exemplars: LXX, L and Jos.

Thanks to the labors of Robert Hanhart and the Göttingen Septuagint editors a critical edition of the two 'biblical' texts (LXX and L) of EG is now available. One of the two was first published from minuscule MS 93 by Archbishop James Usher in 1655.[4] Paul de Lagarde edited the first critical edition of this text tradition in 1883 using three MSS: 19, 93 and 108. In 1940 the Larger Cambridge Septuagint published this Esther text and collated a fourth witness, a minuscule from Mt Athos: y (= Hanhart's 319). In spite of these and a few other publications[5] treating this witness, it has been largely passed over. The relative neglect apparently stems from two causes: scholars have judged, or assumed, this tradition to be inferior; and it does not appear in Hatch and Redpath's *Concordance*, or in the standard hand editions of the Greek Bible, Swete's *The Old Testament in Greek* and Rahlf's *Septuaginta*.

As far as is known this form of Esther (so-called L) has enjoyed neither wide circulation nor canonical status, at least since Jerome produced the Latin Vulgate between 390 and 405 CE.[6] One must remember, however, that before Jerome some form of the Greek Old Testament reigned as canon. As Würthwein points out, 'even Augustine himself was disquieted at Jerome's setting aside the inspired, canonical Septuagint to go back to a [Hebrew] text which no one in the church but himself could understand'.[7]

---

4.   J. Usher, *De Graeca Septuaginta interpretum versione syntagma: cum libri Estherae editione Origenica, et vetera Graeca altera, ex Arundelliana bibliotheca nunc primum in lucem producta* (London: J. Crook, 1655). Cf. H. Swete, *An Introduction to the Old Testament in Greek* (Cambridge: Cambridge University Press, 1902), pp. 192, 258.

5.   For a handy summary, see D.J.A. Clines, *The Esther Scroll: The Story of the Story* (JSOTSup, 30; Sheffield: JSOT Press, 1984), pp. 71-72.

6.   E. Würthwein, *The Text of the Old Testament* (Grand Rapids: Eerdmans, 1979), pp. 91ff.

7.   Würthwein, *Text*, p. 92. It is important to note however that Jerome accepted

In spite of Jerome's reliance on *Hebraica Veritas*, and the eventual popularity of the resultant Latin Vulgate Bible, more than one Greek text tradition of several biblical books somehow survived. One of the survivors is this lesser-known, four manuscript Greek witness to Esther—called A by the Cambridge editors, but L in the 1966 Hanhart edition. Mistakenly dubbed Lucianic since 1890,[8] L contains exactly 4,761 words and is 56.41% longer than EH.

Another survivor preserves a better-known witness to Esther: the Septuagint. Largely supplanted by the canonical Hebrew, LXX nevertheless preserves six larger blocks of material not found in Hebrew. Ignoring smaller differences between Greek and Hebrew, Jerome honored the six larger blocks by placing them as appendices after his translation of EH. Hence these portions of LXX still form part of the Roman Catholic canon; but with regard to either LXX or L it would be a mistake to assume that Jerome bequeathed to the Church all that EG contains.

Hanhart deals with the entire LXX Esther, but labels it with the Greek siglum for '70': o'. His critical text consists of no less than 5,837 words—91.75% longer than EH! A third, 'non-biblical' version, often referred to as a 'paraphrase', appears in the writing of a first-century CE general turned historian, whose works once again are attracting scholarly attention.[9] Flavius Josephus in his *Antiquities* 11.184-296[10] retells the Esther story in 4,423 Greek words—45.30% longer than EH. Thus even though Jos adds his own 'frame narrative' and some 'unscriptural details' (thus translator Marcus), he presents a text shorter than either L or o', principally because he does not mention Mordecai's dream/interpretation, and because he presents only a précis of Esther's prayer. But it is important to say that Jos is still notably longer than the Hebrew text.

However, the percentage figures for the three longer Greek texts—based on word-for-word counts—do not allow for the fact that even a wooden translation of Hebrew into Greek produces a longer text. How

the Septuagint (or Old Greek?) as inspired.

8. R. Hanhart, *Esther* (Septuaginta Vetus Testamentum Graecum Auctoritate Academiae Letterarum Goettingensis editum, 8/3; Göttingen: Vandenhoeck & Ruprecht, 1966), p. 95.

9. Cf. e.g. T. Rajak, *Josephus: The Historian and His Society* (London: Duckworth, 1983); S.J.D. Cohen, *Josephus in Galilee and Rome: His Vita and Development as a Historian* (Leiden: Brill, 1979). For an older work, cf. H.S.J. Thackeray, *Josephus: The Man and the Historian* (repr., New York: Ktav, 1967).

10. H. Thackeray, R. Marcus and L. Feldman (eds.), *Josephus* (9 vols.; Cambridge, MA: Harvard University Press, 1937–65).

much adjustment should be made? A standard *minimum* estimate of 11.45% is based on a careful comparison of three short samples from the Pentateuch (one narrative, two dialogs), judged by consensus to stand in relatively literal relationship to one another. If this 'normal conversion factor' of (rounded) 12% is applied to the core of EG which seems to translate the extant Hebrew, the adjusted extra Greek lengths are: 32.55% for Jos, 45.47% for L and 76.97% for o'.[11]

1. *The Problem*

These three Greek texts do not often receive analysis as whole units. Rather they appear as footnotes in comparisons with EH, or are treated integrally only in the five sections or blocks that Jerome placed at the end of his translation. Since these sections do not exist in EH, and since their assumed purpose is to fill a 'perceived lack' in an earlier EH, they are often denominated with the inaccurate term 'Additions'.[12] Of this commonplace, more later. For now, it is important to recognize that both the o' and L texts are not segmented blocks, and they may not be slavish translations of EH. They are whole documents which may witness to variant but venerable traditions in several faithful Jewish and Christian communities. Why not treat such ancient witnesses as integral works in their own right? Merely to ask that question, or to state that texts as rich and ancient as o', L and Jos have not been treated holistically might alone justify this preliminary essay.

But more justification may be required. Notice this recent quotation

---

11. No allowance was made for the growing consensus that Sections B and E—the two 'epistles'—originate in Greek, while Sections A, C, D and F reflect Semitic originals. For this judgment, cf. R.A. Martin, 'Syntax Criticism of the LXX Additions to the Book of Esther', *JBL* 94 (1975), pp. 65-72; C.A. Moore, *Daniel, Esther and Jeremiah: The Additions* (AB, 44; Garden City, NY: Doubleday, 1977), pp. 180, 193 and *passim*. If one assumes that A, C, D and F are translation Greek and therefore applies the 12% reduction to these sections also, Jos is 31% longer than EH, L is 41% longer and o' is 72% longer—still quite lengthier texts.

12. It is not clear where the term originated, but it may derive from Jerome's treatment of the LXX passages not found in Hebrew. F.W. Schultz uses the term in his introduction to Esther in 1876 ('The Book of Esther', in J.P. Lange [ed.], *Lange's Commentary on the Holy Scriptures* [repr., Grand Rapids: Zondervan, 1960], and so does Paton in his now standard work (1908). Note the use of the term in the popular *Anchor Bible* (see previous footnote). The problem with the term is that it presupposes what has not been proved.

('Additions' refer to the six sections of EG with no Hebrew *Vorlage* as explained above):

> It is a serious mistake to read the Additions out of context, i.e. either *after* reading the canonical portion (as in the Vulgate) or *without* any canonical text at all (as in most 'Protestant' Bibles, e.g. KJ, RSV, NEB, *et alia*). Therefore, in order to provide the reader with some context for the Additions as well as to remind him of how very different in style and spirit they are from the canonical Hebrew text, in the present commentary the Additions will be placed within the context of our English translation of the Hebrew text. (To have put them within the Greek version would not have been as illuminating to the reader, since in the Greek version the canonical parts and the Additions are harmonized and leveled through, the many differences and contradictions between the Hebrew version and the Greek Additions being minimized.)[13]

The value of context will hardly be disputed. What one can dispute— as the author recognizes just below—is the last opinion: that the Greek context would not be illuminating. Apparently that decision was not easily taken: 'This admittedly unorthodox procedure was decided upon by the present writer only after considerable inner debate'. One can sympathize with the intent behind this 'unorthodox procedure', which was to provide 'simultaneously, [to] the reader context *and contrast* and [the writer] can only hope the reader will withhold judgment on this procedure until after its fruits have been tasted'.[14] In fact I did try to withhold that judgment until the end. But in the end the decision must be negative. Filling in between the so-called 'Additions' by translating EH—no matter how well reported the 'Greek variants', no matter how learned and professional the commentator (Moore certainly is)—unavoidably causes the overall impression to be not that of a coherent *text*, but at best that of scattered gems from a now lost pirate chest—gem readings, one is tempted to add, that do not comprise a textual tiara, anything whole or integrated. At worst, the impression is that of scattered segments which sometimes make little sense. Swete went so far as to say that Jerome, by placing the six Greek parts as appendices, had rendered them 'unintelligible'.[15]

Could this problem not be handled by a careful and exhaustive critical

---

13. Moore, *Daniel, Esther and Jeremiah; The Additions*, p. 168

14. Moore, *Daniel, Esther and Jeremiah: The Additions*, p. 168 (emphasis original in all Moore citations).

15. Swete, *Introduction*, p. 257.

apparatus? Although significant in and of themselves, some readings in
the footnoting approach invariably suffer non-mention or, if mentioned,
fail to impress most readers with their just impact. 'Just impact' involves
polar opposites. On the one hand an isolated variant, lacking context for
determining proper denotation and/or connotation, may seem less important than it really is. Conversely there is the lesser, still real, danger
that variants—thus broken out of both text and context—may appear
more weighty than they really are. It simply is not possible to treat a text
in piecemeal fashion without distortion.

Therefore it is 'a serious mistake' (Moore) not to have context for
either EG text. The suggestion offered here is simple: that desired context will best be provided by the Greek itself *in toto*. So much for the
problem of integrated treatment.

Other problems and needs beg consideration. For decades the L text
lacked both translation and scholarly treatment. A major cause behind
the current inferior ranking of this text tradition is its attribution by
scholarship to Lucian of Antioch. Before being martyred in 312 CE he
is known to have worked with Dorotheus, a Hebrew scholar who also
was a student of Greek literature. This association comports well with
Lucian's being credited (by Jerome's day) as editor of a new large scale
koinē version of the Hebrew Bible.[16] But it is not known with certainty
which MSS, if any, are Lucianic. By careful detective work on scholia,
Field (c. 1875) was able to isolate readings credited to Lucian by a marginal siglum in MSS 19, 82, 93, 108 for certain passages in 2 Kings.
Additionally in these four MSS he found many agreements in Kings,
Chronicles and Ezra–Nehemiah with the readings of the Antiochian fathers Chrysostom and Theodoret—presumptive evidence of Lucian's
influence.[17]

The list of Field's findings goes on, but the interest here focuses on
three of those four MSS. Apparently neither Ceriani (1874), Field (1875)
nor Lagarde (1883) attributed the Esther text within MSS 19, 93, 108 to
Lucian. That (dis)credit goes to Jacob's work of 1890, according to
Hanhart.[18] Perhaps this error was perpetuated by the knowledge that
one of Lagarde's life projects was to publish a provisional Lucianic OT.
As Swete says, 'his lamented death intercepted the work, and only the
first volume of his Lucianic LXX (*sic*) has appeared (Genesis–2 Esdr.,

16. Swete, *Introduction*, pp. 80-81.
17. Swete, *Introduction*, p. 83.
18. Hanhart, *Esther*, pp. 94-95.

Esther)'.[19] So Esther does appear within Lagarde's larger work which intended to reflect Lucian, but Hanhart specifically denies that Lagarde intended a Lucianic label for Esther—a designation 'which had already been extended over the book of Esther, and which indeed already demanded special explanation, because two of these witnesses, 93 and 108, carry both texts' (o' and L in separate columns).[20] One is left to assume that Lagarde published both texts of Esther out of thoroughness (i.e., the MSS he was working on contained both), not because he thought one was Lucianic.

Jacob's rubric 'Lucianic' adhered to this Lagarde text from 1890 on, and perhaps contributed to an already existent undercurrent of depreciation. However, scholarly discussion is reversing direction on this question. Notice that the Cambridge LXX—in this case the volume containing Esther, published in 1940—uses quotation marks thus: 'Lucianic'.[21] The rubric was further eroded in 1965 with the publication of Moore's Johns Hopkins dissertation, 'The Greek Text of Esther', and again in 1966 with Hanhart's critical edition which states flatly that the gains of research on the (real) Lucian text so far show that 'der "L-Text" des Esther-Buches nichts zu tun haben kann mit der Textform der Bücher der LXX, die als die "lukianische Rezension" bekannt ist'.[22]

Self-evidently this four-MSS tradition tells us little about the text of Esther before 300 CE if it in fact comes from Lucian's quill. Since evidence is mounting that it does not, a new importance begins to attach to this witness. If it is not a priori nor automatically judged to be inferior in comparison to LXX, questions may be asked of it in a different light. Once freed from the name of Lucian, the L text could derive from an earlier, perhaps a much earlier, period.

Clines's recent work[23] offers a twofold exception to the prevailing non-treatment of this witness: the first published translation in English of L, and a coherent theory of literary stages in the development of 'The Story of the Story', the interrelationship of EH and EG. Thus one translation and a fresh source analysis (along with criticism of previous source theories) are now available. But work remains to be done.

---

19. Swete, *Introduction*, p. 83.
20. Hanhart, *Esther*, p. 95.
21. Brooke *et al.*, *The Old Testament in Greek*, III, pp. v-vi.
22. Hanhart, *Esther*, p. 92.
23. Clines, *The Esther Scroll, passim*.

First, none of the Greek texts has been submitted to the exacting dissection which the International Form Critical Project[24] has demonstrated to be methodologically indispensable: structure analysis. This exegetical tool continues to produce new insights/discoveries, as numerous articles and dissertations now demonstrate. Secondly, o´ and L have not been compared and contrasted with EH from the perspective of a structure analysis.

As for EH itself, various presentations of its structure are available, but a consensus is not. A few examples plus a chart will suffice to show that minimal agreement does exist and wide variations surround the agreement. Wide reading in Esther literature would also show that there is little consistency and no organizing principle behind the agreements and disagreements. Following are a few examples. Schultz's commentary of 1876[25] presents a most compact structure—Esther has two parts: chs. 1–5 and 6–10. However, a closer reading in fact shows that Schultz has three parts (format closely follows Schultz; content is abbreviated):

PART ONE. The origin and increase of danger to the Jews	Chs. 1–5
Introduction. The occasion of the history	Ch. 1
First Section. The rise and meeting of the contrasts	Chs. 2–3
Second Section. The conflict between the contrasts	Chs. 4–5
PART TWO. The removal of the danger	Chs. 6–10
First Section. Haman's downfall	Chs. 6–7
Second Section. The removal of the danger	Chs. 8–9
ADDENDA (*sic*). Authority, consequence and power of	
Mordecai the Jew in the powerful Persian world-monarchy	Ch. 10

Note that ch. 10 is listed twice, once under Part Two, and again after Addenda, which stands, as printed, at the same level of importance as Part One and Part Two, thus three parts.

The Companion Bible (no date, but published after 1885) boasts of its structures as making it unique.[26] This cumbrous annotated Bible presents a running outline which contains scores of subdivisions throughout Esther. But the large, single page macrostructure (my term) used to introduce Esther offers the reader what appears to be a 10-part outline.

---

24. *Forms of the Old Testament Literature* (Grand Rapids: Eerdmans), a projected 24-volume series under the editorship of G. Tucker and R. Knierim; hereafter referred to as FOTL.

25. Schultz, 'The Book of Esther', p. 3.

26. E.W. Bullinger (ed.), *The Companion Bible* (repr., London: Samuel Bagster & Sons, 1964), p. viii.

The somewhat tangled and forced panels (letters overlap each other!) appear in just three major tiers as follows, if the overlapping is ignored:

A1: 1.1. Ahasuerus: Reign, Extent of kingdom.
  B1: 1.2–4.3. Ahasuerus: On his throne.[27]
    C1: 4.4–5.14. Esther: Her intercession.[28]
  B2: 6.1-14. Ahasuerus: On his bed.
    C2: 7.1. Esther: Her banquet.
  B3: 7.2-10. Ahasuerus: At Esther's Table.
    C3: 8.1a. Esther: Her Royal Gift.
  B4: 8.1b–9.28. Ahasuerus: On his throne.
    C4: 9.29-32. Esther: Her Royal Authority.
A2: 10.1-3. Ahasuerus: Reign, Extent of Kingdom.

Under the four B panels one finds four envelope figures (of the pattern A, B, A´), one spanning three chapters, another only eight verses. The primary organizing principle is Ahasuerus' physical location; the secondary one seems to be Esther's actions, and perhaps her status in C4. Admittedly distortion enters into the presentation here when only the titles are given as above, and the subsumed, overlapped subpanels are left out. Still one comes away with the impression that overlapping panels confuse more than clarify. One is further puzzled upon discovering that a portion of *The Companion Bible*'s microstructures which are interspersed throughout its marginal notes to Esther are missing. One must conclude that the original *Companion Bible* structure outline is both incomplete and forced.

There follows in chart form a selection of recent works on EH with their respective structures, or more correctly in most cases, their divisions of the text. (Note that 'Domm.' stands for Dommershausen and 'Gerlem.' for Gerleman.) From the agreements in the chart it should appear that various units of EH have been identified. The divergences show that some integrative, structural explanation is needed. That is, while there remain some problems of unit identification, the principal question is how to integrate from three to 22 blocks. That problem leads into an area closely related to the study of structure.

---

27. Other subjects/titles are assigned within these verses, but their identifying letters D and E are overlapped by B1.

28. Next follows B2, the second of four B panels each overlapping not fully subordinated D and E panels which have their respective subtitles.

Ch.	Hebrew	Paton	Domm.	Clines	Murphy	Moore	Bardtke	Gerlem.
1.	**1-9** **10-15** **16-22**	**1-22** 1-4 5-9 10-12 13-15 16-20 21-22	**1-9** 1-4 5-9 **10-22** 10-12 13-15 16-20 21-22	**1-22** 1-9 10-12 13-22	**1-9** 1-4 5-8 9 **10-22** 10-12 13-15 16-20 21-22	**1-22** 1-4 5-9 10-11 12-15 16-18 19-20 21-22	**1-9** **10-22**	**1-22**
2.	**1-4** **5-20** **21-23**	**1-23** 1-4 5-7 8-11 12-14 15-18 19-23	**1-4** **5-11** 5-7 8-11 **12-20** 12-14 15-20 **21-23**	**1-18** 1-4 5-7 8-11 12-14 15-18 **19-23**	**1-20** 1-4 5-11 12-20 **21-23**	**1-18** 1-4 5-7 8-11 12-14 15-18 **19-23**	**1-20** **21-23**	**1-20** **21-23**
3.	**1-7** **8-15**	**1–4.17** 1-2a 2b-5 6-7 8-11 12-15	**1-7** **8-15** 8-11 12-15	**1-15** 1-7 8-15	**1-7** 1-2a 2b 2b-4 5-6 7 **8-15** 8-9 10-11 12-15a 15b	**1-15** 1 2a 2b-6 7-10 11 12-15	**1-7** **8-15**	**1-15**
4.	**1-12** **13-17**	1-3 4-9 10-14 15-17	**1-3** **4-11** **12-17**	**1-3** **4-17**	**1-17** 1-3 4-17	**1-17** 1-3 4-8 9-11 12-14 15-17	**1-17**	**1-17**
5.	**1-2** **3-14**	**1–9.19** 1-2 3-5 6-8 9-14	**1-8** **9-14**	**1-8** **9-14**	**1-8** 1-3 4-5 6 7-8 **9-14**	**1-8** 1-3 4 5a 5b-6 7-8 **9-14**	**1-8** **9-14**	**1-8** **9-14**

Ch.	Hebrew	Paton	Domm.	Clines	Murphy	Moore	Bardtke	Gerlem.
6.	**1–7.4**	1-3 4-10 11-13 14–7.6	**1-14** 1-5 6-11 12-14	**1-14**	**1-13** 1-3 4-5 6-9 10-11 **14–7.10** 14–7.1	**1-13** 1-3a 3b 4a 4b-5a 5b 6a 6b-9 10 11-13 **14–7.10** 14–7.2	**1-13** **14–7.4**	**1-13** **14–7.10**
7.	**5-8** **9-10**	7-10	**1-10**	**1-10**	2-4 5-7 8a 8b-10	3-4 5 6a 6b-8a 8b-9a 9b 10	**5-10**	
8.	**1-2** **3-6** **7-14** **15–9.4**	1-2 3-8 9-14a 14b-17	**1-8** 1-2 3-6 7-8 **9-17** 9-14 15-17	**1-17** 1-8 9-14 15-17	**1-2** **3-17** 3-6 7-8 9-14 15-17	**1-17** 1-15 16-17	**1-2** **3-6** **7-14** **15-17**	**3-17**
9.	**5-11** **12-19** **20-28** **29-32**	1-10 11-15 16-19 **20-32** 20-22 23-28 29-32	**1-10** 1-4 5-10 **11-15** **16-19** **20-28** 20-23 24-26a 26b-28 29-32	**1-32** 1-19 20-28 29-32	**1-10** 1-4 5-10 **11-19** 11-15 16-19 **20-28** **29-32**	**1-19** 1-10 11-12 13 14 15-19 **20-32** 20-23 24-26a 26b-28 29-32	**1-10** **11-19** **20-28** **29-32**	**1-19** **20-32**
10.	**1-3**	**1-3**	**1-3**	**1-3**	**1-3**	**1-3**	**1-3**	**1-3**
Total parts:	6	22	13	18	13	21	13	

While literary considerations are not entirely lacking in recent treatments of Esther,[29] the second area of need involves narrative questions. Theoretical narrative insights—now becoming finely tuned in recent work on the Pentateuch and the historical books[30]—have not been applied at all to EG. Thus these texts invite an initial investigation.

The case is different with canonical Esther. The work begun on EH in 1981[31] needs now to be updated. That first approach by Murphy in the area of structure analysis and narrativity is meaningful, but falls short of completeness (whole verses are left unaccounted for; narrative components remain uncorrelated). With regard to unity EH stands in 18 coordinate panels according to Murphy's presentation, and one does not find any discussion of how these panels might relate to his genre suggestions. Similarly Dommershausen's careful study[32] of style and forms in EH (often relied on, but not slavishly followed, by Murphy) leaves the book in no less than 22 pieces/parts. One fears that literary critics would simply reject so many unsubordinated parts for a story which carefully builds and releases tension, creates the feeling of considerable artistry and unity, and gives the reader a 'sense of ending'—to borrow from literary critic Frank Kermode.[33] One need only go to Aristotle's *Poetics* or *The Rhetoric* in order to integrate the Esther narrative (used here to include EG and EH) into a half dozen parts or less. One may move beyond Aristotle, but one must offer a rationale for so many unsubordinated parts in a work as short as Esther.

29. D.J.A. Clines, *Ezra, Nehemiah, Esther* (NCBC; Grand Rapids: Eerdmans, 1984); W.L. Humphreys, 'The Story of Esther and Mordecai: An Early Jewish Novella', in G.W. Coats (ed.), *Saga, Legend, Tale, Novella, Fable: Narrative Forms in Old Testament Literature* (JSOTSup, 35; Sheffield: JSOT Press, 1985), pp. 97-113; J.G. Baldwin, *Esther* (TOTC; Downers Grove, IL: Inter-Varsity Press, 1984).

30. G.W. Coats, *Genesis, with an Introduction to Narrative Literature* (FOTL, 1; Grand Rapids: Eerdmans, 1983); also B.O. Long, *1 Kings, with an Introduction to Historical Literature* (FOTL, 9; Grand Rapids: Eerdmans, 1984). Cf. also A. Berlin, *The Poetics and Interpretation of Biblical Narrative* (Bible and Literature, 9; Sheffield: Almond Press, 1983); see the works of J.P. Fokkelman, M. Perry, M. Sternberg and others as listed in Berlin's bibliography.

31. R. Murphy, *Wisdom Literature* (FOTL, 13; Grand Rapids: Eerdmans, 1981).

32. W. Dommershausen, *Die Estherrolle: Stil und Ziel einer alttestamentlichen Schrift* (Stuttgarter Biblische Monographien, 6; Stuttgart: Verlag Katholisches Bibelwerk, 1968).

33. The phrase is taken from the title of F. Kermode's work, *The Sense of an Ending: Studies in the Theory of Fiction* (Oxford: Oxford University Press, 1968).

Perhaps literary critics, whose narrative insights do aid biblical criticism, would conceive structural and narrative investigations as separate operations. However, once these two aspects of the interpretative task are understood, there is no compelling reason not to employ them simultaneously in the exegesis of a text.

A third need involves the question of redaction in Esther. Clines[34] has proposed a redaction history model for o´, L and MT on the bases of literary and source analysis. What effect would the form-critical concerns (structure, genre, setting, intention and function) have on his model, if they were investigated first and then used to undergird a follow-up redactional analysis?

A fourth and last consideration would be that of text criticism: would a comparison among multiple text traditions of the same work produce any guidelines for text-critical method?

The problem/needs which prompt this study can now be summarized: (1) piecemeal analysis of EG, or conversely, lack of integral treatment of texts; (2) lack of a detailed structure analysis of either o´ or L; (3) a need to update the structural work already begun on EH; (4) a need for the coupling of narrative studies with the structuring process; (5) the need to determine a genre, setting and intention for the final forms of EG (not yet attempted in the literature) and of EH (attempted, but consensus lacking); (6) a need to discern any redactional layers in the light of answers produced by working through the above five areas; and finally (7) the necessity for discovering whatever a multiple text situation (such as Esther offers) may speak to current approaches in text criticism.

Taking the texts under discussion as a whole—in their final form, not as 'additions'—and wedding narratology with structure analysis, this study will address those problem/needs as follows. The second chapter will detail the structure of two of the Greek books of Esther (o´ and L; Jos must be limited to occasional citation[35]) and discuss selected similarities and differences. A third chapter will present a fresh structure analysis of the Masoretic text (MT or EH). Chapter 4 will discuss genre,

34. Clines, *The Esther Scroll*, p. 140.

35. Unfortunately this relegates Jos to piecemeal treatment. However, this author (in unpublished work) has also submitted Jos to structural analysis and to the same form critical questions as are asked of o´ and L in this study. For that reason it is deemed not inadmissible to cite from Jos certain elements which clarify the arguments advanced here.

setting, intention, function and redaction. The fifth and final chapter summarizes the earlier chapters and draws conclusions about the possible origins of the Esther story, the textual history of o′, L and EH, the contrast between o′ and L as integral compositions and the implications for text criticism of whatever level of textual integrity is discovered in the course of this study, and the role of community regarding the several books of Esther.

As a guide through the following chapters the following salient questions can be derived from the problems and needs stated above.

1. What of the structure of EG as integral texts:
   a. Do the three texts show the same structure among themselves?
   b. What effect do the sections not found in Hebrew have on the total narrative impact?
2. What of the structure of EG vis-à-vis EH:
   a. How do these structures compare to EH?
   b. Do the longer Greek versions/plots in fact also show precise reversal—peripety—as M. Fox[36] has shown for EH?
   c. Or, as Moore suggests, does the plot of EG 'peak' at a different juncture?[37]
3. Can something be learned about the genre, setting and intention of the Esther texts from comparison of the three textual traditions?
4. Do the texts yield clues to previous redactional layers, either under analysis of their individual structure or in intertextual comparison?
5. Did ancient translators of the Hebrew take 'a liberty which astonishes us'[38] in order to produce these differing Greek texts of Esther? Were Esther scribes simply careless? Or do the texts themselves hint at a more complex explanation?

36. M.V. Fox, 'The Structure of Esther', in A. Rofé and Y. Zakovitch (eds.), *Isaac Leo Seeligmann Volume* (Jerusalem: E. Rubinstein, 1983), vol. 3, pp. 291-304 (non-Hebrew section).

37. Moore's note at D 8 (*Daniel, Esther and Jeremiah: The Additions*, p. 218) says, 'This may well be "the culminating point" and "La l'unique miracle" of the Greek version (so Brownlee, *RB* 73 [1966], p. 182), but it is certainly not the climax of the Hebrew version, where the establishment of Purim in ch. 9 is the main consideration.' Moore's first 'Comment' on this section is this: 'Unquestionably, Addition D is the dramatic climax of the Greek Esther' (*Daniel, Esther and Jeremiah: The Additions*, p. 219). There is a crisis and emotional climax at D 8 (to follow the definitions offered in this study), but it is not the structural crisis/climax of the narrative, nor is the second crisis at 6.1ff. devoid of drama.

38. A. Barucq, *Judith, Esther* (La Sainte Bible; Paris: Cerf, 2nd edn, 1959), p. 78.

2. *Description and Delimitation of the Textual Base of this Study*

2.1. *Description*

This description is complicated by the existence of different MSS sigla in each publication of the text. As stated above, Usher published minuscule 93 in 1655 noting that it represented a tradition quite at variance with all the majuscules and all other minuscules known at that time. Fritzsche's works of 1848 and 1871[39] mention 'the text of two books...according to the best codices' in the title, but since the work is not available to this writer, it is not clear whether his second book, the non-LXX text of Esther, had any MS base other than 93. What is clear is that Paul de Lagarde published a critical edition using MSS 19, 93 and 108 in 1883.[40] Lagarde called this text tradition the 'A Text', and the LXX the 'B Text'.

The Cambridge Septuagint introduced new sigla for Lagarde's three MSS and added a fourth MS standing in the same tradition as 19, 93 and 108, but apparently hitherto unnoticed as such. McLean lists the four MSS as follows: b′ (= 19) Rome, Chigi R. vi. 38 (now in the Vatican); b (= 108) Rome, Vat. Gr. 330; e (= 93) London, British Museum, Royal 1 D. ii; y (= 319) Athos, Vatopethi 513.[41] One is not surprised that 'this recension of Esther differs so much from the B-text (LXX) that we found it necessary to print it in full'.[42] But one is disappointed to learn that the now four-manuscript 'A Text' does not merit placement along-side the standard 'B Text' for easy comparison, but is relegated to an appendix, and that even with the addition of a MS not used by Lagarde, the Cambridge text is Lagarde's text reprinted, although 'a fresh colla-tion was done'.[43] Given the additional MS, the size and scope of the Cambridge project, and Lagarde's slender apparatus for 'A', one would expect a fresh publication of the text.

For the five uncials and many cursives which form the base for McLean's B Text and Hanhart's o′ (both = LXX)—too lengthy to cover

---

39. O.F. Fritzsche, *ΕΣΘΗΡ: Duplicem libri textum ad optimos codices emendavit et cum selecta lectionis varietate edidit* (Zurich: Orel, 1848), cited by Swete, *Intro-duction*, p. 192.

40. P. de Lagarde, *Librorum Veteris Testamenti Canonicorum Pars Prior Graece* (Göttingen: A. Hoyer, 1883).

41. Brooke *et al.*, *The Old Testament in Greek*, III, p. vi. Vatopethi 513 is cited via a transcript prepared by R. Harris.

42. Brooke *et al.*, *The Old Testament in Greek*, III, p. vi.

43. Brooke *et al.*, *The Old Testament in Greek*, III, p. vi.

here—one may refer to their respective introductions. Suffice it to say that both editors use the five uncials, including Chester Beatty Papyrus 967, but Hanhart has taken note of the readings of the first part of the papyrus which is housed at Cologne University's Institut für Altertumskunde zur Verfügung. This first part was either not known or not available to McLean. The Cambridge edition used 17 minuscules; Hanhart accessed 32, plus other 'daughter or sister' MSS only partly collated and cited exclusively in terms of *Sonderlesarten*.

2.2. *Delimitation*

The text base for EG will be Hanhart's edition, and in the case of EH, the Leningradensis of BHS. Strictly speaking, Esther material ends in the o′ text at F 11; this parallels the end in L's 7.59. But o′ boasts a colophon giving historical details of MS provenance —printed as F 11 in McLean and Hanhart. A close variant is found in MS 93 (printed as part of Hanhart's apparatus to the L text). Neither of these colophons will be considered as part of the text to be analyzed. Similarly excluded will be the three-paragraph subscription dealing with the history of copyists which is printed only in McLean's apparatus. These exclusions are not intended as value judgments, rather as matters of expediency.

3. *Definitions and Observations on Method*

3.1. *Basic/Operational Definitions*

What is a *text*? In line with recent communication theory and structural linguistics a text may be

> understood as an organic linguistic entity, as the elementary and self-contained unit of linguistic (oral or written) expression in a communication event. In principle, it supersedes the entities of the word and sentence levels. It is a 'macrosyntactical unit'.[44]

What is a *genre*? Baird's attempt in New Testament criticism to limit form to the 'unitary' term describing the smaller oral or literary units, and genre to the 'collective' term encompassing all such units,[45] must be rejected, at least in the Old Testament field. Even if he based this

---

44. R. Knierim, 'Criticism of Literary Features, Form, Tradition, and Redaction', in D.A. Knight and G. Tucker (eds.), *The Hebrew Bible and its Modern Interpreters* (Chico, CA: Scholars Press, 1985), p. 137 (citing Koch's *Amos*).

45. J.A. Baird, 'Genre Analysis as a Method of Historical Criticism', in *PSBL* II (1972), p. 387.

suggestion on the older distinction between *Form* and *Gattung*, the suggested use introduces terminological confusion into the arena; the first term would be better described now as 'structure'. *Gattung* and genre may still serve as synonyms. Naturally it is assumed here that human communication in general, and biblical materials in particular, are structured in some determinable way, otherwise there would be no communication.[46] Instead, to borrow from Saussure, there would be an incoherent mass of signifiers with few or no signifieds and only one result: no shared meaning.

As Coats recently pointed out, the goal in defining genre is not to defend the 'right' use of a term; 'It is rather to identify a class of literature that will facilitate a functional definition of any given piece that may belong to [a particular] class.'[47] Furthermore, the goals of interpretation are served by associating 'an object with its typical group'.[48] Further still,

> There is consistently a correspondence between the genre that serves to present some particular content to the world and the intention for the content. Indeed, there is a clear correspondence between the typical genre and the unique content of any given piece of literature. To be aware of the genre…will give a precise handle for controlling what the point of the content may be.[49]

A genre, then, will evidence one or more of the five following typicalities: (1) *typical structure* with elements related to each other in a functional pattern; (2) *typical content*, although more variation enters here than under the first typicality; (3) *typical vocabulary*—more variation yet, but keywords on up to whole sentences or paragraphs may recur from text to text; (4) *typical setting*, the place/institution in society where this model 'most naturally belongs, lives'; and finally (5) *typical function*, with this observation: 'the general rule of thumb [is] that genre and content correspond in order to accomplish a particular, recurring goal'.[50]

46. R. Knierim, 'Form Criticism Reconsidered', *Int* 27 (1973), p. 459.

47. G.W. Coats, 'Genres: Why Should They Be Important for Exegesis?' (in *idem* [ed.], *Saga, Legend, Tale, Novella, Fable*), p. 8.

48. Coats, 'Genres', p. 9.

49. Coats, 'Genres', pp. 9-10.

50. Coats, 'Genres', pp. 11-13, but he lists only four points, mentioning content under vocabulary. It was deemed advisable to present content under a separate number.

Coats wishes to register a distinction between intention and function. Within its place or social institution a genre of course fulfills a certain function: it encourages, exhorts, condemns, reports, warns, and so on. 'When the genre is given life by combination with a particular content, the typical function of the genre will meet a particular intention.'[51] The distinction seems a valid one. Perhaps Coats here also responds in part to a felt need in the discipline and moves in the direction of Knight's redefinition of 'setting' into the broader 'matrix',[52] or in the direction of Weis's 'historical situation' (socio-politico-literary-historical context) as distinct from the older term (socio-institutional) setting.[53] At any rate, this study maintains the older meaning of 'setting' and in addition employs 'matrix' or 'historical situation' when areas beyond social institutions must be discussed.

What is *redaction*? If the further question is asked of literary stages (previous 'layers' which existed prior to, and have been combined with, or adapted into, the final text form), whether it is an authorial, redactional or compositional stage, the answer will be inaccurate. The question needs reformulation. Knierim's recent work has shown that a single person may engage in any or all of the above-named activities.[54] Sweeney's definition will both clarify and help reformulate the questions put to the text:

> Redaction is the revision or reuse in writing of previously existing written or unwritten material. Regardless of its intent or purpose, it operates mechanically in that it employs essentially mechanical, editorial operations such as collecting, combining, connecting, framing, inserting, interpolating, glossing, expanding, amending, transcribing, etc., previously existing works. The resulting text may well represent an entirely new viewpoint or serve a new purpose, but the operations which produced that text are still mechanical. Authorial activity is the creation of something entirely new, regardless of whether it is oral or written. Elements of both may occur in a biblical text.[55]

One may quibble over the incidental expression 'entirely new' in light of

51. Coats, 'Genres', p. 13.
52. D.A. Knight, 'The Understanding of "Sitz im Leben" in Form Criticism', in SBLSP, I (1974), pp. 105-25.
53. R.D. Weis, *A Handbook of Old Testament Exegesis* (Claremont, CA: Privately printed, 2nd edn, 1983), pp. 71ff.
54. Knierim, 'Criticism of Literary Features', esp. pp. 151f.
55. M. Sweeney, *Isaiah 1–4 and the Postexilic Understanding of the Isaianic Tradition* (BZAW, 171; Berlin: de Gruyter, 1988).

literary critic H. Bloom's 'anxiety of influence', and offer the term 'fresh' in order not to detract from Sweeney's otherwise undoubtedly correct point. Accepting then his definition, one sees that the question of redaction should not be an absolute, but a relative one: what measure of redaction, and what measure of fresh authorship, does a text present?

The section below on method will offer definitions of *structure analysis* and *redaction criticism*.

3.2. *Narrative Definitions*

It is true that some 'stories' may be so short and direct that they fall short of having a *plot* as that term is being defined in literary cirles. Form-critically these brief pieces would be better labelled 'anecdotes', 'reports', and so on.[56] But any story/narrative the length of Esther implies 'plot' in the classic sense of Aristotle's core definitions: 'imitation of an action' and also 'arrangement of the incidents'.[57] Thus classically plot means a 'causal completion' by which a reader senses unity; 'it produces a synthetic whole carved from the infinite contingency of the world. It is the final end that all the parts are to serve'.[58] This classical approach is certainly correct as far as it goes, and may be understood as a first level of abstraction from the text. This is plot as 'skeleton'. 'At an intermediate stage of abstraction, "plot" is to be understood less in terms of the incidents or elements it organizes, and more in terms of the mind that does the organizing.'[59]

Harmon, editing the fifth edition of Thrall and Hibbard's standard *Handbook*, first confirms a causal/'skeletal' concept of plot, then adds the pertinent observation that plot, 'at least in most modern writing... focuses with one principal idea in mind—character'.[60] This focus probably derives from Henry James's dictum: 'character is action'.[61] Mary

56. See the glossaries in FOTL.

57. Aristotle, *The Poetics*, 6, quoted in K. Egan, 'What Is a Plot?', in *New Literary History* 9:3 (1978), p. 472 n. 4.

58. Egan, 'What Is a Plot?', p. 455.

59. Egan, 'What Is a Plot?', p. 455.

60. W.F. Thrall and A. Hibbard, *A Handbook to Literature* (New York: Odyssey, 3rd edn, 1962) p. 358. Cf. similar words in the 5th edn by C.H. Holman and W. Harmon (New York: Macmillan, 1986), pp. 377-79.

61. H. James, *The Art of Fiction and Other Essays*, quoted in M. Savage, 'Literary Criticism and Biblical Studies: A Rhetorical Analysis of the Joseph Narrative', in C.D. Evans, W.W. Hallo and J.B. White (eds.), *Scripture in Context: Essays on the Comparative Method* (Pittsburgh: Pickwick, 1980), vol. 1, p. 83.

Savage has recently criticized what she views as over-reliance among literary critics in general on the Jamesian model. In particular her suggestive article levels the same criticism at Coats's and Redford's treatment of the Joseph story.[62] Accordingly, one must be aware of literary models other than James's and above all be sensitive to the text, trying not to force a model upon it. That said, either character, or Savage's *ethos* and *pathos* (from Aristotle), in addition to the classic emphasis on action, must figure in any definition of plot.

One or more of the above definitions might seem to be sufficient, but Kieran Egan points out that the use of *plot* is still 'characterized by vagueness and confusion'.[63] He offers other, 'geometric' definitions of plot beyond the 'skeleton' level, then argues with telling logic for the necessity of including 'affective meaning' within the concept of plot. This term concerns reader response and therefore should not be confused with the 'emotion' of formalism which concerns the feelings within the story/characters: 'affective meaning derives from following with our gut, as it were, the rhythms of emotion which resonate from the event.[64]

Going beyond Aristotle, Egan argues that 'plot' both *determines* and organizes meaning in the text as well as one's response to it. He readily admits that the 'set of rules', by which such determination and organization is achieved and any irrelevancies are eliminated, is not yet entirely understood. Recognizing also that one does not have the luxury of prescribing meanings, Egan proposes the following definition: 'plot is a set of rules that determines and sequences events to cause a determinate affective response'.[65] Important for the structural and genre work in our study is this further clarification:

62. Savage, 'Literary Criticism and Biblical Studies', pp. 89ff.
63. Egan, 'What Is a Plot?', p. 456.
64. To illustrate, Egan poses the example 'he shot Tom'; this is 'merely' a semantically meaningful statement. But by adding that 'he' picks his nose in public and uses foul language in front of children, while Tom is a clean, handsome fellow who loves his grandmother, Egan arouses tentative *feelings* in the reader. Subverting these feelings, Egan adds that 'he' is unprepossessing and has a heart of gold, while Tom and grandmother push drugs and live in an unspeakable relationship. Thus one begins, tentatively, to feel first negative disapproval, then positive relief about the killing, especially, one may add, if a hero was threatened by the evil Tom. At or near the end a reader will form a final emotional reaction to the whole—thus moving through tentative to final affective responses.
65. Egan, 'What Is a Plot?', p. 470.

Plots, then, determine and provide rules for the sequencing of narrative units—thereby creating a sense of causality. Classifying plots in a nonarbitrary fashion must involve isolating and classifying kinds of narrative units and the causal effects of juxtaposing them in particular sequences.[66]

Having profited from insights selectively drawn from formalists, structuralists and Egan, I would be quite happy with the last two quotations as working definitions, as long as it be recognized that 'plot' may refer both to the more theoretical and still debated 'set of rules' which ought to operate, and to the more concrete results once those rules have operated to produce a text. The results referred to here include action, character, tension/conflict, crisis, release of tension, closure, unity and such like. With the above in mind, the question can now be asked: What are the basic *units of narrative structure*? What elements combine to create plot—causality and affective response—and how are they defined? These questions can be answered in broad outlines without prejudice to the investigation of Esther. Specific features, however, will await their place as they occur in the narrative.

Robert Alter (apparently) uses only two units or structure elements in his analysis of several Genesis narratives: *exposition* and *narrative event*.[67] Since he focuses more on vocabulary, style and pathos, the bipartite model suffices. But what if the focus centers on the structure per se? The volumes of FOTL so far published exegete texts inductively and thus uncover a wide variety of 'skeletal' and 'geometric' organizations (to borrow from the discussion of plot without equating the terms). The FOTL volume on Genesis, which of course deals with narratives of many kinds, uses a more classical tripartite division—exposition, complication, resolution—for some of the same narratives covered by Alter's two-part model. These three parts are borrowed from 'standard' literary criticism, but stand in need of definition (for purposes of this investigation), and of terminological refinement (relative to that 'standard', non-biblical criticism).

The tripartite 'exposition', 'complication' and 'resolution' may be seen to be correlative with Aristotle's beginning, middle and end.

The beginning initiates the main action in a way which makes us look forward to something more; the middle presumes what has gone before

66. Egan, 'What Is a Plot?', p. 470.
67. R. Alter, *The Art of Biblical Narrative* (New York: Basic Books, 1981), *passim*.

and requires something to follow; and the end follows from what has gone before but requires nothing more. Then we are satisfied that the plot is complete.[68]

Before further definition is undertaken, one can profit from reference to the well-known Freytag's pyramid which 'has been widely accepted as a means of getting at the *plot structure* of many kinds of fiction in addition to drama'.[69]

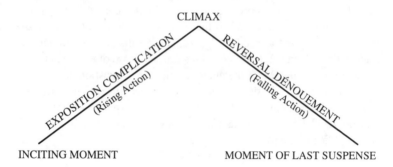

This graphic, originally intended to describe tragedy, does not explain all plots. Nevertheless it highlights a radical element found generally in narrative or storytelling—an element implied in the older three-part model: the phenomenon of tension and release. Freytag's work (1863) may be presumed to underlie Claus Westermann's cardinal point in his approach to biblical narrative: one must ask after 'ein Geschehen zusammenbindenden Bogen..., der eine Spannung zu einer Lösung bringt'.[70] Coats felicitously summarizes by translating what he calls Westermann's key term: 'arc of tension'.[71] One may accept this as a partial definition of plot, or as a key principle among Egan's 'set of rules'—rules which of course are the focus of ongoing discussion.

However, the need for precise definition and refinement enters with

---

68. M.H. Abrams, *A Glossary of Literary Terms* (New York: Holt, Rinehart and Winston, 4th edn, 1981) pp. 138-39. Cf. J.T. Shipley (ed.), *Dictionary of World Literature* (Paterson, NJ: Littlefield, Adams, 1962), p. 310. Aristotle also maintained that plot should have unity and not be episodic (Holman and Harmon, *A Handbook to Literature*, pp. 377-78.

69. Holman and Harmon, *A Handbook to Literature*, p. 216.

70. C. Westermann, *Forschung am Alten Testament* (Munich: Chr. Kaiser Verlag, 1964), p. 34.

71. Coats (ed.), *Saga, Legend, Tale, Novella, Fable*, p. 144.

the application of Green's and Coats's natural translation of *Lösung* as 'resolving' or 'resolution'.[72] Coats's recent article on the tale[73] builds on Westermann and applies the term as follows:

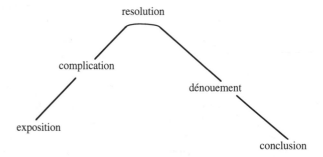

In this scheme, 'resolution' means the turning point of action. Referring to Freytag's pyramid once again, one can see that 'resolution' is not the term used for the apex of tension (whether arc or pyramid matters not). According to the literary manuals, 'resolution' is synonymous with falling action. The peak of tension is the 'crisis' and may or may not coincide with 'climax'.[74] Harmon defines crisis and climax thus:

> Crisis: In fiction or drama the point at which the opposing forces that create the conflict interlock in the decisive action on which the plot will turn…the episode or incident wherein the situation of the protagonist is certain either to improve or worsen. Since crisis is essentially a structural element of plot rather than an index of the emotional response that an event may produce in a reader or spectator, as climax is, crisis and climax do not always occur together.[75]

Thus modern writers distinguish crisis from climax; Freytag may have understood this distinction but rigidly lumped both into the 'third act' of his five-act pyramid for tragedies.

72. Used by D. Green in his translation of C. Westermann, *The Promises to the Fathers: Studies on the Patriarchal Narratives* (Philadelphia: Fortress Press, 1980), p. 29 (which is taken in part from *Forschung*, note 70 above); Coats's article 'Tale', in *idem* (ed.), *Saga, Legend, Tale, Novella, Fable,* pp. 64ff.

73. Coats (ed.), *Saga, Legend, Tale, Novella, Fable*, pp. 64-65.

74. Abrams, *A Glossary of Literary Terms*, p. 138.

75. Holman and Harmon, *A Handbook to Literature*, p. 116. Recent writing has tended to move both crisis (structure) and climax (reader response) away from the middle (see pyramid) toward the end of the work.

Comparing the previous graphic for tale with Coats's earlier work in Genesis, it would appear that he is refining his own paradigms. And if the above suggestion of 'crisis' for the apex or turning point of action be accepted, another refinement is achieved. Thus 'resolution' becomes—as it already is in literary parlance—a synonym for dénouement or falling action.

Drawing on Coats and the manuals, more definitions may now be offered. As Coats points out, the narrative use of 'exposition' must not be confused with its use in composition. There it stands as one of four types, the others being argumentation, description and narration. When applied to structure, 'exposition is the introductory material which creates the tone, gives the setting, introduces the characters, and supplies other facts necessary to an understanding of the play [or work]'.[76] Or, in other terms, 'in some cases [it is] a brief presentation of the situation that holds these characters together in an interesting and significant combination of events'.[77] One may add that these statements tally well with Alter's use of the term. Succinctly, then, the breakdown of an exposition may contain general circumstances, principal characters, and events that create 'relationships'.[78] All this is helpful when it comes to distinguishing briefer elements such as report, notice, and so on, which do not create relationships and do not usually serve as building blocks for narrative complication.

The *complication* 'stirs the mixture enough to suggest that the "relationships"…are not simple. To the contrary, there is some kind of problem, a crisis in relationships, a threatening turn of events, a hostile confrontation.'[79]

The critical turning point, the *crisis*, which may well provide 'insight into the goals of the story…or at least a signpost toward that end'[80] has just been defined. Thus the three-part model, beginning–middle–end, has been refined into three parts up to the 'middle' of Aristotle's middle. Two parts remain: dénouement and conclusion.

The fourth common narrative element, *dénouement*, has been hinted at above. Here the consequences of the crisis/climax begin to unfold or

76. Holman and Harmon, *A Handbook to Literature*, p. 194.
77. Coats (ed.), *Saga, Legend, Tale, Novella, Fable*, p. 64.
78. Coats (ed.), *Saga, Legend, Tale, Novella, Fable*, p. 65.
79. Coats (ed.), *Saga, Legend, Tale, Novella, Fable*, p. 65.
80. Coats (ed.), *Saga, Legend, Tale, Novella, Fable*, p. 65, but using the term 'resolution'.

'unwind'. 'It addresses the natural concern of the audience to know what difference the breaking point makes for the principals of the plot.'[81] If falling action is an apt term, then the dénouement will move toward either a 'moment of last suspense' (Freytag) or 'from excitement to calm' (Olrik).[82]

The final narrative unit in this basic scheme will of course be the *conclusion*. Here is reached that difficult to define, yet commonly perceived or felt, phenomenon called closure.[83] Suffice it to say that the close/conclusion 'wraps up all the loose ends, rounding off the plot with observations [or actions] that bring the concerns of the audience to a natural conclusion', or in some modern works, an unnatural one.[84]

Although a discussion on possible subunits within the five major narrative units just mentioned was not found in the works consulted, a preliminary inquiry into Esther's structure led to the following observation. The structure within any of those larger narrative elements may also be organized on the order of exposition, complication and (temporary or partial) release of tension. With regard to the first two, no better terms than exposition and complication could be found. 'Conflict', an established synonym for complication in literary parlance, was disallowed on the grounds that complication is already used in FOTL and that 'conflict' may connote a personal confrontation of characters when this facet of the narrative may rather involve pressure from the situation—forces outside the personae. So within the major exposition or complication of the whole narrative one may find two or three subunits: minor exposition, minor complication, and possibly a pause or release of tension/complication.

But what to do in such cases with the third subunit, the temporary or partial release of tension? Some term is needed to label these pause-like plateaus within the rising action. (Outside of Esther such plateaus may also occur within the falling action.) The term 'conclusion' is impertinent here because of its sound of finality and its lack of precision in describing

81. Coats (ed.), *Saga, Legend, Tale, Novella, Fable*, p. 65.

82. Coats (ed.), *Saga, Legend, Tale, Novella, Fable*, p. 65. See A. Olrik, 'Epic Laws of Folk Narrative', in A. Dundes (ed.), *The Study of Folklore* (Englewood Cliffs, NJ: Prentice–Hall, 1965), p. 132.

83. See Kermode, *The Sense of an Ending*; N.R. Petersen, 'When Is the End Not the End? Literary Reflections on the Ending of Mark's Narrative', in *Int* 34 (1980), pp. 151-66; B.H. Smith, *Poetic Closure: A Study of How Poems End* (Chicago: University of Chicago Press, 1968).

84. Coats (ed.), *Saga, Legend, Tale, Novella, Fable*, p. 65.

the answer, plan or solution found by the character(s). Thus 'solution' was chosen.

The seemingly simple term *scene* was deleted from earlier drafts of the structure diagrams, for two reasons. First, beyond certain rudiments, the concept is slippery, and would require discussion and careful definition. Secondly, the application of 'scene' to EG in some cases would be problematic. Not only some narrative seams, but also some diverse genre elements, resist the imposition of 'scenes'.

3.3. *Observations on Method*

Hermann Gunkel, following a then new thrust in literary studies of oral composition, introduced form criticism to biblical scholarship. He searched for the smallest identifiable unit constitutive of biblical materials: the genre.[85] Probing into cultic, narrative and, to a lesser extent, prophetic materials, his interest was to relate genres to their oral *Sitz im Leben* or setting in life (institutional sense). Stimulating as was the work of Gunkel, Gressmann and others, the fact remains that what survives of the Bible is literary, not oral. The units

> appear before us now in a literary setting together with many other units and supplementary materials which did not belong together in the oral setting. Furthermore, we can never be sure that the small units contained in the present literary context appear in their original oral form.[86]

I agree, therefore, with Knierim[87] that to focus on the 'short, originally independent' components of a text at the opening stage of exegesis is questionable, and that an earlier form of the text must not be assumed a priori, but must be proven. Thus the evidence of the text's final form must be the starting point for study. Structural work begins on the final form because 'in addition to meriting its own investigation, it is in most cases our only evidence for any earlier stages and so deserves our full attention to its construction in order to avoid misconstruing that evidence'.[88] Once the synthetic task of tracing the final shape of the text is

---

85. J.H. Hayes (ed.), *Old Testament Form Criticism* (San Antonio, TX: Trinity University Press, 1974), p. 129.

86. Sweeney, 'Isaiah 1–4', p. 81.

87. Knierim, 'Criticism of Literary Features', p. 155; *idem*, 'Form Criticism Reconsidered', pp. 457-58.

88. R.D. Weis, 'A Definition of the Genre Maśśā' in the Hebrew Bible' (PhD diss., Claremont Graduate School, 1986), p. 33.

completed, the analytical inquiry of seeking redactional layers can be undertaken.

3.3.1. *Structure analysis.* The goals at this entry level of exegesis are to discover how the text is organized, how the parts interrelate, what it says, its 'setting' (in the socio-politico-historical sense),[89] and its genre and intention, to name several of the most important ones. The operating method is to present the text in a graphic or diagrammatic form in such a way as to show its hierarchical organization. This is done by first defining the limits of the text—beginning and end—and secondly, determining how many parts it has. Thirdly one looks at the grammar and syntax of each part in order to determine which phrases and sentences are subordinate to which. In this fashion, clues such as formulaic expressions, changes of subject, person, tense, scene (in the basic sense of time or place), plot, differences in vocabulary, style, meter, strophic patterns and figures of speech, and so on, help to determine the units and subunits of meaning.[90] Each unit or element is labelled primarily as to function in the text,

> and/or its generalized literary nature…and only secondarily specifying its content if at all (sometimes labels specifying both are used). The reason for this is that in structure analysis we want to describe the way the various elements of the text function together within the whole pericope.[91]

Two hermeneutical guiding principles must be observed in the above process. Grammar is never to be violated, but logic prevails over grammar. In practice that means the researcher must always reflect grammatical indicators in the schema, but may insist on joining or separating grammatic units under larger or smaller logical groupings.

3.3.2. *Redaction/earlier stages of the text.* In order to find previous layers of composition, one looks for tensions or inconsistencies in the text;

89. For the distinction between 'setting in life' and 'socio-political setting/ situation', I am indebted to R.D. Weis, 'Old Testament Exegesis: An Outline of the Procedures Involved' (unpublished handout for BS308: Jeremiah at the School of Theology at Claremont, Fall, 1979); see *idem, A Handbook of Old Testament Exegesis*, pp. 71-81. The three-part term socio-politico-historical is mine and is intended not as a rejection, but simply as another expression, of the broad conception of setting; cf. Knight's convenient term 'matrix', in 'The Understanding of "Sitz im Leben" in Form Criticism', pp. 105-25.
90. Weis, *A Handbook of Old Testament Exegesis*, p. 23.
91. Weis, *A Handbook of Old Testament Exegesis*, p. 23.

to find these one looks for the same clues/changes as listed above for detecting elements/units of meaning. One should have recourse here to Knierim's insightful discussion on competing methods.[92]

3.3.3. *Textual integrity*. A recent thrust in text-critical circles involves a major shift in the way a critic approaches the intra- and inter-manuscript evidence. No attempt is made here to trace all the roots of the new approach, but a summary of an incipient and growing consensus in this field of study will set the stage for the reader to assess the import of multi-text Esther evidence.

The multi-manuscript finds at Qumran, which in some cases included more than one text tradition of a single book, have helped scholars to recognize a relative textual fluidity in pre-Masoretic times,[93] the existence of 'independent witnesses' which do not neatly fit within previous classes of MS 'types',[94] and therefore the necessity of looking at the character of an entire document before extracting readings for a critical apparatus or a reconstructed *Vorlage*. As Sanders remarks, 'text criticism as formerly practiced made pillaging of ancient and medieval manuscripts a righteous act done in the service of an imagined original'.[95]

Perhaps more influential in altering that former practice (which in tendency hastened to reconstruct a forerunner text from any witness that could be pirated and pressed into service) are the Hebrew University Bible Project and the United Bible Societies' Hebrew Old Testament Text Project. Both of these Project committees independently reached remarkably similar conclusions regarding a four-stage transmission history of the Hebrew Bible manuscripts,[96] and each is fostering in its own way a greater respect for the integrity of every individual apograph.

The concern here for textual integrity is not a foppish preservationism; rather it is the recognition of the wider issue of hermeneutics involved in text criticism, and the conviction that a hermeneutic of respect will

92. Knierim, 'Criticism of Literary Features', *passim*.

93. Thus J.A. Sanders can say, 'the earlier the date of biblical manuscripts the greater variety there are in text types and text characteristics' ('Text and Canon: Concepts and Method', *JBL* 98 [1979], pp. 13-14).

94. E. Tov, 'A Modern Textual Outlook Based on the Qumran Scrolls', *HUCA* 53 (1982), pp. 11-27.

95. J.A. Sanders, 'The Hermeneutics of Text Criticism and Translation' (SBL paper, Boston, 1987), p. 4. See his forthcoming 'Apographs, Suspicion and Scripture'.

96. See Sanders, 'Text and Canon', pp. 10ff.

enhance the common goals of accuracy and certainty in this field, whether it involves interpreting a single concrete witness, or reconstructing a hypothetical forerunner.

4. *The Role of this Study*

The role of this study involves a two-step process. The first step will be to investigate the structure, genre and intention of the Greek and Hebrew traditions of Esther, using the texts listed above as bases. The twofold second step will be relating the results of that investigation to redactional questions, especially of the two 'biblical' EGs, and issues of textual history and integrity.

The structural inquiry will be pursued under two aspects: an internal, 'intratextual' search for the organization of each text as a whole and in its final form; an external, intertextual comparison of the texts vis-à-vis each other. In order to facilitate both internal and external comparisons, two levels of synchronic analyses have been provided as follows.

First, given the need to see likenesses and dissimilarities between the Greek text traditions of L and o´, a detailed microstructure will be presented for each of these texts (Chapter 2). It will not be possible in this study to present Jos in any detail; an integral treatment must await a separate study. However, notes regarding a few of Jos's differences, pluses and minuses will be appended to successive microstructural panels of L and o´. Following this material a microstructure of EH will be found (Chapter 3). These three schemata have been laid out with an eye to intertextual comparison.

(A second schema, which could be termed a midi-macro level, will not be printed here for reasons of space, but could easily be extracted down to whatever detail is desired by listing panels from the microstructure so that each text could be compared and contrasted within a span of three to five pages.)

Next, as a conclusion to Chapter 3, each text will be summarized in a one-page macrostructure. The redactional inquiry (Chapter 4) will concentrate on EG and will begin with the final text level, then insofar as possible will proceed chronologically, in regressive fashion, from latest to earliest layers. Finally, the work of previous chapters will be summarized and conclusions will be drawn, especially regarding a proposed text history of o´, L, and EH, and the implications of the various Esthers for the concept of textual integrity and text criticism (Chapter 5).

Chapter 2

GREEK ESTHER

The procedure for presenting the microstructures of EG in both o′ and L texts is as follows: first a determination of where the unit begins; secondly a discussion of the extent and structure of each subunit; finally the microstructure itself. This will be followed by a discussion of selected differences between the two; some divergences will be left without comment in the microstructure for the reader to find. When 'exposition' or 'complication' (as subelements) occur within larger units, they will initially be labelled 'minor'. The term 'solution', of course, needs no other designation. Later on in the Esther microstructures, when 'minor' is dropped, the reader is asked to distinguish between *major* and *minor* expositions and complications. Observation of these subunits will help to resolve questions of function and interrelationships between smaller and larger units. In terms of structure, the proper identification of subunits helps to resolve questions of the relative importance of blocks of material—superordination and subordination (a major problem with EH, as mentioned above)—and to determine how many parts there are in Esther.

In the chain of subordination, with space at a premium, resort to the shortest possible structural labels became mandatory, so that three spaces would never be required to label panels. Thus the subordination runs: I., A., 1., a., 1), a), α, αα, α1 and, if further subdivisions are required, they continue as α2, α3, α4, etc. Note that the siglum // connects parallel passages of o′ and L, and the siglum -I means 'up to (including) the last word', as in 3-I standing for words 3-10.

A final reminder: the minute detail of these microstructures intends to aid the comparison of the two texts read in the original; it is not intended to substitute for that reading. A yet more minute study of the comparative vocabulary would require separate treatment and, with the help of

Thesaurus Linguae Graecae,[1] would no doubt advance knowledge appreciably. Nevertheless, the diagrammatic presentations account for many small units in order to move the comparison of EG texts out of the grip of misstatement, and beyond its current state of judgment by broad and sometimes fuzzy comparisons.

Therefore an attempt has been made here to present every structural element down to minutiae, every sentence of both texts, and almost all the grammatical units within those sentences, whether the texts show differences or not. Conjunctions, especially opening ones, are generally ignored, as are occasionally some small syntactical units such as adverbs, short prepositional phrases or interjections. These arbitrary omissions were judged as minor in the realms of structure, content and cross-textual comparison.[2]

However, the presentation is frequently so detailed that commas are added within structural panels (an unusual procedure) in order to indicate that the underlying Greek sentence is not yet complete. To help the reader capture the fine narrativity of the original, present tense has replaced the aorist where action is involved.

The presentation will begin in each case with the longest text (o′) and then proceed to L. When the presentation of both these microstructures is complete, EH will be covered. Regrettably, text criticism has to be held to a few cases which directly affect the argument or hold special interest.

The Superscription. At the outset the determination of an overall beginning is greatly facilitated by the superscription Εσθηρ, Αισθηρ and the like (see the superior apparatus of Hanhart; the superscription is

---

1.   A massive project under the direction of Theodore F. Brunner at the University of California, Irvine; its present goal, which may be expanded, is to collect and computerize all ancient Greek materials extant from the period between Homer and 600 CE—approximately 62 million words.

2.   One will probably not be able to remove the misnomers 'Lucian' and 'Additions' already objected to above. Note the misleading statement of Bissell: 'The general scope of the narrative in both (o′ and L) is the same, and not infrequently there is literal agreement...the changes (in L) are always clearly recognizable as such [!], and, by a careful comparison, the reasons which might have suggested them generally discoverable' (E.C. Bissell, 'Additions to Esther', in J.P. Lange [ed.], *The Apocrypha of the Old Testament* [Commentary on the Holy Scriptures, 15; repr., Grand Rapids: Zondervan, 1960], pp. 199-200. Clines opines that in this area 'misleading statements abound' (Clines, *The Esther Scroll*, p. 190 n. 40).

not accounted for in the microstructure). Furthermore, the text proper begins—'Dream Report: Introduction' (o′ A 1-4 // L A 1-2)—with a date and the introduction of two new characters: King Artaxerxes (o′) or Assueros (L), and Mordecai. They are new because they differ from 'Esther' above. Thus the superscription has ended.

1. *Mordecai's Dream (LXX A 1-11)*

The appearance of a date (A 1a), a third-person *statement* (as defined in the glossaries of FOTL) concerning Mordecai's dream (v. 1b[1-3]), and a brief biography (vv. 1b[4-13]–3), lead up to the report of the dream proper. A new subunit begins with the announcement 'And this is...', which is a *report* formulary functioning as modern quotation marks, not to introduce speech (as in Nebuchadnezzar's first-person dream report in Dan. 4.4ff.), but as if to document the authenticity of what follows (v. 4a). The dream proper extends from v. 4b to v. 10 (L A 3b-9); then a conclusion reports in the third person the end of the dream and its effect on Mordecai, and gives a statement of narrated time in both o′ and L (vv. 11 and 10 respectively, but expressed differently). A new action of Mordecai (again expressed differently), the introduction of new characters (but with widely variant names), and a (new?) location clearly mark a new unit (or scene): o′ A 12ff. // L A 11ff.

o′ Text

I. DREAM REPORT (Mordecai)	A 1-11
A. INTRODUCTION: Date, Statement, Biography	1-3
1. Date	1a
a. Year: 2nd	1a(1-2)
b. Reference: reign of Artaxerxes	1a(3-6)
c. Day (1) & month (Nisan)	1a(7-10)
2. Statement	1b(1-3)
a. Object: dream	1b(1)
b. Action: he saw	1b(2)
c. Person: Mordecai	1b(3)
3. Biography	1b(4-13)-3
a. Genealogy	1b(4-13)
1) Patrimony	1b(4-10)

L Text

γ Act: every nation prepares ... 6cα
δ Complement: to fight ... 6cβ
b. Episode 2: We cry to Lord; response ... 6d-8
  1) Setting ... 6d
    a) Subject: we (!) ... 6dα(1-2)
    b) Act: cry/appeal ... 6dα(2)
    c) Object: to κύριος ... 6dα(3-5)
    d) Reason: sound of their roar ... 6dβ
  2) Development: 4 (?) symbols appear ... 7-8
    a) small spring becomes much water ... 7a
    b) = great river ... 7b
    c) light ... 8aα
    d) sun ... 8aβ(1)
    e) Act 1: rises ... 8aβ(2)
    f) Subject: rivers ... 8bα
    g) Act 2: are exalted ... 8bβ
    h) Act 3: swallow up ... 8cα
    i) Object: the honored ones ... 8cβ
3. Conclusion ... 9-10
  a. Mordecai, rising/awaking from dream ... 9aα
  b. Act 1: ponders ... 9aβ
  c. Objects ... 9b
    1) the dream's meaning ... 9bα
    2) what the Mighty One is preparing ... 9bβ
  d. Act 2: dream hidden in heart ... 10a
  e. Act 3: seeks to understand ... 10b

The basic structures of both o′ and L in the 'Introduction' (o′ A 1-3 // L A 1-2) are identical, but some differences of detail occur:

1. for the royal name, o′ has Artaxerxes, while L has Ahasuerus;
2. in L the corresponding Greek is inserted for the time correlation ('Adar–Nisan, that is Dystros–Xanthikos');
3. o′ stresses the ethnicity of Mordecai as Jewish in a foreign surrounding by adding 'a Jew dwelling in Sousa', which is lacking in L;
4. similarly, o′ notes specifically that Mordecai was taken from Jerusalem, whereas L leaves this for readers to fill in.

The third-person status of the section qualifies it as a report (see FOTL). The introduction to Mordecai gives the reader only the knowledge of his present position along with his ethnic background. It is constructed to move immediately to the dream report itself and functions more as a prelude to the dream rather than as an introduction of Mordecai.

One is struck initially with the fact that the introduction to both o´ and L is not an introduction to the book of Esther. Rather, the reader is asked to focus upon Mordecai and the king as the main characters in the story. That Mordecai is designated 'a great man' (= a noble?; Moore opts for 'prominent man') is said to put him in a place of prominence. One must question how this introduction functions thematically and formally within the whole. Is a measure of androcentricity at work here, diminishing the glory of Vashti and Esther by spotlighting Mordecai and the king?

Most certainly this introduction intends for the reader to sympathize with Mordecai, perhaps to applaud him for attaining such a position under difficult circumstances. His Jewishness is no doubt emphasized as foreshadowing the events yet to unfold, and to increase the reader's anticipation of the plot against the Jews.

In the 'Dream Report Proper' (o´ A 4-11 // L A 3-10), the dream itself is divided into two episodes, giving the setting and development. Some differences appear between o´ and L:

1. o´ anticipates the appearance of the dragons in having 'voices' in the setting, while L has only noise;
2. o´ uses the third person throughout the report, while L has the first person in the phrase which opens episode 2, 'And we cried to the Lord' (A 6d);
3. o´ has θεός, while L has κύριος.
4. in o´ 'the lowly are exalted and devour the honorable', while L personifies the river which devours the honorable;
5. in o´ the cry uttered forth (v. 6a[1]) is a summons to the nations to rally against the just nation, while in L the cry evokes 'fear in everything';
6. in o´ the just nation prepares to be killed (= defeated), whereas in L no mention of defeat occurs.

The setting is reminiscent of the chaos in the creation epic. The darkness, along with the voice of Tiamat (?), combines to give a very ominous picture. The darkness of the surroundings is dispelled by the dividing of the waters and the breaking forth of the light[3]—an appropriate reference

---

3. Benefit can be derived here from the judicious approach regarding comparison and contrast of ancient Near Eastern materials in a programmatic article by W.W. Hallo, 'Biblical History in Its Near Eastern Setting: The Contextual Approach', in C.D. Evans, W.W. Hallo and J.B. White (eds.), *Scripture in Context: Essays on the Comparative Method* (Pittsburgh: Pickwick Press, 1980), pp. 1-26.

versus fire in a Persian or post-Persian context (see J.A. Sanders's creative account of Genesis[4]).

The 'Conclusion' of the dream report (o′ A 11 // L A 9-10) returns to narrative, announcing Mordecai's awaking from his dream—a typical element in the 'frame' of ancient Near Eastern dreams, according to Oppenheim.[5] The differences are these:

1. L returns to the third person, which o′ never left;
2. o′ has θεός again, while L has 'Mighty One';
3. o′ has Mordecai ponder the dream until night time, while L gives no specific time frame, though it, like o′, assumes no delay in the fulfillment of the dream;
4. o′ gives no advance indication that the chamberlains will be the key to the dream's interpretation, whereas L specifically states that Mordecai's desire to find the meaning of the dream would come when he slept in the king's courtyard.

The differences in the royal names can be left to the commentaries except for the observation that L's use of 'Ahasuerus' is usually taken to mean that the translator is revising toward MT. This conclusion, however, is not a necessary one when Dan. 11.1-2 is taken into account: the fourth Persian king will be 'far richer than all of them'. The date of the Daniel passage does not weigh heavily since Persian lavishness and Xerxes' wealth were already known to Herodotus in the fifth century BCE. Since Esther also uses the richness motif, L could have an early, even the earliest, tradition here (from within or without the Danielic line); or, if L is late, he could be revising toward consistency with a tradition that stood against Josephus' and LXX's 'Artaxerxes' or a Hebrew *Vorlage* which, although reading 'Ahasuerus', nevertheless differed in many ways from MT.

Note L's double name for the month in A 1αβ, and the correlation with Greek month names in A 1αγ, not in o′. Just as the text gives clues to early month name changes from Hebrew to Babylonian ('Adar, which is Nisan'), L shows the process of relating this important ritual matter to its Greek-speaking audience. L's double month name is difficult: the Hellenistic 'Dystros' provides a critical correlation with the Jewish calendar which could be dropped once these dates were generally

---

4.　J.A. Sanders, 'God Is God', *Foundations* 6 (1963), pp. 343-61.
5.　A.L. Oppenheim, *Dreams and Their Interpretation in the Ancient Near East* (Transactions of the American Philosophical Society, New Series, 46, Part 3; Philadelphia: American Philosophical Society, 1956), pp. 186-87.

known, but is difficult to explain as a late addition. Therefore L appears to have the earliest reading.

Does the use of 'we cried' (L A 6) hint at some use in the cult? Mordecai is associated with 'Jeconiah, king of Judea', probably for purposes of public image, and the author/editor's legislative program. Other changes involve motifs in the dream which do not seem to derive from textual variation, but from authorial/editorial intention. Since the dream's interpretation occurs at the end of both texts, just above the subscription Εσθηρ (*mutil*), inclusio or frame enters the picture, but discussion of frame types and functions can be delayed until the end.

2. *First (Partial) Fulfillment of Dream (LXX A 12-17)*

Without delay the o´ text thrusts Mordecai into the royal court with no transition, but the last words τῆς νυκτός and the verb 'rested/slept' immediately following probably intend to compress the action into a single day–night sequence. L leaves no doubt and says that the meaning was made clear (διασαφηθήσεται [+ ἕος, from עד in a Semitic *Vorlage*?]) 'on the day that he slept'.

That is to say, one text implies while the other states that what follows is some level of dream fulfillment. Therefore the unit may provisionally be called 'Dream's First (Partial) Fulfillment'. All this has major implications for the rest of Esther's structure: the main plot is also dream fulfillment, a second (complete) fulfillment.

Returning to the dream's first outworking, the unit of A 12-16 logically falls into three subunits which serve to (1) set the stage, (2) uncover a plot and thus bring Mordecai and the king together, and (3) spell out the results: thus 'Introduction', 'Body' and 'Conclusion'. Although a problem is reported here, this third-person presentation of action by two or more parties without developed tension (in the narrative sense) is called 'report'. Other reports with three parts will also be found in Esther; yet A 17, introducing a new character, Aman, has only two parts. Again because it only presents or reports a problem and does not *develop* the conflict/tension, it could be called either 'report' or 'statement'. This single verse joins with the previous material and not with the following section on the king and his kingdom, power and banquet, and so on. Since it introduces a new character and sets the stage for tension to develop in the later narrative, and since the narrative will offer up many pairs, this segment can also be called a 'report'.

oʹ Text

L Text

    d. King's act 2: (Introduction of Aman the Antagonist)

Aman given to Mordecai	17
1) gives	17aα
2) to Mordecai for these things	17aβ
3) Object	17b
α Name: Aman, Macedonian .	17bα
β Job: works in king's presence	17bβ
B. STATEMENT: Aman's Reaction = Plot	18
1. Act: seeks	18aα
2. Purpose: to harm	18aβ
3. Dual Objects	18aγ
a. Mordecai	18aγ(1-2)
b. & his people (Jews)	18aγ(3-7)
4. Dual Reason	18b
a. for reporting the eunuchs	18bα
b. because they were executed	18bβ

The dream is immediately translated into reality and thus fulfillment. Here oʹ is less smooth, L giving a smoother transition by telling the reader that the interpretation would be discovered by Mordecai as he slept in the king's courtyard.

The differences in the 'Introduction' to Mordecai's discovery (oʹ A 12 // L A 11) are:

1.   oʹ has Gabatha and Tharra (Semitic), while L has Astaos and Thedeutes (Greek).
2.   oʹ is more detailed in describing the eunuchs as guards of the king, whereas L simply calls them eunuchs.

It would appear oʹ feels the need to make the plot more apparent, leaving less to the reader's imagination, since it gives the job description of the eunuchs, which L omits.

In the 'Body' of the report (oʹ A 13-14 // L A 12-14), Mordecai, by his close proximity to the eunuchs, overhears their plans. The two texts show some slight differences:

1.   oʹ credits Mordecai with an active role in searching out their plans, while L simply has him passively hear the plot of the eunuchs;
2.   oʹ has λογισμούς/μερίμνας, whereas L has διαβολάς (the allusion seems intentional).

The oʹ text is abrupt in its style, juxtaposing Mordecai's actions to the king's. Yet oʹ uses a more emotive verb, ἐξαιτέω ('demand', but the noun form means 'torture'). On the other hand, L carefully shows the actions of Mordecai, then of the eunuchs, then of Mordecai, the king, and finally the eunuchs. It appears that L is more concerned with literary style, while o′ simply reports.

In the 'Conclusion' to the discovery (vv. 15-16 in both texts), the legal aspects are apparent. The king writes in an official way the memorial of Mordecai. The general flow in both texts is the same: Mordecai testifies, the eunuchs are examined (L's restraint shows), the king judges, the eunuchs are condemned, and Mordecai is promoted. Differences—one major—may be noted in the texts:

1. o′ has Mordecai involved in the actual writing of the record in addition to the king, while L only has the king writing/recording;
2. o′ has the king giving Mordecai gifts, but not Aman specifically, while L specifically makes Aman a gift to Mordecai for Mordecai's good service (major tension for the plot);
3. o′ introduces Aman abruptly without any apparent added tension to the plot, while L increases tension by introducing Aman as a subordinate to Mordecai (note that it happens by the king's action);
4. The PN designation differs (contemporizing exegesis), with o′ having Αμαν Αμαδαθου Βουγαῖος, whereas L has Αμαν Αμαδαθου Μακεδόνα.

3. *Second (Complete) Fulfillment of Dream (LXX 1.1–10.3)*

A. *Frame Prolog (LXX 1.1-3)*

A clearcut transition phrase, καὶ ἐγένετο μετὰ τοὺς λόγους τούτους, plus a change of subject—the king and his kingdom—mark off a new unit in EG. But the apparent simple directness masks some problems and points up real differences between o′ and L, which beg discussion. This unit must be looked at closely, but its relation to EH will be delayed until later.

How far does the unit extend? The complement needed after the transition phrase does not come until after two clauses, one independent and one dependent; it is δοχὴν ἐποίησεν in 1.3b ('reception/feast', as opposed to πότος, 'drinkfest'). Verse 4 opens with another transition phrase and introduces a second 'social', in this case a drinkfest—possibly another unit. Through this second transition the reader learns two major things: that the first reception lasted 180 days (v. 4c), and that it was a marriage celebration (v. 5αβ). Contrastingly, the new drinkfest lasts six days (v. 5cβ, but it becomes seven days in v. 10), and is given to 'the peoples/races in Sousa' (v. 5cα). Contrast the five recipients of the reception in v. 3b.

Clearly within vv. 1-3 and 4-5 the time, locale and action are focusing, narrowing. The question is whether these two verse groups and their 'socials' *function* in the same way, or are functionally—and therefore structurally—distinct. The question may be answered by three different approaches in addition to the one of content just mentioned: first, an intratextual search for the (re)use of phrase or motif in o′ as a possible clue to its function here; secondly, intertextual comparisons with L and EH; and thirdly, 'extratextual' or contextual parallels from Israel's neighbors (the ancient Near Eastern context).[6]

The 180-day motif does not recur, but the king ruling 127 provinces from India (so v. 1) surfaces in the texts of B 1b and E 1b, where his power and authority are stressed for purposes of the letter/decrees. What might be missed in a concordance search is the unit 10.1-3, where 127 provinces do not occur. However, the king and the extent of his realm over land and sea (a new, possibly climactic element), his power and ἀνδραγαθίαν (possibly 'strength and courage'),[7] plus his wealth and kingdom glory, are explicitly foregrounded. At another place the meaning and probable generic derivation of this closing can be explained. Now it only need be noted that these four passages stress royal power and splendor, and that on grounds of internal structure and content 1.1-3 and 10.1-3 mirror each other.

L differs in sentence length and verses. The complement occurs after the transition plus introductory prepositional phrase in 1.1b: 'provinces were subject to him' (ὑπετάγησαν). A new sentence begins in v. 2 and runs—one could say rambles—through v. 5. Note the different syntax and content in L, which do not appear to derive solely, or at all, from purely text-critical considerations. L has '180 days' also, but knows nothing of a marriage; the seven-day drinkfest celebrates the king's deliverance (σωτηρία).

Differences aside, however, both texts mention a show of wealth and power and two separate audiences involved in the two 'feasts'; both close with a reflex or inclusio glorifying the king. Through shorter or longer means, both texts exhibit the same function in the two verse

6. Cf. footnote 4 above. Further evidence, drawn from ancient Near Eastern parallels, that the two feasts do function separately must await Chapter 4.

7. This double expression is chosen by J.C. Dancy, *The Shorter Books of the Apocrypha* (CBCNEB; Cambridge: Cambridge University Press, 1972), p. 166.

groups. The first historicizes and introduces the king, stressing his legendary majesty. The second presents necessary scenic backdrop and narrows the focus, thus readying the hearer or reader for action—action which does develop out of the second unit. For the relation between the two banquets, see the full treatment of EH and the chapter on redaction.

EH, if it may be cited here before it is treated *en bloc*, evinces the same phenomenon, and perhaps more crisply than EG. After the introductory וַיְהִי (which usually takes a complement after this introductory position), the finite preterite עָשָׂה in 1.3 serves as complement; thus the first complete sentence is vv. 1-4. The same preterite again in v. 5 serves as anchor for the next section, vv. 5-8, in which no other preterite occurs in an independent clause. One finds the third preterite in v. 9 with the introduction of Vashti. Thus separate assertions are made for the 180-day and seven-day feasts. Verses 1-3 of ch. 10 of course end the EH text, and they do so in the same way as has been remarked for EG, except that the latter are non-final sections. Likewise Jos uses two different verbs and phrases for the two 'feasts' and separates the second one with ἔπειτα and puts the verb postpositively in penultimate position.

Returning to o´, one can see that 1.1-3 do of course give background and context for the Esther narrative, do introduce the king (note the mention of his name already in A 13), and do broach the banquet motif. But the 180-day element does not recur, and the unit does not serve to introduce other characters or plot. Verses 4ff. do serve to develop narrative action. Therefore vv. 1-3 are to be marked as structurally distinct from the seven-day drinkfest with its characters and actions. The same applies to L 1.1.

So a cumulative case—supported by innertextual and intertextual argument—can begin here, with the extratextual evidence yet to come. The thesis is that the third unit of o´ and L (o´ 1.1-3 // L 1.1) and Jos, and the first unit of EH—on the basis of syntax, content and function—is structurally distinct, and has a reflex immediately preceding the dream interpretation (EG) or at the end (EH and Jos); that is, an inclusio or frame. Further argument supporting this second frame concept can wait until o´ 10.1-3 // L 7.50-52, and the thesis that this particular genus of frame has a heretofore unrecognized generic model can profitably be broached in the chapter on redaction.

Even if another frame does not exist here, as argued above and below, the present form of the EG texts presents the core of Esther as a further fulfillment of the dream, a 'second (complete) fulfillment'. Hence the next title.

B. *Novella Proper (LXX 1.4–9.19)*

1. *Exposition (LXX 1.4–2.23)*

The next units, 1.4ff. in o′ and 1.2ff. in L, do introduce characters and
action, and are thus apparently 'exposition'. But the exposition is not
flat. A mild 'arc of tension' develops, which leads to a plan which in
turn leads to a temporary release or pause. By its early position in the
narrative, before the principal conflict or complication has begun, this
pause must be a partial or transitory kind that will be called 'solution'
until a better term can be found. But that is to anticipate.

Verses 4-5 give a focused background for action, and are thus 'setting'. Verses 6-8 give us an asyndetic string of participial and prepositional phrases describing the lavish arena for what one would expect was
a debauch. Interestingly, L, which is usually described as 'closer to its
MT or Hebrew *Vorlage*', is further away than o′, because it inserts the
finite verb, ἦν, thus rendering all that follows rather properly syndetic. It
is o′ that is closer to Hebrew, of whatever *Vorlage*! A statement (in the
form-critical sense) in v. 9 (in both o′ & L) suddenly presents Astin/
Ouastin without portfolio and the fact of her drinkfest (o′) or reception
(L).

The next signal is the transitional time phrase in v. 10 and the report
of speech which follows. The queen refuses, and tension enters the narrative. Direct speech introduces a unit in which the king seeks counsel
(two different groups in EG) and a plan is proposed to solve a crisis (of
buffoons?) of empire-shaking proportions: wives will now disobey husbands! L, it must be admitted, puts it first in a positive context of government and authority by example before mentioning the family, but the
irony is not obliterated, only softened. In terms of plot, not all the
characters have entered, and the major complication and plan lie yet
ahead. Therefore the plot remains within the background or 'exposition'
stage; both the complication of Astin's refusal and the plan to 'solve'
her disobedience are structurally 'minor'. Nonetheless, the counsellor's
plan is implemented and a narrative unit closes. That content close is also
marked by grammar: a major time-transition phrase in o′ 2.1, or a summary linking phrase in the case of L, both serving to start a new subunit.

In 2.1ff. a new (minor) plan, flowing logically from the completion of
the 'solution' to the first plan (banish Astin), is again proposed by (different) counsellors: find a wife (or a replacement as chief concubine?) for
the king. This second suggested plan leads to the introduction of the last

principal character, Esther. Execution of the plan and artistic expansions (flashbacks) follow quickly: lo and behold, Esther is chosen, and becomes queen. The section closes with another drinkfest, possibly an intentional inclusio to mark off the exposition.

However, ancient narrative art was not always averse to what modern readers would call anticlimax. Three structurally troublesome digressions serve as a transitional *entr'acte*: Mordecai's success, Esther's success, and Mordecai's discovery of a regicide plot. In o′ this second plot by high-placed eunuchs appears at first blush to be a doublet of A 12-14, presumably because it translates EH, which in fact has the unit here. Closer inspection, however, shows that, in its final form, o′ wants the reader to understand this as a second and separate episode of Mordecai saving the king's life. In addition to the general observation that all texts of Esther contain numerous twos or dualities which are not true doublets, the discreteness of this episode can be established by the following considerations: (1) the lack of the eunuchs' PNN here versus the naming of Gabatha and Tharra in A 12; (2) the designation of ἀρχισωμα-τοφύλακες ('chief bodyguards') here versus 'guarding the court' in A 12; (3) the eunuchs are 'offended by Mordecai's promotion', which had not taken place in the narrative time of section A; and (4) Mordecai here notifies Esther (who then tells the king), something he did not do in A 12-14. Clearly o′ presents two different regicide plots, one for which Mordecai receives a reward, and one for which he does not.

L, on the other hand, does not have the digressions on success here, nor does it have or repeat the regicide plot here. However, since o′ is frequently thought to mistakenly present a doublet, L's minus here can be used to support Tov's contention[8] that L is an intentional rewrite of LXX in the (corrective and conforming) direction of a different Hebrew *Vorlage* (see the discussion of this theory in Chapter 4 below).

Regarding structure and plot development, one notes that the digressions in o′ 2.19-23 (an L minus) do not move the reader into the major narrative complication. Both o′ and L mark that entry with yet another time-transition phrase in 3.1.

Interestingly, Jos presents these digressions in developed and reasoned form, explaining Mordecai's presence as a change of residence from Babylon to Sousa and noting Mordecai's filial affection (thus giving us one of the infrequent character insights concerning the heroes). Josephus

---

8. E. Tov, 'The "Lucianic" Text of the Canonical and the Apocryphal Sections of Esther: A Rewritten Biblical Book', *Textus* 10 (1982), pp. 1-25.

also has a colorful paragraph here describing the law against entering the king's presence and the axe-wielding royal guards who back up that law with summary justice (11.203-205).

That this much, o′ 1.4–2.23 // L 1.2–2.18, should be grouped as exposition is shown by four principal items: (1) the last character is now introduced; (2) the two proposals of the two councils have been completed (thus Esther is 'narratively' in place for plot development); (3) the digressions flow from the preceding material and provide 'pause'; and (4) the weighty time phrase (itself an important divider) introduces the principal conflict of the narrative beginning immediately after 3.1. Thus the narrative exposition extends from 1.4 to 2.23 (1.2–2.18 in L).

o′ Text

B. NARRATIVE PROPER	1.4–9.11
1. EXPOSITION: New Feast & Astin's Fall; Esther Made	
Queen & New Feast; Concluding Statements & Report	1.4–2.23
a. New feast/Astin's fall; statement	1.4-22
1) Exposition minor: setting, description & statement	
dual 6-day (+1) drinkfests	4-9
a) Setting (old & 1st new feasts)	4-5
α Transition: (1st flashback)	4aα
β 2 purposes (2nd flashback)	4aβb
αα after showing riches	4aβ
ββ & glorious festivity of riches	4b
γ Duration: 180 days	4c
δ 3rd purpose, 3rd flashback	5a
αα Time (specific)	5aα
ββ Purpose: marriage	5aβ
ε Act: makes new drinking bout	5b
αα Recipients	5bα
ββ Duration: 6 days (+1)	5bβ
γγ Place: court	5bγ
b) Description (= luxury)	6-8
α Decor	6a
αα being decorated	6aα(1)
ββ with fine linen, flax	6aα(2-4)
γγ tied white/purple cords	6aβ
δδ on gold/silver studs	6aγ

β Hall: pillar   6b
    αα marble   6bα
    ββ stone   6bβ
γ Furniture: couches   6cα
    αα of gold   6cα(2)
    ββ & silver   6cα(3-4)
δ Hall: pavement   6c
    αα of emerald   6cβ
    ββ pearl   6cγ(1-2)
    γγ marble   6cγ(3-5)
ε Furniture (?)   6d
    αα couches/beds   6d(1-3)
    ββ flowers   6d(4-5)
    γγ roses spread around   6e
ζ Service/drinking vessels   7ab
    αα gold & silver   7a
    ββ cupstand (worth 30,000
        silver talents [!])   7b
η Drinking   7c-8
    αα much sweet wine   7cα
        which king also drinks   7cβ
    ββ no pre-set limits   8a
    γγ so king willed it   8b
    δδ dual command of king   8c
        α1 to do his will   8cα
        β1 & will of guests   8cβ
c) Statement: expansion (intro of Queen Astin)
    & women's drinkfest   9
    α Transition (καί)   9aα(1)
    β Subject: Queen Astin   9aα(2-4)
    γ Action: hosts drinkfest   9aβ
    δ Indirect object: the women   9bα
    ε Place: king's palace   9bβ
2) Complication minor: Astin disobeys king   10-12
    a) Time and setting   10aα
    α Time: day 7   10aα
    β Setting: king 'high'   10aβ

γ1 Reasons (dual)   17ab
    α2 her words have spread   17a
    β2 she resisted king   17b
δ1 Result (analogy)   17c-18
    α2 as she did to king   17c
    β2 so wives will dare   18a
      to dishonor husbands   18b
ββ Proposed plan/antidote   19-20
    α1 protocol of politeness   19aα
    β1 publish (royal decree)   19aβ
    γ1 as Medo-Persian laws   19bα
    δ1 let it not be altered   19bβ
    ε1 queen must be banished   19cα
    ζ1 replaced by a better woman   19cβ
    η1 Manner   20a
      α2 let law be heard   20aα
      β2 however he decides   20aβ
        (or: whatever he does)
γγ Result   20b
    α1 wives will honor   20bα
    β1 from poor to rich   20bβ
4) Resolution minor: statement: verdict   21-22
  a) speech pleased king and all   21a
  b) king did as Muchaeus said   21b
  c) sent (decree) throughout land   22a
    α to each province   22bα
    β in each language   22bβ
  d) Purpose: men to be respected   22c
b. Search for queen: Esther crowned & new feast;
concluding report   2.1-23
  1) Exposition minor: king's anger subsides   1a
  a) transition: ('After . . . ')   1aα
  b) king ceases from anger   1aβ
  2) Complication minor: king mentions Astin no more   1b
  a) bearing in mind her words   1bα
  b) & how he condemned her   1bβ
  3) Plan minor: proposal/expansions/execution   2-16
  a) Proposal: speech of servants   2-4a
    α Introductory quotation formula   2a

L Text

αα of gold   7aα
ββ each different   7aβ
η Drinking   7b-8
αα royal wine   7bα
ββ which king also drinks   7bβ
γγ according to law   8a
δδ Reason: king's order   8b
α1 to do   8bα
β1 will of guests   8bβ
c) Statement: expansion: intro of Queen Ouastin:
women's drinkfest   9
α Transition (καί)   9aα(1)
β Subject: Queen Ouastin   9aα(2-4)
γ Act: hosts big drinkfest   9aβ
δ Indirect Object: all women   9bα
ε Place: king's palace   9βb
2) Complication minor: Ouastin disobeys king   10-12
a) Time and setting   10a
α Act: came to pass   10aα(1-2)
β Time: day 7   10aα(3-6)
γ Setting: king 'high' on wine   10aβ
b) Act: tells servants   10b
c) Object: to bring Queen Ouastin   11aα
α to συμπόσιον   11aβ
β with crown (royal garb?)   11bα
d) Purpose: (to show her) to his army   11bβ
e) Reaction: Ouastin   12
α does not will   12aα
β to do king's will   12aβ
γ by eunuchs   12aγ
f) Results (dual)   12bc
α when king hears   12bα
β that Ouastin disobeyed   12bβ
γ he is much grieved   12cα
δ & his anger burns   12cβ
3) Plan minor: king calls; council advises;
trial in absentia   13 14,16,18,20

a) king summons wise & lawyers   13
  α Intro. quotation formula = summons   13a
  β Indirect speech = accusation   13b
    αα Indirect question   13bα(1-2)
    ββ Object: to queen   13bα(3-4)
    γγ Reason = accusation   13bβγ
      α1 she doesn't will   13bβ
      β1 to do king's will   13bγ
b) council (3) convenes   14
  α rulers come   14aα
    αα of Persians   14aβ(1)
    ββ & Medes   14aβ(2-3)
  β intimates (who see king)   14b
  γ officials (sit in palace)   14c
                   [no v. 15]
c) Counsellor Bougaios' speech   16,18,20
  α Introductory quotation formula: advised   16aα
  β Speech proper   16aβ,18,20
    αα Effects of Ouastin's 'crime'   16aβ-18
      α1 Object 1: not king only   16aβ(1-4)
      β1 Subject: Ouastin   16aβ(5-8)
      γ1 Object 2: also princes   16bα
        α2 of Persians   16bβ(1)
        β2 & Medes   16bβ(2-3)
      δ1 Object 3: all peoples   16cα
      ε1 her 'crime' spread   16cβ
      ζ1 that she disobeyed   16cγ(1-2)
      η1 king's decree   16cγ(3-6)
                   [no v. 17]
    ββ Proposed plan/antidote   18,20
      α1 Protocol: politeness (2)   18a
        α2 if good   18aα(1-3)
        β2 to our lord   18aα(4-6)
        γ2 & pleasing   18aβ(1-2)
        δ2 to him   18aβ(3-5)
      β1 publish (royal decree)   18bα(1)
      γ1 Addressees   18bα(2-5)β
        α2 all provinces   18bα(2-5)
        β2 all nations   18bβ

δ1 let it be known — 18cα

ε1 she refused king's word — 18cβ

ζ1 royalty given to better woman — 18d

[no v. 19]

η1 Manner — 20a

α2 let her be shown — 20aα(1-2)

β2 to be obedient — 20aα(3)

γ2 to king's voice — 20aβ

γγ Results (2) — 20b

α1 Subj./Act: he/it will benefit — 20bα

β1 Object: all kingdoms — 20bβ

γ1 Subject/Act: wives give — 20cα

δ1 Object (2) — 20cβγ

α2 honor/glory — 20cβ(1-3)

β2 to husbands — 20cβ(4-6)

γ2 great & small — 20cγ

4) Resolution minor: statement: verdict — 21

a) speech pleased king — 21a

b) king did so readily — 21b

b. Search for queen: Esther crowned
& new feast — 2.1-2,4-5,7-9,14,17-18

1) Exposition minor: king forgets Ouastin — 1

a) Transition: ('And thus') — 1aα(1-2)

b) Summary: (impersonal) it stood — 1aα(3)

α re Ouastin's memory — 1aβ

β & what she did — 1bα

γ Object: to King Assueros — 1bβ

2) Plan minor: new (?) council advises king:
proposal /expansions/execution — 2,4-5,7-9,14

a) Proposal: servant speech — 2-4a

α Introductory quotation formula — 2aα

β Speech proper (3) — 2aβ-4b

αα search for virgin beauties — 2aβ

ββ entrust to eunuch Gogaios — 2bα

γγ guard of women — 2bβ

δδ whoever pleases king — 4a

εε reigns instead of Ouastin — 4b

γ Result: search begins quickly — 4c

η Manner (for Esther): evening: taken in;
    morning: released

(or: Digression [for all virgins])	14
3) Resolution minor: results (3)	17-18
a) Result (of 'contest'): Esther wins	17a
α Transition	17aα(1)
β king examined all virgins	17aα(2-8)
γ Esther's success	17aβb
αα appears outstanding	17aβ
ββ finds favor & mercy	17bα
γγ with him	17bβ
b) Coronation: king acts	17c
α king puts crown	17cα
β on Esther's head	17cβ
c) Celebration: marriage [no summary statement]	18
α Act: king celebrates	18aα
β Object: marriage of Esther	18aβ(1-4)
γ Manner: elegantly	18aβ(5)
d) Gift to empire (to cause celebration)	18b
α makes release (tax?, holiday?)	18bα
β to all provinces	18bβ

The fulfillment of the dream continues in good narrative fashion. The activity of Mordecai in pursuing the dream is temporarily laid aside for preparation within the confines of the court, where much of the dream's outcome will take place.

While the general thrust of the 'Setting' (o´ 1.4-5 // L 1.2-5) is similar in both texts, notable differences exist:

1.   o´, incorporating the common transitional phrase 'and it came to pass after these things', proceeds awkwardly, with Artaxerxes appearing at first blush to be a new character (οὗτος ὁ Ἀρταξέρξες cannot be understood as 'the same Artaxerxes who...')—it appears that existing sections have been joined, since there is no reason for this kind of biographical introduction unless a new character is being introduced—and L creates the same question, even with its straightforward syntax, and it *stands farther from MT than o´* (the power motif, of course, heightens plot tension, in that the destiny of Mordecai ['and his people', A 18] will be in the king's hand);

2.   L adds 'great king' after Artaxerxes/Ahasuerus (cf. A 1), while o´ omits this appellative,

3.   L gives more definitive boundary designations, 'from India to Ethiopia' (cf. MT), while o´ has only 'from India';

4. o′ puts the throne of 'this Artaxerxes' in Sousa, parallel to the opening biography (A 1-2), while L omits the reference to Sousa here, but includes it in the later description of the royal feast (2.5);
5. o′ carefully notes the time frame as specific ('the third year'), while L gives only a general reference ('when Ahasuerus sat upon his royal throne');
6. o′ enumerates the guests of the feast with an extended list ('friends, and other nations, and to the nobles of the Persians and Medes and the chief of the satraps'), whereas L's feast serves 'the chiefs of the court of the Persians and Medes, and the chiefs of districts', with 'all the city of Sousa' only enjoying the action later;
7. further divergencies occur regarding the motivation for the feast, with o′ offering both the reason of showing the kingdom's wealth and power and the reason of celebrating a marriage, while L offers the unique 'celebrating his deliverances' (τὰ σωτηρία—from the assasination plot? or from war?);
8. o′ states that the second feast lasts six days, then has a seventh (more reminiscent of Ugaritic and Hebrew counting patterns), while L directly states 'seven days';
9. the second feast is characterized by drinking and as being 'not according to the appointed law' (not under the restrictions of court drinking rules?) in o′, whereas L has the banquet 'according to law'.

The 'Description' of the palace (1.6-8 in both texts) is similar but not congruent:

1. o′ has the fine hangings on 'parian marble' pillars, a detail which is omitted in L;
2. L has the awning connected to 'gilt marble' (= parian marble?);
3. o′ has both 'gold and silver couches', while L only has gold;
4. o′ describes the pavement as 'emerald stone, and of pearl, and of parian stone', while L only has emerald;
5. o′ has the roses as worked upon the coverings, while L is less specific;
6. o′ is more specific about drinking vessels, labelling them as of gold, silver and carbuncle, even giving the specific value of the carbuncle cup, whereas L has them only of gold and indicates each as being different.

One has the distinct impression that the account of o′ is that of an eye-witness, while L is not. At least o′ wants the reader to be aware of the greatness of the king's palace by indicating very specifically the grandeur of the surroundings. L is likewise hopeful that the reader will see the majesty of the palace, but from a more general vantage point.

In the 'Statement' (1.9), the women's drinkfest is introduced in both texts by the transitional καί. The movement of both is parallel, with the exception of the queen's name (Astin in o′, but Ouastin in L).

Now to the 'Complication Minor' (1.10-12). At the point where the king commands his servants to fetch the queen, o′ lists the names of the eunuchs with an interesting twist (Aman is included!), whereas L leaves the servants unnamed. One has to notice the degree of intensity that o′ strives for in order to draw the reader into the plot. The inclusion of Aman with the eunuchs involves real irony. It works to strengthen the fear of the reader that Aman will be able to accomplish the evil he has planned. Also note that, if L is later than o′, it makes little sense to delete the PNN; if L is earlier, one can understand that L has not yet 'developed' the only secondarily important names.

There are some further differences in the calling of the queen and in the king's vexation at her refusal to come:

1. in o′, the calling for the queen is stated as being to install her as queen (an annual ritual?), to crown her, and to show off her beauty, while in L it is just to show her to the army (sexual overtones);
2. o′ has ἐλυπήθη ('vexed' or 'grieved') and ὠργίσθη ('angry')—a double expression is found here in MT, but the Greek of o′ is smooth—while L has ἐλυπήθη σφόδρα ('greatly vexed') plus ὀργὴ ἐξεκαύθη ἐν αὐτῷ ('anger burned in him'), which sounds Semitic in its closeness here to MT.

In the 'Plan Minor' (1.13-20), when the king convenes his counsellors to determine the proper course of action, the following differences may be noted:

1. o′ refers to the counsellors as φίλοι ('friends'), while L has σοφοί ('wise men'), a Hellenistic versus Semitic color;
2. in o′ the counsellors are named, while in L they all remain anonymous, save one Bougaios (credited with showing the king the ramifications of the queen's actions), who is Muchaeus in o′;
3. the character descriptions of the counsellors differ, in that o′ has 'those near the king' (οἱ ἐγγὺς τοῦ βασιλέως), while L has the more Semitic 'those who see the king's face' (οἱ ὁρῶντες τὸ πρόσωπον τοῦ βασιλέως);
4. while the plot is identical and the 'crime' is ἀδικέω in both texts, the language and tone differ in such a way as to make a single *Vorlage* for o′ and L unlikely:
   a. o′ uses the legal-sounding 'necessary to do' (δεῖ ποιῆσαι) in relation to sentencing her, while L has only the storylike 'what to do' (τί ποιῆσαι);
   b. in o′ the legal language of indictment is found twice in οὐκ εἰσήκουσεν αὐτοῦ Αστιν κτλ. (1.12) and in οὐκ ἐποίησεν τὰ ὑπὸ τοῦ βασιλέως προσταχθέντα διὰ τῶν εὐνούχων ('things commanded by the king through the eunuchs', 1.15), whereas L, with only one statement, leans toward personal ethos rather than legality, with μὴ τεθεληκέναι αὐτὴν ποιῆσαι τὸ θέλημα τοῦ βασιλέως ('her not having consented to do the king's will').

The viewpoint of both texts appears quite different. LXX gives more detail and is thus more discursive and flowery (perhaps in good Alexandrian style). Does one detect that L, with obvious storytelling economy, preserves an earlier form of Esther, and/or intends to stir the hearts of his Jewish readers?

The speech of counsellor Muchaeus/Bougaios differs between the two texts in these respects:

1. in o´, Muchaeus speaks directly, while L has the speech only indirectly (introduced by λέγων);

2. the queen's crime in o´ extends beyond the court to 'all the rulers and princes of the kingdom', while L has 'the rulers of the Persians and Medes' (o´ seems to be more history-oriented vis-à-vis L's ethnic and socio-political emphasis, as L marks the distinction between foreign peoples and the Jews in this story);

3. o´ has the queen 'resist the king' (ἀντεῖπεν τῷ βασιλεῖ), while L softens to 'she refused the word (command) of the king' (ἠθετηκυῖα τὸν λόγον τοῦ βασιλέως Ουαστιν);

4. o´ specifically details the possible effect of the queen's 'crime', that the wives of the princes of Persia and Media will rebel against their husbands in similar fashion, whereas L only implies a copy-cat rebellion by noting the story has leaked to the populace at large (L says that the queen has wronged the princes in her crime, but the wrong may be in undermining their authority in the eyes of the general public).

The chief counsellor now proposes a plan of action (o´ 1.19-20 // L 1.18-20). With characteristic protocol he gives it to the king. It involves a decree to the entire kingdom, announcing and condemning the queen's 'crime' and giving official notice that she is to be replaced. The differences are:

1. o´ specifies the royal decree to be in accord with the laws of the Medes and the Persians (i.e., 'let him not alter it'), while L refers to the decree simply as a letter;

2. o´ generalizes the content of the decree in two items—the queen is prohibited (sexual?) access to the king (καὶ μὴ ἄλλως χρησάσθω) and she is to be replaced—whereas L's two items are that the crimes of the queen are to be published and she is to be replaced (both indicate the decree is to be widely published).

With regard to the first of these points, it may be commented that o´ casts the speech in more legal terms, the language of the court. It is difficult to say which is earlier. L moves quickly to the main plot, while o´, in introducing the legal-sounding phrase here, establishes that motif early on. On balance, it seems L would retain this motif if it were the later text. L may evidence the hand of someone telling or slanting the story for the purpose of drawing national and cultic lessons from it, perhaps evidencing less interest in reporting the minutiae of the events themselves.

The proposed outcome or 'Result' (v. 20b in both texts) is heightened in L. In o′ it is said that benefit will come to husbands, in that all wives will honor their husbands, while L additionally says that the king will benefit the entire kingdom; that is, he will appear to all as a good, benevolent king (note 'from poor to rich' = 'all'). L is more rational, and the irony is softer.

In the 'Resolution Minor' (o′ 1.21-22 // L 1.21), the counsellor's speech results in the adoption of his plan. Again, o′ is more specific from a legal standpoint:

1. L has the simple statement that the king liked the proposal and did accordingly, while o′ specifies not only the king's acceptance of the plan, but also its specific outworking:
    a. send a decree to all provinces in the kingdom;
    b. cast the decree in the appropriate, corresponding language of the people in each province;
    c. give the general purpose for the decree, that husbands should be respected by their wives;
2. in o′ the proposal is agreed upon not only by the king, but also by the other princes, whereas in L the king acts independently.

o′ fleshes out the legal–administrative procedures within the court (presumably of interest to uninitiated readers) and heightens the irony of a royal decree needed for Persian husbands to have fear and thus control at home!

As we move into the second part—subsection b (o′ 2.1-23 // L 2.1-18)—of the exposition, it can be seen that the personal results are noted in both texts (namely that the king ceased to view Astin/Ouastin as queen), but that they diverge markedly in the manner by which this is expressed:

1. o′ emphasizes first that the king's anger is pacified, while L has no parallel;
2. o′ takes the activity of forgetting and remembering in a legal sense in v. 1b (the king no longer mentions her [οὐκέτι ἐμνήσθη τῆς Αστιν] because he remembers the things she said and his verdict of condemnation),[9] whereas L uses 'remember' in the covenant (Semitic) sense of Hebrew זכר in covenant

---

9. Feminine subject is to be preferred in light of v. 13, though the reader is never treated to hear Astin's words.

passages of the Pentateuch, Psalms and Second Isaiah (to 'cease to remember'—so the unusual ἔστη τοῦ μνημονεύειν τῆς Ουαστιν—is to sever
covenant ties).[10]

Interestingly, o′ follows the MT in its use of 'remember'. On the one
hand, 'to remember' here may stress the fact that the king remained
firm in his decree against Astin, while 'to forget' (in L) may emphasize
the broken marriage or political contract between the queen and the
king. In all cases (including MT and Jos's embellished explanation where
counsellors advise him to 'cast out memory and love'), the king's
upholding the decree and/or breaking relations with the queen leaves not
only a political void (i.e. the need for a new queen as figurehead of the
female population) but also a personal (sexual?) one . In o′ and MT the
king remembers (= 'longs'), which prompts the court to suggest a
method for replacing the queen. Likewise, in L, the fact that the king
'did not remember the queen' (= officially severed the legal contract/
covenant) prompts the need for a replacement.

Now to the 'Plan Minor' (o′ 2.2-16 // L 2.2-14 [with L vv. 3, 6, and
10-13 lacking]). A new (?) council advises the king, outlining a plan for
him to find a new queen.

In the 'Proposal' (2.2-4a in both texts), the same characteristics distinguish the two texts:

1.   o′ is detailed by additional legal perspectives (the appointment of governors
     in every province, the bringing of the maidens specifically to Sousa, their
     being under the care of appropriate court officials, and the prescription of the
     ritual of purification), while L specifies Gogaios as the one in charge of the
     virgins, but gives no other details;
2.   in o′ the king acts, whereas in L the servants carry out the plan.

In regard to the first point, one could surmise that L did not want to cast
the Gentile court as having any ritual of purification, and thus gives only
the general scheme of seeking virgins, a fact obviously integral to the
plot. L distinquishes the Jewishness of his perspective. Does the author
hint here that only Jews are clean, and all others are unclean?

There follows an 'Expansion' (2.5-7). The plot, in order to continue,
necessitates a refocusing upon Mordecai. For this reason, Mordecai is

10. On זכר in the context of covenant language, see M. Weinfeld, 'Berit', in
TDOT, II, p. 261; *idem*, 'Covenant Terminology in the Ancient Near East and Its
Influence on the West', *JAOS* 93 (1973), p. 194; *idem*, 'The Covenant of Grant in
the Old Testament and the Ancient Near East', *JAOS* 90 (1970), pp. 187ff. I am
indebted to Tim Hegg for these references.

reintroduced with biographical notes. Both texts give his genealogy, tracing him to the tribe of Benjamin. But there are some variations:

1. L only tells us that Esther was related to Mordecai as a niece (omitting her father's name) and adds the fact that Mordecai was faithful in raising Esther (a legal duty?), while o´ is more detailed:
    a. Mordecai is noted as a prisoner brought from Jerusalem by Nebuchadnezzar;
    b. the adopted child, Esther, is more specifically identified as the daughter of Aminadab;
    c. Esther's parents are both described as deceased;
    d. Mordecai's motivation for raising Esther is specifically stated to be that of marriage to her.
2. Both texts describe Esther as beautiful, but L emphasizes this by the additional 'very beautiful and lovely to behold';
3. L adds the anticipatory or summary statement, 'and the maiden was taken into the king's palace', which o´ omits.

The additional facts surrounding the captivity in o´ could perhaps be due to a Hellenistic millieu where specifics of Jewish history might have been less known, and the plus of 'faithful' (πιστῶς) Mordecai (L v. 7aα) may be due to concern for halachic obedience.

The 'Execution' is resumed in o´ 2.8-11 // L 2.8-9. The manner in which the search for virgins is worked out is extended in o´, but only summarized in L. The result of L is marked: only the information specifically necessary regarding Esther is included. Further, the detailed custom of purification outlined in o´ is absent from L. If L is later than o´, as commonly assumed, then L may have omitted material in order to cast the Gentile court as not having commendable laws which even approach the Jewish attitude of cleanliness and purification. If L is earlier than o´ the same possible cant exists if these purification details existed in an earlier Semitic *Vorlage*. With L earlier than o´, the additional possibility exists that the legend-like motif of a year-long cleansing was not yet available. The variations are:

1. o´ lists Gai as specifically in charge of overseeing the virgins in Sousa, while L makes no mention of such an official here, having previously identified Gogaios (v. 1; cf. Gog in Ezekiel 38) in this capacity;
2. o´ has Gai giving Esther the things necessary for purification, while L has no equivalent;
3. o´ notes that Esther did not relate her nationality to the officials (anticipating the plot), while L makes no mention of this;
4. o´ notes Mordecai's continuing 'faithfulness' to Esther and his concern for her welfare (v. 11), which L does not mention;

5. o′ specifically details twelve months for purification (six months relating to myrrh and six months relating to spices and feminine hygiene), for which L has no parallel;

6. o′ tastefully outlines the specific procedure of how a virgin is tested by the king (going from one apartment to the king in the evening, then leaving in the morning to a second apartment to await the king's decision), while L only vaguely notes the evening/morning aspect of the procedure;

7. o′ gives specific details as to Esther (her genealogy is repeated, her attendance to the instructions of the eunuch is noted, her purification time is fulfilled, her acceptance in the eyes of all is recorded, and so is the specific time of her going in to the king—the twelfth month of the seventh year of the king's reign [cf. Hebrew 'tenth month'), while L compresses all of this into one statement, noting only that Esther found favor (χάριν) and mercy (ἔλεος) in his eyes;

8. o′ has 'the king loved Esther' (καὶ ἠράσθη ὁ βασιλεὺς Εσθηρ), whereas L has the less personal 'and the king married Esther' (καὶ ἤγαγεν ὁ βασιλεὺς τὸν γάμον τῆς Εσθηρ).

The two accounts portray differing viewpoints of the marriage: o′ is more Greek; L more orthodox/Jewish. o′ has a sexual sense in ἐράω, which translates the Hebrew אהב. אהב is translated by ἐράομαι at only two other places: 1 Esd. 4.24 and Prov. 4.6 (both may be seen in a conjugal sense, though less so in the latter). Normally, the Hebrew would express sexual intercourse with ידע, though Ugaritic texts employing the root 'hb[11] lend a sense of sexuality to אהב. It appears very probable that o′ simply translated the MT (or its *Vorlage*) at this place, using a word which would allow the idea of sexual relations. On the other hand, L seems predisposed to keep the text from suggesting outright that Esther had sexual relations with the king. L gives the more formal (legal?) expression for marriage, not found elsewhere in the LXX, ἄγειν τὸν γάμον.[12]

11. G. Wallis, 'אהב, III', *TDOT*, I, pp. 107ff. For the Ugaritic root '*hb*, see *UT* 51.IV.39; Anat.III.4; 67.V.18. Citing Quell and Hirshberg, Wallis presents a translation of Herdner's *CTA* 4[II AB].IV-V.38-39. which seems preferable to Driver's (*Canaanite Myths and Legends*, p. 97), 'Truly, the male organ of King El will have intercourse with thee, the love of the bull will stimulate thee', where Ugaritic *yd* is a euphemism for penis, much like Isa. 57.8 and the Hebrew use of יד. It may well be that in a context of conjugal relationship, אהב carries with it a sexual overtone. It would certainly appear that the LXX translator(s) thought so, in employing ἐράομαι to translate אהב. The form ἠράσθη is not found elsewhere in the LXX. This reference is again due to the kindness of Tim Hegg.

12. This unexpected fact can be verified by comparing Hatch and Redpath's *Concordance* with Liddell and Scott.

In regard to point 3 above, it appears that L intends Esther to be viewed by the readers as thoroughly Jewish throughout the narrative. On this view, to have her concealing her Jewishness would go contrary to the author's (apologetic and homiletical?) purpose. The only specifically Jewish element in o´'s plus is Esther's genealogy; all other elements can be understood as good narrative backgrounding technique, akin to the Homeric type described by Auerbach.[13]

The 'Coronation' and 'Celebration' of Esther (2.18 in both texts) varies. The o´ text once again fully expands the details, while L is nearly silent:

1. o´ mentions a banquet in Esther's honor, for seven days, while L has no such mention;
2. o´ emphasizes the fact that Esther did not disclose her ethnic origins, and that she remained faithful to her 'manner of life' (= Hellenistic ἀριστεία, or Jewish laws of cleanliness, purification, diet, etc?), while L has no equivalent at this point;[14]
3. o´ has an entire account of an assassination attempt by two of the king's chamberlains, Mordecai discovers the plot, informs Esther, she informs the king, and the two are executed, but all this is lacking in L;
4. o´ has the king officially recording a commendation for Mordecai (as a result of the thwarted attempt on the king's life), for which L has no parallel.

The o´ text seems particularly tangled at this point. This second assassination account, entirely lacking in L, is too close to the first account in section A not to be seen as a near duplicate—but, as explained above, o´ intends them to be different. The question of whether one or the other is original in EG (o´ has a surplus), or whether both are original (L is defective), will be treated in Chapter 4 of this study. The labels in the microstructure attempt to account for the text as it stands.

2. *Complication (LXX 3.1-15 and B 1-7)*

As one crosses the time bridge of 3.1, found in all four texts, the ground becomes narratively smooth and the action rises. The king promotes Aman, who is then provided with a brief biography, and the ancient reader is alerted by the ancestry: (H)amedatha the Bougaian. In case one's genealogical recall needs tuning in this area, EH and Jos ring in

---

13. E. Auerbach, *Mimesis* (Princeton, NJ: Princeton University Press, 1974), ch. 1 *passim*.

14. One wonders if the Messianic Secret motif might be somehow related to Jews in Diaspora and this secrecy element regarding both Mordecai and Esther.

the changes with chilling force: Amalek! 'The Amalekite race' (Jos) transports one to the first enemy of Israel in the exodus (Exod. 17.8ff.), the prophesied tyrant (Num. 24.7), and the dreadful incident with Agag (1 Sam. 15.8) which triggered the fall of King Saul. L, at least in MS 93, has Γωγαιον, the eschatological Gog of Ezekiel 38–39.

In v. 2a the king has ordered all to worship Aman. From this background and introduction the tension comes to the fore in v. 2b: Mordecai refuses to worship. One must hear the resonance with Astin's refusal to obey the king—the conflict/complication has begun. The tension mounts as Aman plans a way to avenge himself: the narrative content regarding his plan, including his 'decree of death', carries through section B to 3.14. The story then focuses on Mordecai, thus beginning another unit. The progress in L is similar, but note the differences between o´ 3.14–4.1 and L 3.19–4.1.

o´ *Text*

2. COMPLICATION: King Promotes Aman (Who Provokes	
Crisis) and Approves Pogrom Empire-Wide	3.1-15
a. Exposition: Aman's promotion & results	1-2a
1) Transition: passage of time	1aα
2) Promotion proper & Aman's biography	1aβb
a) Artaxerxes promotes him (1st verb)	1aβ
b) Aman's biography (Amalek/Bougai)	1bα
c) Promotion (2nd verb)	1bβ
d) Promotion (3rd verb): above friends	1bγ
3) Result: all in court bow to him	2aα
4) Reason: so king commanded	2aβ
b. Complication: hero/villian confrontation	2b-5
1) Mordecai's 1st refusal (1 act)	2b
2) First reaction of co-workers (speech)	3
a) Quotation formula & introduction of workers	3a
b) Appeal-speech proper	3b
α Vocative: O Mordecai	3bα
β Question: why disobey?	3bβ
c) Frequency of reaction: daily	4aα
3) Mordecai's 2nd refusal (resoluteness)	4aβ
4) Second reaction of coworkers (report)	4bc

a) Act: they inform Aman   4bα
b) Object: Mordecai's words of resistance   4bβ
c) Addition: Mordecai reveals he is a Jew   4c
5) Aman's reactions: confirmation & anger   5
   a) 1st: witnesses Mordecai disobey (sensual)   5a
   b) 2nd: great anger (emotional)   5b
c. Plan (of villain): Aman plots pogrom empire-wide:
conception, preparation, proposal, approval
& initial execution   6-15a
  1) *Conception*: 'final solution': 3rd reaction
    (volitional): kill all in Artaxerxes' land   6
  2) *Preparation*/Decree (council vote?): lots cast to find
    pagan polytheistic propitious pogrom point (2 acts)   7
   a) Act: Aman's decree (by vote/die?)   7aα
   b) Date: king's 12th year   7aβ
   c) Act: casting lot   7bα
   d) Manner: day by day, month by month   7bβ
   e) Purpose: to destroy Mordecai's race   7c
   f) Result: lot fell on 14th of month Adar   7d
  3) *Proposal*: plan presented by prosecutor   8-9
   a) Introductory quotation formula, to Artaxerxes   8aα
   b) Plan proper: speech   8aβ-9
    α Accusations & conclusion   8aβb
     αα a scattered people   8aβ
     ββ with different laws   8bα
     γγ they do not obey king   8bβ
     δδ (therefore) not worthy   8c
    β Prosecutorial request   9
     αα Protocol form   9a
     ββ Request proper: kill all   9b
    γ Incentive/result: money   9c
  4) *Royal approval*: king's dual reaction   10-11
   a) Report of act: transfers ring (power) to Aman   10
    α king removes royal seal   10a
    β gives it to Aman   10b
   b) Royal speech: dual judgments   11
    α Introductory quotation formula   11aα
    β 'have [keep] the money'   11aβ
    γ 'do as you desire'   11b

5) *Execution*: plan begins/*decree* text   12-15a

   a) Preparation of decree   12

      α Action: royal scribes called   12aα

      β Time: 1st month, 13th day   12aβ

      γ Object: (decree) written   12bα(1-2)

      δ Author: Aman in control   12bα(3-5)

      ε Recipients: (2) satraps & rulers   12bα(6-l)

         αα Detail: India to Ethiopia   12bβ

         ββ Detail: 127 provinces   12c

      ζ Manner: in ruler's speech   12dα

      η Validation: in king's name   12dβ

   b) Publication: mail/bookcarriers   13aα

   c) Area: to Artaxerxes' kingdom   13aβ

   d) Contents: description   13bc

      α Act: annihilate   13bα(1)

      β Object: Jewish race   13bα(2-5)

      γ Duration: one day   13bβ(1-3)

      δ Time: 12th month (Adar)   13bβ(4-8)

      ε Reward: take booty   13c

   e) Contents: *decree* documentation   B 1-7

     [shown in detail later in this study]

   f) Distribution (dual)   3.14

      α copies of decree issued in every province   14a

      β order given to nations   14bα

   g) Purpose: ready 11 months ahead   14bβ

   h) Compliance   15

      α matter was hastened   15aα

      β & at Sousa   15aβ

6. Reactions: (dual)   15b

   a) king & Aman beginning to drink   15bα

   b) Sousa in confusion   15bβ

L Text

2. COMPLICATION: King Promotes Aman (Who Provokes
Crisis) and Approves Pogrom Empire-Wide   3.1-13

   a. Exposition: Aman's promotion & results   1-2a

     1) Transition: passage of time   1aα

     2) Promotion proper (3) & Aman's biography   1aβb

α Mordecai	5cα(4-5)
β & all his people	5cβ
c) in 1 day	5cγ
2) Further reactions (seeing Mordecai refuse?)	6
a) Aman agitated	6aα
b) disturbed in wrath	6aβ
c) becomes red (in face)	6bα
d) fires?/banishes? Mordecai	6bβ
3) *Proposal*: prosecutor presents plan	
(= 1st half of dialog)	6c,8-9
a) Introduction	6c
α with evil heart	6cα
β speaks to king	6cβ
γ evil about Israel	6cγ
b) Introductory quotation formula	8aα(1)
c) Indictment & plan: speech	8aα(2-8)-9
α Accusations	8aα(2-8)βbc
αα 'a scattered people'	8aα(2-8)
ββ warlike & disobedient	8aβ
γγ with different ways	8bα
δδ not having your ways	8bβ,δ
εε O king	8bγ
ζζ known by all as evil	8cα
ηη setting aside your decrees	8cβ
θθ to diminish your glory	8cγ
β Prosecutorial request	9
αα Transition: therefore	9aα(3)
ββ Protocol (dual)	9a
α1 if good	9aα
β1 & decision is good	9aβ
γγ Request proper	9b
α1 give nation to me	9bα(1-4)
β1 for destruction	9bα(5-6)
γ Incentive/result: money	9bβγ
αα I will give	9bβ
ββ 10,000 silver talents	9bγ

[v. 10 follows after v. 11]

4) *Royal* approval: king's triple reaction (= 2nd half of dialog); statement (= author interruption)	11,10

a) Royal speech: dual judgments 11

    α Introductory quotation formula 11aα

    β 'have [keep] the money' 11aβ

    γ to the people 11bα

    δ do as you desire 11bβ

b) Statement of act: transfer ring (power) to Aman 10a

    α king removes royal seal 10aα

    β gives it to Aman 10aβ

c) Royal speech resumed (2) 10aγbc

    α Introductory quotation formula 10aγ

    β write to all lands 10bα

    γ & seal [decree] 10bβ

    δ for none will reverse seal 10c

[here follows v. 7]

5) *Religious preparation* for date of decree: lots cast to

find pagan polytheistic propitious pogrom point (2 acts) 7

    a) Act: Aman goes to gods 7aα

    b) Purpose: to learn day of death 7aβ

    c) Act 2: casts lots 7bα

    d) Date: 13th day; Adar/Nisan (sic) 7bβ

    e) Purpose 1: to kill 7cα(1)

    f) Object 7cα(2-4)βγ

        α all Jews 7cα(2-4)

        β male & female 7cβ

    g) Purpose 2: to plunder young 7cγ

[here follows v. 13]

6) *Execution*: plan begins: distribution; *decree* text 13-19

    a) Distribution of decree 13

        α Act: (Aman = implied author) hastens 13aα

        β Act 2: gives 13aβ

        γ (Object: decree) —

        δ to swift horsemen 13b

    b) Contents: *decree* documentation 14-18

    [shown in detail later in this study]

    c) Distribution of decree (continued) 19

        α in Sousa 19aα

        β was published 19aβ

        γ this decree 19b

The following differences may be noted in the 'Exposition' and 'Complication' (3.1-5 in both texts):

1. in o´ the refusal of Mordecai to bow to Aman is identified as repeated for a period of time ('daily'), while L has no such detail;
2. in o´ the eunuchs approach Mordecai twice regarding his failure to obey the king's command regarding Aman, while in L Mordecai's refusal issues in his revealing his Jewishness (L is simply more compact at this point);
3. o´ describes Aman as angry at the report of Mordecai's defiance, while in L the anger of Aman is heightened by the additional phrase 'his wrath burned in him'.

This last plus of L is Semitic in its flavor (see Deut. 29.20; 2 Kgdms 24.1; Pss. 77[78].38; 88[89].46 etc.). Note that this same expression has occurred already in L at 1.12 (most interestingly, a variant in o´ at 1.12 includes the same expression) and that L adds 'in one day'—also Semitic in flavor—as part of Aman's plan to exterminate the Jews, while o´ puts no such description upon Aman's plan. Perhaps here L is reminiscent of the dream in section A, and echoes the phrase 'a day of darkness and gloom' in the phrase 'in one day', or else L anticipates the edict about to be described, in which a day for the execution of the nation is set.

The 'Plan' outlined by Aman is now introduced (3.6-13). L continues to stress the anti-Semitic viewpoint of Aman in a more dramatic way than o´:

1. o´ describes the Jews as being scattered among the nations, having laws differing from all other nations, and disobeying the laws of Artaxerxes, while L describes them as scattered among all the kingdoms, warlike, disobedient, possessing strange laws, not obeying the laws of the king, being reckoned by the nations as wicked, and disregarding Ahasuerus' commands in order to diminish the glory of the king (the more strident anti-Semitism in L could, of itself, derive from earlier or later Diaspora times, but would certainly be at home in an audience more Jewish than Hellenistic);
2. o´ simply asks for a decree 'to destroy' the Jews, while in L Aman asks that Jews 'be given to him for destruction' (thus o´ is 'historical', while L is personal/dramatic);
3. L has a plan in which the king gives his ring to Aman and instructs him to seal the letter, noting that no one will go against the king's seal, to which o´ has no parallel;
4. L has Aman inquiring of the gods to determine the date for execution, but this is not paralleled in o´;
5. o´ has the court recorders come in to draft the edict at Aman's command, while L makes no mention of court recorders;

6. in o′ the edict is written on the 13th day of the first month, whereas in L
    Aman casts lots on the 13th of Adar–Nisan.

Considering together points 4 and 5, the court recorders of o′ may be
seen as continuing the descriptive/'historical' tone, while L's inquiry of
the gods continues the personal/dramatic tone—possibly preserving an
ancient element of the story here. In regard to point 6, note L's ambiguity: καὶ βάλλει κλήρους εἰς τὴν τρισκαιδεκάτην τοῦ μηνὸς...
φονεύειν πάντας κτλ. The question is, does this phrase give the time
of his casting lots, the date determined by the lots, or the date hoped for
in the lot casting? Note also L's use of 'Adar–Nisan': Does this preserve
a concern (older than o′'s generic, adaptable term) for the crossover
from Hebrew to Babylonian month names?

Following the decree itself (on which see below) is a notice pertaining
to the publishing of it. The o′ text (vv. 14-15) is much longer at this
point than L (v. 19). o′ tells us that copies were published in every province, the order was specifically given to all nations to prepare for the day
of the decree's execution, the matter was taken up quickly (particularly
in Sousa), the king and Aman drank together festively, and in contrast
the city was troubled. L is much more brief, with only the notification
that the decree was exhibited in Sousa.

The Decree Documentation (LXX B 1-7)

The next unit in the text is usually called 'addition B', but since its
'additive' nature and the 'original' to which it was first appended are
items to be proved, not assumed, I prefer to label it with the neutral
'section' B (likewise the other sections). The text in turn labels the section B material as *epistole*, yet it functions (as most readers would
recognize) as *prostagma* (or synonym): a decree. One is left with a
question of genre classification.

The situation is similar with Josephus. Few would criticize Josephus'
translator, R. Marcus, even if he had not *diatagma* in the preceding sentence (215), for translating the section's opening and only verb γράφει
not as 'writes' but as 'the decree of'. Thus Josephus' text in a sense
uses both 'decree' and 'epistle', and leaves one with a question of terminology.

Can the terms decree and epistle be distinguished, or do they col-
lapse into synonyms? Recent advances in epistolography (both in publication of cuneiform tablets, papyri, ostraca, etc. and in theoretical

understanding)[15] cannot even be summarized here, but salient points can be drawn upon in order to classify sections B and E in o′, and parallels in L.

Although letters are known as far back as the second millenium, one can begin with the Greek phenomenon because most of the investigative work has been done there. Hellenistic letters are extant from roughly 300 BCE to Byzantine times and may be variously classified (see Dahl).[16]

Improving on Exler's standard classification, White[17] suggests a refined, but still fourfold typology: (1) letters of introduction and recommendation; (2) letters of petition; (3) family letters, with a sub-species 'letters from soldiers'; and (4) memoranda. Yet seeing some value in the designation 'official' (Exler), White suggests a subdivision called *diplomatic* or *royal* correspondence for benefactions and other messages which emanate from Hellenistic kings and Roman emperors.[18] Presumably this latter category also contains decrees, edicts, orders, plans and official decisions—categories which may apply to either or both *epistolai* in Esther.

If a classification attempt is to succeed, it must take into account purpose and function. Recent discussion enjoys a broad consensus—if

15. A few examples and the bibliographies therein will suffice. A major publication thrust began with U. Wilckens, *Aegyptische Urkunden aus den Koeniglichen* (later *Staatlichen*) *Museen zu Berlin, Griechische Urkunden* (1895), and B.P. Grenfell and A.S. Hunt, *The Oxyrhynchos Papyri* (London: Egypt Exploration Fund, 1898). Since that time publication has not ceased, with an estimated 25,000 published texts of Roman date and roughly twice that number from the same period still waiting as of 1981 (N. Lewis, *Life in Egypt under Roman Rule* [Oxford: Clarendon Press, 1983], pp. 1-8, cited in J.L. White, *Light from Ancient Letters* [Philadelphia: Fortress Press, 1986], p. 5). For theory in addition to A. Deissmann's works, see the bibliography for Exler, Winter, Welles, Kim and White. For texts and tools, see J.F. Oates, R.S. Bagnall and W.H. Willis, *Checklist of Editions of Greek Papyri and Ostraca* (Chico, CA: Scholars Press, 2nd edn, 1978); J.L. White (ed.), 'Studies in Ancient Letter Writing', *Semeia* 22 (1982). For Semitic examples, see J.D. Whitehead (comp.), 'Handbook of Early Aramaic Letters: Preliminary Presentation', for the Ancient Epistolary Group, SBL Annual Meeting, 1975; D. Pardee and S.D. Sperling (eds.), *Handbook of Ancient Letters* (SBLSBS, 15; Chico, CA: Scholars Press, 1982).

16. N.A. Dahl, 'Letter', in K. Crim (ed.), *IDBSup*, pp. 538-41; cf. the same entry by O.J.F. Seitz in *IDB*, III (1962), pp. 113-15.

17. White, *Light from Ancient Letters*, p. 5.

18. White, *Light from Ancient Letters*, p. 5. My study supports the need for the existence of White's proposed subdivision.

expressed with some variation—regarding the purpose of the ancient letter, its three parts, and their functions. From Deissmann to the present it has been understood that letters serve to take the place of personal conversation—in the words of Koskenniemi, 'to turn *apousia* into *parousia*'.[19] The latter scholar presents letter functions as follows: (1) a demonstration of friendship, *philophronesis*; (2) a mode of spiritual presence in a time of bodily absence, *parousia*; and (3) a conversation, in the sense of an intimate personal relationship, *homilia*. The major function, as it emerges from actual letters, is that of continuing an interpersonal relationship.

The latest definition of letter purpose—one which will serve as an operating definition here—is White's:

> Letter writing was invented because of the writer's need to inform (or to be informed by) those at a distance about something they (or the writer) should know. In the earliest stage of writing, the messages appear to have been official injunctions of a military or diplomatic [or royal?] nature.[20]

The discussion here has focused on the Hellenistic letter, but one needs to be aware that the Esther *epistolai* could derive from the Persian period (where Aramaic was the lingua franca). Recent work by P. Dion demonstrates that *if* the Greeks originated the idea that the familiar letter (the letter of friendship) is the most authentic form of correspondence, they did not invent the letter genre itself. Dion identified

> a number of ancient Near Eastern letters between family members which, though not so selfconsciously literate as the [Greek/Latin] rhetoricians' letters of friendship, are characterized by analogous epistolary sentiments and were written for the enhancement of the correspondents' personal relationship, not out of specific need.[21]

That means that the Esther material could stem from an Aramaic original in the Persian Period.

The question naturally arises whether one is dealing with a Semitic model or a Greek one in EG sections B and E. The application of R.

---

19. H. Koskenniemi, *Studien zur Idee und Phraseologie des griechischen Briefes bis 400 n. Chr.* (Helsinki: Annales Academiae Scientiarum Fennicae, 1956), pp. 18f.

20. White, *Light from Ancient Letters*, p. 192.

21. P. Dion, 'The Aramaic "Family Letter" and Related Epistolary Forms in other Oriental Languages and in Hellenistic Greek', *Semeia* 22 (1982), p. 69.

Martin's 17 criteria[22] for detecting translation Greek (i.e. from a Semitic *Vorlage*) fail to detect Semitic influence in sections B and E. I am compelled to agree with Martin because of the additional discovery in the present study that retroversion is difficult in the extreme. A close comparison of Targum Sheni in these sections leads to the same conviction. I conclude, then, that sections B and E are Greek creations.

Given this conclusion, and given the fact that B and E seem unlike the few available Persian materials (Behistun inscription, examples in Ezra and Chronicles, Aramaic letters from Egypt), structural comparison can now be made with Greek exemplars. The Hellenistic letter typically falls into three structural divisions: opening, body and close, roughly corresponding to salutation, message and farewell. In his 1971 dissertation, 'The Body of the Greek Letter', J. White[23] argued for an analogous tripartite division within the letter body: body opening, body middle, body close. But his recent investigation[24] does not insist on a tripartite body, though numerous examples do exist. White also has abandoned the three terms 'body opening', 'body middle', and 'body close', in order to avoid imposing a too rigid model on material that may fall into two parts, or possibly only one.

Nevertheless, using the above understanding as a guide, one finds three parts in the text at hand (section B). Respecting both the three content divisions (marked by clear transitions) and White's lead, I have decided to use only 'opening', 'middle' and 'close' under 'Body' in order to retain some label for the structure elements found in the text.

Taking the text's term *epistole* seriously and combining that with current terminology, section B exhibits either an 'embedded letter'[25] or an 'embedded decree'. Contrary to the procedure so far, a generic title will be withheld until the discussion following the structure analysis, where a final determination can be made.

Note that for completeness and convenience of presentation, section B

---

22. R.A. Martin, *Syntactical Evidence of Semitic Sources in Greek Documents* (SBLSCS, 3; Missoula, MT: University of Montana Press, 1974).

23. J.L. White, *The Body of the Greek Letter* (SBLDS, 2; Missoula, MT: University of Montana Press, 1972), pp. 7-66.

24. Private communication; and see White, *Light from Ancient Letters*, *passim*.

25. Examples are found in Esther, the Macabbees, Pseudo-Aristeas, Josephus, Eusebius, etc. J.L. White's *Light from Ancient Letters* does not cover this ground, but by private communication he has provided an unpublished paper in this area, entitled 'Royal Correspondence in Pseudo-Aristeas and Parallel Letters in Josephus and Eusebius'. Further work is hoped for.

(o′ B 1-7 // L 3.14-18) will stand outside the sequential indentation, but noted above (in the last structure diagram) is its proper numerical panel and function in the text. In o′ it repeats and expands the 'Contents' panel, and intensifies the major narrative 'Complication' of Esther; in L it stands within a report of distributing horsemen headed to the ends of the empire and the distribution/publication in Sousa. In both texts, it appears to be an insertion into an earlier narrative.

o′ Text of the 'Epistle' (B 1-7)

I. INTRODUCTION: Statement: 'This is a copy'	1a
II. TEXT PROPER	1b-7
A. OPENING	1
1. Titulature	1b
a. Title & addressor: Artaxerxes	1bα
b. Addressees & areas	1bβ
1) Addressees	1bβ(1,12-15)
a) rulers	1bβ(1,12)
b) subordinate governors	1bβ(13-15)
2) Areas	1bβ(2-11)
a) from India to Ethiopia	1bβ(2-7)
b) 127 provinces	1bβ(8-11)
2. Opening proper ('King...writes thus')	1c
B. BODY	2-7
1. Opening: Background: Persian Government, Royal Plan; Circumstances: Council; Prosecutor Aman's Credential 'Letter'; Indictment/Problem	2-4
a. 1st-person report of background: plan	2
1) Manner: how I (king) rule	2aα
a) many nations & whole world	2a
b) not elated by power	2bα
c) with moderation & gentleness	2bβ
2) Intent (3-part plan)	2cd
a) ensure undisturbed lives	2c
b) (future) providing a kingdom	2dα,γ
α civilized	2dβ(1)
β & wholly traversable	2dβ(2-5)
c) re-establish the peace that all want	2e

L Text of the 'Epistle' (3.14-18)

c) uncooperative (hostile)   16cγ(1)

d) laws dispute with all nations   16d

e) & continually evade decrees of the kings   16e

4) Result: government will never reach peaceful stability 16f

2. Middle: Result of Royal Investigation: Decision/Verdict,

Decree   17-18e

 a. Decision/Verdict (negative)   17

  1) Transition (οὖν)   17aα(2)

  2) Decision/verdict proper   17aα(1,3-5)

   a) Act: (we) realizing   17aα(1)

   b) Verdict detailed (Object)   17aα(3-5)bcd

    α people (to be) unusual   17aα(3-5)

    β standing opposed to all   17aβ

    γ foreignize perversity by their laws 17b

    δ resisting/being incorrigible to our decrees 17c

    ε always plotting heinous crimes   17d

   c) Result: monarchy skilfully managed by

   us can't be established   17e

 b. Decree/Sentence (positive)   18

  1) Transition (οὖν)   18aα(2)

  2) Decree/Sentence proper   18aα(1,3)βγbcd

   a) Act: we have decreed   18aα(1)

   b) Sentence detailed: (1st)   18aβγbd

    α The condemned   18aβγ

     αα named to you   18aβ

     ββ in Aman's (accompanying?) letter 18aγ

    β Executioner: Aman's authorization 18b

     αα chief administrator   18bα

     ββ 2nd father   18bβ

    γ Execution   18c

     αα kill completely   18cα

     ββ extent (woman/child)   18cβ

     γγ manner (2)   18cγδ

      α1 by sword   18cγ

      β1 no mercy/sparing   18cδ

    δ Date of execution   18d

     αα 14th day, 12th month   18dα

     ββ this is Adar   18dβ(1-4)

     γγ which is Dystros   18dβ(5-7)

c) Sentence repeated (2nd)	18e
α kill	18eα(1)
β all Jews	18eα(2-4)
γ seize/plunder young	18eβ
3. Close: New Plan; Intended Result	18fg
a. Plan: one-day destruction	18f
1) Transition: (ἵνα)	18fα(1)
2) Object: ones former hostile, now	18fα(2-6)
3) Duration: one day	18fβ
4) End: may all go to hell/hades	18fγ
b. Intended results (2)	18g
1) so from there on	18gα
2) they may be quiet (!)	18gβ
3) cease to thwart our affairs/government	18gγ

Some observations about the text itself as now laid out and a few comparisons with non-biblical material will bring a determination of typicality and hence genre and function.

Opening clues of typicality are the title 'Great King PN', the addressees being all officials (contrast E 1c and parallel καὶ τοῖς τὰ ἡμέτερα φρονοῦσιν, which can extend to all citizens), and finally the lack of epistolary greeting, χαίρειν. 'Almost all papyrus letters have "A to B greeting" as their initial formula and ἔρρωσο as the word of farewell'.[26] But as White also points out, legal texts usually omit greetings and opening phrases of friendship and cordiality (though such is possible where blood relationship or companionship actually existed). The farewell frequently falls out, but frequently included are the date and specification of the official's titles. In the case of known decrees the infinitive χαίρειν disappears and a third-person indicative verb—usually λέγε— serves as the only finite action of the opening. See for example the two edicts of Germanicus which begin with name, titles and 'writes': Γερμα-νικὸς Καῖσαρ Σεβαστοῦ υἱὸς θεοῦ Σεβαστοῦ υἱωνὸς ἀνθύπατος λέγει.[27]

In o´ and L γράφει substitutes for the normal 'official' verb 'says'. Notice the 'Letter of Claudius to the Alexandrians', which itself attests χαίρειν (proper to a letter) after a lengthy list of titles, but is preceded

26. White, *Light from Ancient Letters*, p. 200.

27. A.S. Hunt and C.C. Edgar (eds.), *Select Papyri*. II. *Non-Literary Papyri. Public Documents* (LCL, 1956), pp. 76-77.

by a 'Proclamation' or decree of Lucius Aemilius Rectus: Λούκιος Αἰμίλλιος Ῥῆκτος λέγει.[28] Thus it appears that the preceding decree or edict follows the usual pattern, while Claudius, though a supreme authority, wishes to deal with the Alexandrians on the plane of polite appeal and thus uses the typical greeting of a letter. Other examples can be adduced showing that λέγει belongs with a decree, edict or proclamation.[29]

Moving on to the body, this material in o´ has only three finite indicative verbs, plus a present subjunctive in the final clause; the introductory clause at B 3a stands outside of this count because it is syntactically dependent as a genitive absolute. With γράφει of the opening, there are thus only four major assertions in the entire 239 words of this text (the literary introduction, 'this is a copy', is excluded from both counts—if counted it would add another assertion and seven words). In the case of L, excluding the introduction, the body has the same three finite indicatives but has two subjunctive verbs in the final clauses. Thus with the opening verb there are also only four major assertions, but this time in 244 words. The 'plus' words come mostly from 3.18e, φονεύειν κτλ.—a second killing order.

From the point of view of syntax and content the two instances of οὖν must be considered major transition markers. The first one (B 5aα[2] and parallel) introduces the transition from background to business, or from circumstances to main message. The message has dual elements—called here 'verdict/decision' and 'decree/sentence'. The second 'therefore' (B 6aα[2] and parallel) is resumptive of the first and stands importantly with the major, and final, indicative of the entire unit: 'we have decreed'.

The purpose of the decree is introduced by ὅπως (B 7aα[1]). One could argue that this purpose clause is not a third part of the body, but it can hardly be argued that it does not close the unit under consideration. On the analogy of other letter forms (although not decrees), and relying on the presence of the three conjunctions and the lack of any normal letter close, it is has been chosen here to divide the body into three parts.

Josephus offers a close parallel but in different vocabulary. The verb of the opening is also γράφει. The next finite verb is a duplicate of EG

---

28. Hunt and Edgar, *Select Papyri*, II, pp. 78-79.

29. The standard work in this area, by a Yale University classicist and still unsurpassed, is C.B. Welles, *Royal Correspondence in the Hellenistic Period: A Study in Greek Epigraphy* (New Haven: Yale University Press, 1934).

ἐβουλήθην but is construed as his fulfilled desire of ruling nations, while the point of seeking 'peace and good government' is expressed with a participle. EG's third verb, ἐπέδειξεν, which documents Aman's showing, becomes a participle in Josephus, while the subordinate proposition about understanding διειληφότης, which introduces the verdict, is passed over. The 'we decree' of EG becomes κελεύω, 'I order' (11.217). Another major proposition, βούλομαι, introduces the date for the pogrom, so that Josephus also comes out with four principal assertions. Interestingly, the Jewish historian uses ὅπως—far more common in decrees than L's ἵνα—to introduce the purpose clause (11.219). This last clause has two verbal elements (almost like L): a subjunctive and a participle.

The above, coupled with the lack of the normal letter close, or conversely the abrupt break-off of literary and inscribed decrees, causes the tentative judgment regarding genre to lean away from letter and toward a royal edict.

A further clue toward classification comes from a work by Welles[30] which is still unsurpassed. His collection of 75 texts (76 with the transcription of a fragment in a late footnote) come principally from the Attalid and Seleucid kingdoms, but also from the Asiatic dependencies of the Ptolemaic kings of Egypt and the minor kingdoms of Asia Minor.[31] Most turn out to be written by chancery secretaries to foreign city states. After arrival these letters were inscribed on stone. Suggesting that the formal characteristics divide into two groups, Welles points out that even the official letter to an individual 'was originally in form a private letter'.[32] The second group—an official letter to a community—may have only a statement (sometimes quite long, apparently run-on by modern standards) or may follow the statement with an 'order'.[33] This latter type, addressed to dependent city states, seems dependent on the city decree—a prevalent form of communication between communities. Like a decree, it consists of one long sentence in two parts, an ἐπεί clause clause followed by the statement of a decision, κρίνομεν διὰ ταῦτα.[34]

Welles mentions that a decree's first part comprises a number of

30. Welles, *Royal Correspondence*.
31. Welles, *Royal Correspondence*, p. xxxviii.
32. Welles, *Royal Correspondence*, p. xlii.
33. Welles, *Royal Correspondence*, pp. xlii-xliii.
34. Welles, *Royal Correspondence*, p. xliii.

clauses in at least logical parataxis, and ἐπεί may be supplanted by a participle (an absolute); in the second part κρίνομεν is followed by a purpose clause introduced by ὅπως. The fragment referred to just above, too broken to establish a subject, attests the ἔκρινον verb and the ὅπως conjunction of purpose, but in reverse order![35] At any rate Welles claims two parts for his royal letters, which in no case *constitute* decrees. In four or five cases, however, the letters *mention* real royal edicts; Welles's exemplars, then, must be forwarding or cover letters. While the core of an edict may show up in these letters, unfortunately the edicts themselves are lost. Yet he remarks on decrees (as quoted) from what appears to be his knowledge of actual texts.

At last the comparative material comes close to the EG texts, if more by discussion than example. In addition, even from the limited materials it can be noted that the purpose conjunction, if expressed, either belongs with the edict (thus there are only two parts [Welles]) or it may be classed, when it occurs, as a third part. Therefore one sees either a bipartite form—background plus decree—or a tripartite background, decree and purpose, the latter being chosen here. In regard to the run-on, paratactic style, it may be commented that what seems already 'loaded' in section B becomes almost 'bloated' in section E, so that both texts in both sections amply demonstrate a parataxis often associated with Hellenistic decrees.

Two more points of comparison. First, if some formal typicality may be noted concerning Hellenistic decrees, it is the distinctive opening: βασιλέως προσταξάντος ('by decree of the king'; or loosely, 'a royal edict'), as in BGU 1211 (third century BCE); or again, βασιλέως καὶ βασιλίσσης προσταξάντος ('by decree of the king and queen'), as in BGU 1211 (50 BCE).[36] The form of the opening is title plus decreeing participle. What that means is this: from the examples available so far EG section B texts can be labelled 'Royal Decrees' but they do not conform to Persian decrees (cf Ezra 1; 7; Behistun) and do not seem to be as close to Hellenistic decrees as they do to decrees in the Roman period. Secondly, the few decretory texts available consistently exhibit compactness in a laconic or telegraphic style. One is not so impressed with section B, which, while not chatty, is not spare with qualifiers, especially pro Aman and contra the condemned.

In summary, the evidence points to a decree, but one with more

---

35. Welles, *Royal Correspondence*, p. xxxviii n. 6.
36. Cited by J.L. White in private communication.

narrative diffuseness than official decrees outside the Bible. As for the designation 'epistle', a possible explanation would be the older use in Herodotus meaning 'oral command' or the like.[37] Perhaps as the oral aspect of royal decrees gave way to more frequent writing (with greater availability of papyrus and greater need for record keeping), the word 'epistle' moved with this technology so that its general semantic range included both true letters and genuine decrees.

Clearly the B 'epistle' does not fall within the letter categories of current discussion. Clearly also more study must be done in the area of decrees. For now a classification must be attempted. If a term may be coined to typify the example(s) under discussion, these texts—in both o′ and L—appear to be embedded, (slightly) 'narrativized' royal decrees.

3. *Plan and Two New Complications (LXX 4.1–C/D–5.14)*

The next units constitute a well-known narrative element which frequently follows the *complication* in tales and novellas. When the heroes face the complication they often form a *plan* in order to avoid or solve the conflict. Typically the plan they form runs into one or more *new/further complications*, as Van Seters points out.[38] In o′ the new predicament turns out to be dual, one for Esther and one for Mordecai; L has Esther facing yet a second trial for a total of three. The dual complication for Esther herself is not necessarily evidence of later expansion, and may stem from an early narrator's desire to show that Esther's first survival was no fluke, but due to strong character; other possible implications cannot be explored here.

As with some of the tales of Abraham and narratives of the prophets, the new complications in Esther lead to total impasses which only divine intervention can solve. A predicament or impasse such as these would be called *crisis* in classic literary analysis. But in his discussion of Gen. 12.10-20 Van Seters does not use the term 'crisis'; he also presents different terms and structural categories as well. Granting that his passage lacks the length of Esther, it compares so closely in outline that his terms and structure elements must be looked at here.

According to Van Seters, the Genesis 12 narrative was at first 'clearly

37. Herodotus, 4.10, 6.50, as noted by M.L. Stierwalt, 'A Classified Index of Terms used in reference to Letter-Writing in Greek Literature' (unpublished essay, 1975), cited in White, *Light from Ancient Letters*, p.192 n. 27.

38. J. Van Seters, *Abraham in History and Tradition* (New Haven: Yale University Press, 1975), pp. 169ff.

told for entertainment'; its function was to celebrate the patriarch's cleverness, the beauty and submission of his wife and the faithful help of Yahweh. This story and others like it have a simple structure which, in Van Seters's view, would consist of the following elements:

a. a situation of need, problem or crisis;
b. a plan to deal with the problem (wise or foolish);
c. the execution of the plan with some complication;
d. an unexpected outside intervention;
e. fortunate or unfortunate consequences.[39]

Van Seters points out that this story structure constitutes a self-contained unit and fulfills the requirements of Olrik's ten epic laws.[40] Whether those 'laws' find fulfilment in Genesis or Esther is not a concern here. What does concern this discussion is the difference between content and structure on the one hand and, on the other, Van Seters's use of the terms 'setting' and 'crisis' for what he labels 'part a', ('a situation of need') in his later recapitulation.[41]

The need, problem or crisis is akin to Freytag's 'inciting moment (or action)'. But some cautions must be registered regarding Van Seters's terms. First, the 'setting' he refers to is the same as the narrative analysts' *exposition*. This structural element may or may not present a need/crisis, which in actuality is a matter of content. In a story as compressed as these tales of Abraham, the exposition may present a problem some, most, or even all of the time. But such 'problems' are material and function in diverse ways as background for narrative action. Whether one employs the term 'exposition' (preferable in my opinion) or 'setting' (used by some literary critics), it is best to let this term signify the formal, compositional element, and to let the text's content be described as (mere) background, or as (more tensive) need, problem, or the like. If Van Seters is distinguishing form from content here, his terms do not make it clear.

Similarly, and secondly, the term 'crisis', if it must be used in the *exposition*, has to then be distinguished from the larger narrative *crisis*. Because 'crisis' at this point may introduce confusion, and because 'setting' lends itself to confusion with the form-critical setting in life, the *Sitz im Leben*, these terms have not been chosen here for Esther.

39. Van Seters, *Abraham in History and Tradition*.
40. A. Olrik, 'Epic Laws of Folk Narrative', in A. Dundes (ed.), *The Study of Folklore* (Englewood Cliffs, NJ: Prentice–Hall, 1965), pp. 129-41.
41. Van Seters, *Abraham in History and Tradition*, p. 170.

Thirdly, in the case of Gen. 12.11-13, which Van Seters designates as 'plan', vv. 11bγ-12 actually state a *complication* in the words כי אשה יפת־מראה את והיה כי־יראו אתך המצרים ואמרו אשתו זאת והרגו אתי ואתך יחיו. Of course this flows out of Abraham's fear and foresight; therefore it is potential, not actual. Nevertheless, 'they will kill me' is a *complication*, and a reason for planning, not the plan itself. What follows in v. 13 is a *plan*. A plan is formed and executed after a complication in tales and presumably in longer works. That this plan may run into a further complication for the hero(es) can be accepted; I am indebted to Van Seters for the insight.

Van Seters, however, might insist on not combining plan, execution and new complication(s) in a macro-panel, as has been done in this study. The rationale for doing so is that the new complication takes its significance from the plan (and its execution of course), and whereas plan execution is isolable in the Abraham tale, in Esther it interweaves with first one and then another complication. The conclusion must be that the narrative structure itself should determine the combination into one, or separation into two units. Another clarification is needed: does the divine intervention comprise a structural or a content element? Its repetition in the Abraham tales, the Tower of Babel tale, and others can be mistaken for a (necessary) structural element. Not so. The element itself is *crisis*; how the crisis is created and how it is solved are matters of content. Fate, the gods (the original *deus ex machina*), blind luck, circumstances or the act of some character or Yahweh's intervention— and no doubt many more—have all been used within the *crisis* to pivot it one way or the other.

Again, Van Seters's last element, the consequences, certainly exists in most stories, but in this study the term *dénouement* has been chosen as more appropriate for structure. The positive or negative results contained within the falling action or resolution fall under the rubric of content.

Van Seters's 'part d' ('an unexpected outside intervention') may now be discussed with specific regard to Esther. The first subunit narrates a lament of Mordecai and the people (o′ 4.1-3 // L 4.1-2) upon learning of the death plan. These verses serve as exposition for four speeches. But 'speech' alone is not precise enough here because Mordecai and Esther do not see each other directly; rather they exchange spoken messages through intermediaries. Why these mediated exchanges exist at all, or why the narrator did not develop them into direct dialog and/or encounters between the principal characters, is not clear. The term 'exchange' will serve here to describe the part indirect discourse, part direct, mediated conversation which is distinct from dialog.

The exchanges arrive finally at the same narrative juncture, but they do so in narratively distinct combinations. In o′ the first exchange (4.4) is initiated by servants and comprises only third-person report of commands spoken. L's first exchange is initiated by Mordecai and Esther comes to speech (4.3b). The second exchange in o′ contains reports of speech and a direct speech by Mordecai (4.5-9). On the other hand, L with different content and vocabulary presents the whole segment as speech. The curious statement in v. 6, καὶ ἀπήγγειλεν αὐτῇ τὴν ὀδύνην τοῦ Ισραηλ, may be taken as summary of the preceding speech, or as compliance by the eunuch, in that he carries Mordecai's message to Esther. Based on completion and compliance statements in this text and in o′ and EH, it is understood here as the eunuch's report to Esther, and thus as a closure to this segment of the exchange.

Tension increases with the third exchange as Esther refuses Mordecai's plan for her to intercede (o′ 4.10-12 // L 4.7-8), and with Mordecai's insistence (the rebuttal in o′ 4.13-14 // L 4.9-10). This means that the speeches of the third exchange could be called a 'complication'. Alternatively, because of the brevity, lack of elaboration, quick disappearance of tension between Mordecai and Esther and the continuing greater tension of the death threat, this unit may be expressed in, and grouped under, the more neutral term 'development'. Development, following upon an exposition, may best capsulize material which focuses on character development or ancillary actions in any of innumerable ways, but prepares for important action more than transmitting 'rising action'.

This exposition and development leads to a *result*: (o′ 4.15-17 // L 4.11-12. Both texts show a speech in which Esther acquiesces to Mordecai's plan and a statement of compliance, but this time not the compliance of the messenger; Mordecai accedes to Esther's part of the plan. A title expressing this 'narrative transformation' would be 'Mordecai Proposes to Thwart Death Through Esther'.

o′ Text

III. B. (*continued*)

    3. PLAN & 2 NEW COMPLICATIONS: Heroes' 3-Step

      Plan; 2 Prayers; Entry; Banquets; Aman Plots   4.1–C/D–5.14

      a. Problem discovered & plan proposed: Mordecai

        tries to thwart death by Esther: 4 mediated exchanges   4.1-17

1) Exposition: Mordecai, people learn of plot
& lament bitterly   1-3
   a) Report: Mordecai learns, reacts   1-2
     α Setting: Mordecai, finding plot   1aα(1)
     β Body: 2 reactions   1aα(7-l)-2a
       αα Lament described (2)   1aα(7-l)β
        α1 rips clothes   1aα(7-l)
        β1 dress: sackcloth/ashes   1aβ
       ββ Itinerary (2)   1b-2a
        α1 Departure: to city   1bα(1-7)
        β1 Travel mode: crying   1bα(8)
         α2 cry/yell proper   1bα(8)
         β2 Detail: loud   1bα(9-10)
         γ1 Message: injustice!   1bβ
          α2 genocide threat   1bβ(1-2)
          β2 against innocent   1bβ(3)
         δ1 Arrival: king's gate   2a
       γγ Digression: law of gate   2b
   b) Description: people learn & lament   3
     α Place: where letters issued   3a
     β Act: Jews (learn)   3bα(7-8)
     γ Reaction: lament (2)   3bα(1-6)β
       αα emotional signs (3)   3bα(1-6)
        α1 crying   3bα(1)
        β1 lamentation   3bα(2-3)
        γ1 great mourning   3bα(4-6)
       ββ Physical signs (2)   3bβ
        α1 sackcloth   3bβ(1)
        β1 ashes   3bβ(2-3)
        γ1 Act: they spread   3bβ(4-5)
2) Development: 3 exchanges on plan: problem
reaches Esther; plan proposed by Mordecai;
rejection by Esther   4-14
   a) Statement: 1st exchange, 3rd person: problem
   reaches Esther (part disclosure)   4
     α maids/eunuchs enter/tell Esther   4aα
     β queen's distress   4aβ
     γ she sends to Mordecai (2 purposes)   4b
       αα to clothe Mordecai   4bα

β
β to remove his sackcloth   4bβ

δ he refuses   4c

b) Reports, speech, Mordecai: 2nd exchange by
eunuch Achrathai (indirect discourse; speech):
problem further described (full disclosure),
plan proposed   5-9

α Report   5

αα Act 1: Esther calls Achrathai   5aα(1-5)

ββ Job description   5aα(6-8)β

α1 her eunuch   5aα(6-8)

β1 who waited on her   5aβ

γγ Act 2: sends him   5bα

δδ Purpose: learn facts from Mordecai 5bβ

[no v. 6]

β Report 2: conversation (6)   7-8

αα Mordecai tells what happened   7aα

ββ & the promise   7aβ

α1 Act: promise to pay   7bα(1-2)

β1 Agent: Aman   7bα(3)

γ1 Beneficiary: king   7bα(4-8)

δ1 Amount: 10,000 tally   7bα(9-l)

ε1 Purpose: kill Jews   7bβ

γγ Proof: gives decree copy   8aα

δδ Object: show Esther   8aβ

γ Speech   8bcde

αα Introductory quotation formula   8bα

ββ Speech proper   8bβcde

α1 Command 1: order Esther   8bβ

β1 Message   8bγcde

α2 Command 2: (3) go,
ask king, seek   8bγ(1-7)

β2 Recipient: people   8bγ(8-l)

γ2 Motivation: remember   8c

α3 humble days 8cα(1-4)

β3 I reared you 8cα(5-9)

δ2 Reason: Aman: position
& act against us   8d

α3 2nd to king   8dα

β3 spoke for death   8dβ

α Orders to arrivee: (2) return, saying	15a
β Introductory quotation formula	15b
γ Speech proper	16
αα Order	16a
α1 Commands: hurry, gather & fast	16aα
β1 Prohibitions (2)	16aβ
α2 do not eat	16aβ(1-3)
β2 or drink	16aβ(4-5)
γ2 duration: 3 days & nights	16aβ(6-l)
ββ Self-commitment: Esther/maids	16bα
γγ Acceptance of Mordecai's plan	16bβ
δδ Declaration: self-sacrifice	16c
b) Compliance statement: plan prepared: Mordecai hurries, does as Esther commands	17
b. Plan initiated: Mordecai begins executing plan	
1) 1st step: 2 prayers (Mordecai & Esther) [shown in detail later in this study]	C 1-30
2) 2nd step: Esther's entry to the king; 1st new complication & crisis minor [shown in detail later in this study]	D 1-16

L Text

III. B. (*continued*)	
3. PLAN & 2 NEW COMPLICATIONS: Heroes' 3-Step Plan; 2 Prayers; Entry; Banquets; Aman plots	4.1–5.24
a. Problem discovered & plan proposed: Mordecai tries to thwart death by Esther: 4 mediated exchanges	4.1-12a
1) Exposition: Mordecai, people learn of plot & lament bitterly	1-2
a) Statement: Mordecai, Sousa & Jews learn & react	1
α Mordecai learns all	1a
β Sousa troubled	1b
γ Jews	1c
αα all	1cα
ββ much bitter grief	1cβ
γγ in every city	1cγ

α2 But God will be   9cα

α3 help   9cβ(1)

β3 & salvation   9cβ(2-3)

β2 you & family perish   9d

δ1 Motive: who knows?   10

3) Result: speech & report: Esther agrees to plan
& orders preparation: 4th 'exchange'

(Esther's speech; Mordecai's compliance)   11-12

    a) Introduction & Esther's acceptance speech   11

        α Sending formula   11aα

        β Introductory quotation formula: saying   11aβ

        γ Speech proper   11b-e

          αα Dual command   11b

          α1 proclaim service   11bα

          β1 pray fervently to God   11bβ

        ββ Self-commitment: Esther/maids   11c

        γγ Acceptance of Mordecai's plan   11d

        δδ Declaration: self-sacrifice   11e

    b) Compliance: Plan prepared: Mordecai hurries,

    does as Esther commands   12a

b. Plan initiated: Mordecai begins executing plan

    1) 1st step: 2 prayers (Mordecai & Esther)   4.12b-29

    [shown in detail later in this study]

    2) 2nd step: Esther's entry to the king;

    1st new complication & resolution minor   5.1-12

    [shown in detail later in this study]

The general flow of the 'Problem Discovered and Plan Proposed' (o′ 4.1-17 // L 4.1-12a) is similar in each text, but there are some notable differences:

1. o′ has no mention of Mordecai going to his house upon learning about the decree, though he does in L (in o′ he immediately puts on sackcloth, etc.);
2. in o′ the content of Mordecai's cry is given (implies 'injustice', a reflex of crying המס?), while L omits both the fact and the content of the cry;
3. in o′ Esther's attendants tell her of Mordecai's actions, while in L Mordecai specifically calls a eunuch and sends him to Esther;
4. in o′ all Jews in every province likewise put on sackcloth and ashes—great mourning on the part of the Jews as a whole—to which L has no parallel;

5. both texts have Esther and Mordecai sending mediated messages (see the microstructure for variations, especially regarding the 'truth of the situation', not paralleled in L);
6. the o′ text is more detailed and psychological at this point, showing Esther to be disturbed, giving details of how Mordecai explained the situation to the chamberlain Achrathai, including the devious plot of Aman, while L has no parallel, but moves right to Mordecai's message (speech) to Esther;
7. o′ mentions Achrathai by name five times, in line with the Greek style of foregrounding more than Hebrew, whereas L, more in line with the Hebrew style of backgrounding lesser details, never names the eunuch—not even once.

In regard to the first two points, it may be commented that the element of going home seems more in keeping with an early form of the story. o′ appears to speed up the narrative by skipping this detail and propelling Mordecai into the streets. Yet L speeds the story even more, by not having Mordecai's cry or its content, in order to arrive at the narratively more important exchanges between Mordecai and Esther. Compare Mordecai's 'great and bitter cry' in MT, which however has no narrated content; o′ has either created Mordecai's cry summary, or found it in an Old Greek or pre-MT Semitic tradition. At the literary level, o′, even with its greater drama (words of the cry) appears closer to the Greek style pointed out by Auerbach,[42] because details are filled in—less is left to the reader's imagination. L seems simpler, more interested in plot progression. Point 4 above also shows less being left to the imagination in o′, yet the drama is not much heightened; if L addresses a Jewish audience, readers would identify more and would assume that their relatives/ancestors mourned.

Note that v. 6 is missing in the o′ text. The variant listed in Rahlfs suggests that v. 6 may have contained a simple assertion that Achrathai went to where Mordecai was.

The speech of Mordecai to Esther via the eunuch (o′ 4.8 // L 4.4-5) is parallel in the two texts, though L has it as direct discourse (more like Hebrew narrative, where the main point comes in the conversation), while o′ shows it primarily as indirect (more like a historian's approach). Knowing the tendency of the ancients to place speeches in the mouths of leading characters as a literary device, one is impressed with the verbal agreement between the two texts. This agreement leads one to believe that the speech of Mordecai was sufficiently known within the

---

42. Auerbach, *Mimesis*, ch. 1.

community or communities to prohibit much change.

Similarly to the speech of Mordecai, the speech of Esther (o´ 4.10-12 // L 4.7-8) shows remarkable similarity between the texts. All elements are consistent in both texts. Such is not the case with the rebuttal by Mordecai (o´ 4.13-14 // L 4.9-10):

1. o´'s argument stresses logic and looks to Providence:
   a. you are Jewish, so you will not escape the decree;
   b. if you refuse, other Jews will be helped (but what good will that do you?);
   c. moreover (δὲ καί), both you and your family will die (you have everything to gain by the attempt and nothing to lose);
   d. perhaps Providence made you queen for this reason.
2. L, more pointed and compact, stresses duty/family and specifically calls on God:
   a. if you neglect *your* (a plus in L) people/duty (as Jew and queen?, you are not indispensable), God (a plus in L) will save them (even if you won't; but what good is that to you?);
   b. moreover, both you and your family will die (the same implication as 'c' above);
   c. perhaps Providence made you queen for this reason (= 'd' above).

At the risk of overexplaining differences, it may be said that o´ uses logic which presumably would appeal to Hellenistic communities accustomed to Socratic reasoning. L appeals to national and family loyalty/ duty which suits a more cohesive and specifically Jewish community. This difference is not easily nor most likely explained as owing to textual variants, nor to a single, rewriting editor deriving one of these texts from the other. It is most naturally explained as arising from a separate traditional, communal base.

Admittedly the restraint regarding the deity in o´ and MT is not easy to explain. However, one can note that the threat of Esther's death occurs in both texts, it appears more as (divine?) judgment than as inevitable consequence, and this concept stems from a Semitic concept, *viz.* corporate personality. Esther's response to Mordecai's rebuttal is found in both texts and is quite parallel. Both texts end this section with notification that Mordecai did what Esther requested.

It may be noted that in L Esther comes to speech in the first exchange. Direct speech continues in each of L's subunits so that a dynamic directness is achieved. But the artistic progression from background to foreground, and from exposition to the narrated intensity of climactic speech, as in o´, is lost. In both texts, however, introductions and compliance formulas are prosaically present until the end of the third exchange, when compliance is dropped for narrative urgency. The fourth exchange begins with a commissioning formula, but one senses the urgency in o´ and foreshortening in L. This sets the stage for the prayers of both Mordecai and Esther.

The Prayers and Entry to the King (LXX C 1-30 and D 1-16)
The reader assumes that some assembly was called at o´ 4.17 and parallel, but neither it nor the fast are narrated. One learns that Esther fasted in o´ C 13 // L 4.18. The first narrated step of the plan had not been mentioned in o´, but L 4.11bβ does specify prayer: 'pray to God fervently/extensively'. And pray they do.

The structure of both prayers is straightforward and together they make an interesting combination. Beginning with o´, one detects three parts: an opening and closing narrative frame (C 1-2aα and C 11) and the prayer proper (C 2aβ-10). The prayer itself yields four parts: Invocation (C 2aβ[1-2]); Ascriptions of praise (C 2aβ[3-4]); Protestation of Innocence (C 5-7); and Address and Petitions (C 8-10). L is different: a narrative introduction opens, but no narrative frame closes. Hence there are only two parts, 4.12b and 4.13-17. The subunits of the prayer proper manifest differences in vocabulary and content, but the same structure. Differences can be located easily in the following presentations.

Note that, as was done above in the case of section B, the contents of these sections, the two prayers and the entry scene—not found in Hebrew—will stand outside the strict sequence of structure for completeness of presentation. The reader will understand from the last structure diagram above that these three segments continue the narration of the 'Plan and Two New Complications' sequence as the 'Plan Initiated' panel.

o´ Text of the Prayers and Entry (C 1-30 & D 1-16)

I. MORDECAI'S PRAYER: Protestation of Innocence & Petitions	C 1-11
A. NARRATIVE FRAME: opening	1-2aα
1. Act: He Besought the Lord	1aα
2. Description: Remembers Magnalia/Torah Story	1aβ
3. Introductory Quotation Formula	2aα
B. PRAYER PROPER	2aβ-10
1. Invocation: 'Lord, Lord'	2aβ(1-2)
2. Ascriptions of Praise/Power	2aβ(3-4)

---

43. Cf. N. Avigad and Y. Yadin (eds.), *A Genesis Apocryphon* (Jerusalem: Magnes Press, 1956), col. XX, where Sarah's beauty is praised by the Egyptian prince Harkenosh in similar but more lengthy and erotic terms: '(how) beautiful the look of her face...all the radiance of her face'. For further development of the beauty/radiance motif, see G. Vermes, *Scripture and Tradition in Judaism* (Leiden: Brill, 2nd edn, 1973), pp. 110-13.

1. Report: King's Reactions   8a
    a. agonizing   8bα(1-2)
    b. springs from throne   8bα(3-7)
    c. takes her up in arms   8bβ
    d. Duration: until she revived   8bγ
    e. Purpose: trying to comfort her   8d
2. Dialog (3 pairs + 1 royal speech D 9–5.8); Statement, Report   9–14
    a. Speech: king's reassurances/comforts   9–11
        1) Introductory quotation formula   9aα
        2) Speech proper   9aβ–11
            a) Question: what is it?   9aβ
            b) Comforts/immunity: personal   9b–11
                α I am your brother   9bα
                β 1st imperative: courage!   9bβ
                γ Grant of immunity & reason   10
                    αα you will not die   10a
                    ββ we share the decree (?)[44]   10b
                δ 2nd imperative: come!   11
    b. Statement: Comforts/immunity: official   12ab
        1) raising gold sceptre   12aα
        2) touches her neck   12aβ
        3) embraces her   12bα
    c. Speech resumed, king   12bβc
        1) Introductory quotation formula   12bβ
        2) Speech: 3rd imperative: speak!   12c
    d. Speech: Esther's praising answer   13–14
        1) Introductory quotation formula   13aα
        2) Speech: answer & reason (2 + 2)   13aβ–14
            a) you, lord, as God's angel   13aβ
            b) troubled/fear of your glory   13b
            c) you, lord = awesome   14a
            d) face full of grace   14b
3. Report: Suspenseful Transition to Further Dialog: Esther,
    King, Servants   15–16
        1) Circumstance: while talking   15a
        2) Act, suspense: collapses in faint   15b

---

44. The meaning of the Greek is uncertain; it may mean that an 'entry rule' protects us both, or that our rule applies (only) to the people, or that our ruling is openly (declared).

1) every adornment/delight of head	18eαβ
2) covered with humiliation	18eγ
B. PRAYER, with 2nd Introduction	19-29
1. Report of Prayer and Introductory Quotation Formula	19a
a. Act: besought the Lord	19aα
b. Introductory quotation formula	19aβ
2. Invocation & Introductory Call for Help	19bcd
a. Invocation proper (O Lord, King)	19bα
b. Ascription: praise/power (only help)	19bβ
c. Introductory petition & 3 reasons	19cd
1) Petition 1 proper: help!	19cα
2) Reasons (3)	19cβγd
a) identity: I am humble(d)	19cβ
b) identity: I have no help but you	19cγ
c) need: life in danger now	19d
3. Recital: Biography of Israel (Torah Story)	20
a. Oral testimony: 'I heard from book'	20aα
b. Content	20aβbc
1) Redemption: Lord redeemed Israel from all nations	20aβ
2) Election (?): our fathers from ancestors	20bα
3) Purpose: eternal inheritance, Israel (Promised Land)	20bβ
4) Theology	20c
a) you 'kept covenant' (Fulfiller of Promise)	20cα
b) you provided their requests (Sustainer)	20cβ
4. Confession & Vindication: we sinned; you are righteous	21-22aα
a. 1st confession & result	21
1) we sinned before you	21a
2) you handed us over	21b
b. 2nd confession: if we honored other gods	21c
c. Vindication (= 3rd confession): 'you are righteous'	22aα
5. Lament	22aβcdef
a. Transition ('now')	22aβ
b. Lament proper/accusation of enemy	22aγbcdef
1) not content with our slavery (negative)	22aγ
2) made pact with their idols (positive)	22b
3) Purposes (6)	22cdef
a) destroy your oath/decree	22cα
b) 'vanish' your inheritance	22cβ
c) seal mouth of praises	22d

The Books of Esther

  d) quench glory of your house & altar (!)   22e

  e) open mouth of gentiles to praise vanities (idols)22fα

  f) & to idolize mortal king   22fβ

6. Petitions: to act, turn/notice, act   23-25d

  a. Core petition (= act! 2 negative, 2 positive)   23

   1) Invocation (κύριε)   23aβ

   2) Petition 1: do not betray   23aα

    a) Object: Sceptre!   23bα

    b) Indirect object: enemies hating you   23bβ

   3) Petition 2: let not rejoice in our fall!   23c

   4) Petition 3: turn (reverse) counsel!   23d

   5) Petition 4: make example of evil plan author!   23e

  b. Petitions to turn attention (2)   24ab

   1) Invocation (κύριε)   24aβ

   2) Dual petitions   24aαb

    a) Petition 5: appear for us!   24aα

    b) Petition 6: make self known: trouble!   24b

  c. Further petitions to act   24c-25

   1) Petition 7: do not grind us up   24c

   2) Petition 8: dual request: speech   25ab

    a) give me persuasive speech!   25a

    b) grace my words!   25bα

    c) (as I am) before the king   25bβ

   3) Petition 9 & purpose   25c

    a) Petition proper: change!   25cα

    b) Purpose: end to fighter & his cohorts   25cβ

   4) Petitions 10-11   25d

    a) rescue us! (for people)   25dα

    b) help me! (for self)   25dβ

7. Protest of Innocence: reason for above petitions 25e-28

  a. Reason: causal ὅτι   25eα

  b. Asseveration 1: God has all knowledge   25eβ

  c. Asseveration 2: God intuits Esther's

  [Torah-led] attitudes; dual denials   25f

   1) You know (Act)   25fα

   2) Denial 1: I abhor bed of uncircumcised (Object 1)   25fβ

   3) Denial 2: I hate splendor of lawless ones

   & of any alien (Object 2)   25g

III. ESTHER'S ENTRY TO KING; Intervention   5.1-12

    A. SETTING: Final Call on God; Preparing Entry   1-2a

        1. Transition   1a

            a. Time: on 3rd day   1aα

            b. Act: Esther ceases to pray (προσεύχομαι)   1aβ

        2. Preparation for Entry   1b-2a

            a. dress   1b-2aα

                1) sheds garments of worship   1bα

                2) adorns self in majestic attire   1bβ

                3) having become glorious   2aα

            b. prayer   2aβ

                1) Act: having called on God (ἐπικαλέω)   2aβ(1-3,8)

                2) Ascriptions (dual)   2aβ(4-7)

                    a) all-knowing   2aβ(4-5)

                    b) & Savior   2aβ(6-7)

    B. PLAN INITIATION: 2nd Step: Entry Proper   2b-6

        1. Departure   2b-4

            a. Act: takes along (with her)   2bα

            b. Accompaniment: two maids   2bβ

            c. Manner   2c

                1) leaning daintily on one   2cα

                2) other follows carrying Esther's train   2cβ

        2. Description of Esther   3

            a. she being radiant   3aα

            b. at peak of beauty   3aβ

            c. her face   3bα

            d. as beloved   3bβ

            e. yet heart frozen   3c

        3. Entry proper   4a

            a. passing through doors   4aα

            b. she stands before the king   4aβ

         4. Description of king   4bc

            a. king is seated on royal throne   4bα

            b. formally dressed with garments of glory   4bβ

            c. covered with gold & precious stones   4cα

            d. he was terribly frightening   4cβ

    C. FIRST NEW COMPLICATION: King's Unreceptive Anger   5-6

        1. King Acts   5

            a. Act 1st: raises face   5aα

---

45. The meaning of the Greek is uncertain; see the previous footnote.

2) Speech: response	11aβb
a) Act	11aβ
α I saw you	11aβ(1-2)
β as God's angel	11aβ(3-5)
b) Result	11b
α heart melted	11bα
β· at glory of your wrath	11bβ
γ O lord	11bγ
3. Report: Suspenseful Transition to Further Dialog:	
Esther, King, Servants	12
a. Description: on face, sweat	12a
b. Result (2)	12bc
1) king & servants troubled	12b
2) they try comforting her	12c

Mordecai's prayer (oʹ C 1-11 // L 4.12b-17) is generally very similar in the two texts. The main thoughts are found in each, and the flow of the prayer is similar in both versions. However, there are differences, some quite obvious:

1. as divine appelatives, oʹ has κύριε κύριε βασιλεῦ (v. 13) where L has δέσποτα παντοκράτορ, κύριε (v. 15) where L has δέσποτα, and no parallel (v. 15) where L has τοῦ ἀληθινοῦ;
2. in the description of Aman, oʹ has 'haughty' (ὑπερήφανος, v. 15) where L has 'uncircumcised' (τὸν ἀπερίτμητον);
3. in the grounds of supplication, oʹ has 'God of Abraham' (v. 16) where L has 'O Lord, who did make a covenant with Abraham'.

It appears again that L has a more Semitic flavor: Aman is far more than haughty, he is uncircumcised; God is the God of Abraham because of the covenant made with him. It appears that the author of L purposes with greater intensity to convince his readers of the honor of being a Jew. He does this by appealing to the righteousness of the Jew as distinct from the unrighteousness of the Gentile. Whenever L's author has the opportunity, he shows the glory of being the covenant people.

Esther's prayer (oʹ C 12-30 // L 4.18-29) has two parts in both texts—the same two as Mordecai's prayer. Curiously Esther's long narrative introduction is followed in both texts by a second, though brief, introduction. The prayer itself falls into eight segments which can be seen well enough in the outline above. Perhaps it should be noted, however, in view of the significance of numbers among the ancients, especially here the number seven, that it is possible to consider the 'Final Ascription and Petitions' as extensions of their respective previous sections, or as subordinate closures of section 7, the 'Protest of Innocence', and thus a heptad.

The introduction to Esther's prayer is close in both traditions with the exception that o′ appears to have Esther actually cut her hair, while L simply states that every sign on her lovely head she covered with humiliation. It may well be that L could not bring himself to have Esther cut her hair, a possible sign of lack of humility in later Judaism (cf. 1 Cor. 11.15).

As in Mordecai's prayer, so also in Esther's, the witnesses are similar in the overall perspective, but differ in details:

1. o′ has 'O my Lord, you alone are king' where L has 'O Lord, King, you alone are a helper';
2. o′ has 'I have heard from my birth, in the tribe of my kindred' where L has 'I have heard from my father's book';
3. o′ has 'they have laid their hands on their idols' where L has 'they have covenanted with their idols';
4. o′ has 'do not surrender your scepter to those who are not' (i.e. those who do not really exist) where L has 'do not surrender your scepter to enemies who hate you' (note that since Greek σκήπτρων translates Hebrew שֵׁבֶט ['tribe'] in 1 Sam. 2.28; 9.21 where Saul speaks of his tribe being the smallest, 'tribe' rather than 'scepter' may be the meaning here);
5. o′ has 'encourage me, O King of gods, and ruler of all dominion' where L has no parallel;
6. o′ has no parallel where L has 'do not break us in pieces';
7. o′ has 'put harmonious speech in my mouth before the lion' where L has 'put eloquent speech in my mouth, and make my words pleasing before the king';
8. o′ has 'I hate the glory...abhor the couch...every stranger' (this seems to have been truncated somehow, the final 'every stranger' not attaching well to 'abhor the couch' but attaching better to 'glory of the wicked' [= Gentile]) where L has 'I hate the bed...splendor of wicked...any alien' (a better construction);
9. o′ has 'which is upon my head in the days of my splendor' where L has 'I do not wear it except on the days when I appear in public';
10. o′ has 'I abhor it as a menstruous cloth' where L has 'I abhor it like the rag of a woman who sits apart';
11. o′ says that Esther did not eat at the table of Aman, whereas L says that she did not eat at 'their' table (a more general policy, absolving her of possible impurity);
12. o′ has 'not rejoiced...except in you, O Lord God of Abraham' where L has 'no joy...except in you, O Master'.

Other minutely divergent matters in the prayer may be observed by the reader, but some of the above points merit further comment here. In regard to the first difference noted, one wonders either if there has been a deliberate shuffling of the words by L, or if o′ has been affected by scribal error. Actually, L makes more literary sense, since the prayer continues to focus on God as helper. It may well be that o′ has transposed the text of an original which L reflects. On the other hand, if Esther is filled with fear at approaching Artaxerxes, to be reassured that Yahweh alone is king makes good sense. If o′ reflects an original, it could be that L adapts the text literarily, to enhance the theme of 'helper', which Esther takes up immediately in her prayer.

The second difference indicated above is a most interesting one. o′ functions in an oral tradition setting, while L takes the same idea as from a written source. One wonders why L does not change the verb 'heard' to 'read'—if L is rewriting o′—since strictly 'to hear from a book' is neither idiomatic Greek nor Hebrew.

The third difference is one of idiom, with the meaning being obviously the same. In an informative article on 'hem/border' ('The Ancient Significance of *Sisith*'),[46] F. Stephens says:

> The pious worshipper in making a petition to his god is often said to have seized the *sisiktu* of the god. Apparently the act had some magical power by which the man could be the more certain of receiving the blessing which he sought… We may picture the suppliant as before the statue of the god, placing his hand upon the representation of some portion of the god's garment, or possibly as grasping some part of an actual garment with which the statue may have been clothed.[47]

Martin's[48] criteria for translation Greek confirm the consensus of various scholars and this author that this section of o′ and L had a Semitic *Vorlage*.[49] Unfortunately it is not possible to know what phrase underlies the two widely different renderings noted in point 3 above. Both texts appear to understand the general phenomenon as Stephens explains it in the quotation just given, but each in a special way. L appears to follow the Semitic/biblical tradition in presenting a contemporary

---

46. F.J. Stephens, 'The Ancient Significance of *sisith*', *JBL* 50 (1931), pp. 59-70.

47. Stephens, 'The Ancient Significance of *sisith*', p. 61.

48. Martin, *Syntactical Evidence of Semitic Sources in Greek Documents*.

49. H.J. Cook, 'The A Text of the Greek Versions of the Book of Esther', *ZAW* 81 (1969), pp. 367-76; Moore, *Daniel, Esther and Jeremiah: The Additions*; Clines, *The Esther Scroll*.

Jewish (Palestinian?) audience with the understandable 'covenant with' (whether or not writer or hearer knew of a prior 'laid their hands on'). On the other hand, o′, which may well be faithful to a Semitic tradition, chooses the phrase which probably had a wider, Hellenistic (i.e. part Jewish, part Gentile) audience appeal.

Point 10 above is is a telling sign: the author of L is Jewish. He uses a euphemism rather than the more vulgar expression, and does so no doubt because he intends that his story be read and accepted by a more conservative Jewish community (as distinct from and perhaps in opposition to the LXX [o′], which originated in the Diaspora and in its several forms became the popular standard used by the Gentile community in the early centuries of the Common Era).

Another straightforward narrative, concerning 'Esther's Entry to the King' (o′ D 1-16 // L 5.1-12), follows her prayer. In this unit Esther faces the possible wrath of the tyrant and her consequent personal death. The style is largely paratactic, with multiple participial phrases depending on one finite verb. Narratively there is more description than action. Possibilities for structuring are several. First, Esther's preparation for departure to the king is narrated in vv. 1-2a (in both texts). This is clearly stage-setting exposition. Exposition could be extended through the subsequent Departure (vv. 2b-4), Description of Esther (v. 5), Entry proper (v. 6a) and Description of the king (v. 6bc). At v. 7 the king and Esther begin to interact and a *new complication* immediately ensues. Esther's life now hangs in the balance and delay can be no more: this is clearly a narrative *crisis* (v. 8). The situation is saved: God acts on the king (note that this is the 'reverse' of his acting on Pharaoh). From here on (vv. 8b-16) the action slows somewhat, while tension is still maintained through descriptive reports and dialog: this subunit could begin the *dénouement*, or a *solution* as defined earlier, and as found in the exposition of chs. 1–2.

However, it is important to keep the overall 'arc of tension' in mind. Such mindfulness leads to a second alternative. The major *crisis* of the plot, set up by the major *complication*, has not yet taken place —the pogrom is still programmed: extinguish Israel! Esther has been but temporarily spared. Working backward from that continuing complication and a turning point yet to come, one can see that the *dénouement* proper has not begun with this intervention. Rather it sets the stage for Mordecai and Esther's plan to take effect; this is only the second step in a three-step plan. So even though Esther has passed through a *crisis* (and the reader may have experienced an emotional *climax* by identifying with Esther's danger), the following material merely carries the plan forward. Hence D 8b-16 can best be called 'plan continues'. Verses 7-8 retain their labels of *new complication* and *crisis*. With D 1-2a clearly seen already as *exposition*, only vv. 2b-6 remain as a question. This subunit also gives background and leads up to the *complication*, but another agenda is already in place: the *plan*. Esther is carrying out the agreed-upon attempt to thwart Aman's death decree. Thus D 2b-6, using the literary technique of description, actually presents the second step of the heroes' plan (the first step having been the prayers): Esther enters the king's presence at risk. No grammatical indicators would be violated in either scheme of presentation, but the second is more logical and integrated with the 'rising action'.

In the 'Preparation for Entry' (vv. 1b-2a in both texts) there is a variation in the divine appellations, with Esther calling upon 'God the Overseer (ἐπόπτην) and Savior' in o′ and on the 'all-knowing (γνώστην) God and Savior' in L. The reason for the variation is not clear, but no doubt the respective appellations were important to the different communities that o′ and L seem to be addressing.

A slight difference exists in the 'Description of Esther' (o′ D 5 // L 5.3), in that her face is described as ἱλαρὸν ὡς προσφιλές ('cheerful, as benevolent') in o′, while L lacks ἱλαρόν and simply describes her face as προσφιλές ('benevolent, beloved').

There are some further differences in the remainder of this section (o′ D 7-16 // L 5.5-12):

1. in describing the king's unreceptive anger, o′ simply has 'he looked with intense anger', while L expands with a simile, 'he looked upon her like a bull in fierce anger' (one may note the imagery of 'bulls' in the context of tense and adverse situations elsewhere, as in Pss. 22.12, 21; 68.30, and it may be that 'bulls' in these contexts became, at some stage of the tradition, symbolic of Gentiles in contrast to Israel as the chosen people—cf. the parallel of 'bulls' with 'nations' in the Psalm 68 text);[50]
2. o′ notes the change of Esther's color and her fainting, while L specifically adds that she was terrified, for once leaving less to the reader's imagination;
3. o′ has the king consoling Esther with the words 'our command is openly declared' and 'draw nigh'(?), while L expands this somewhat nebulous

50. אבר in Hebrew is a curious word of obscure origin. The root occurs in Akkadian, Ugaritic and Aramaic. In Akkadian it means 'power, strength', though it is not often linked with 'strong animal/bull'. In Ugaritic, the meaning is certainly 'bull' (*TDOT*, I, p. 42) and is found in compound names.

statement with 'our business is mutual', 'the threat is not against you', and 'the sceptre is in your hand';

4. in o′ the heart of Esther is 'troubled' (ἐταράχθη) in explaining her fainting to the king, while in L her heart 'melts' (ἐτάκη);

5. o′ expands the description of the king as an 'angel of God;' with the added 'you are to be wondered at' and 'your face is full of grace', while L omits such a description (it appears that L hesitates to attribute glory to this Gentile king, preferring the sovereign changing of his heart by God to be the platform for his benevolent actions);

6. in o′ Esther faints a second time while speaking to king, while in L the king wipes a bead of sweat from Esther's face but there is no mention of a second fainting spell;

7. in o′ the king is troubled and his servant attempts to comfort Esther (apparently responding to the king's agitation), whereas in L both the king and his servants attempt to comfort Esther.

In regard to the third difference listed above, it may be noted that at that point L is explaining, spelling out, what is left ambiguous in o′. The question is: does L intentionally explain o′, or does o′ compress L into nebulosity, or are they two separate traditions? 'Our command is openly declared' (κοινὸν τὸ πρόσταγμα ἡμῶν ἐστιν) or 'our command is mutual' (i.e. therefore the rule is only for our subjects) may well correspond in meaning to 'our business is mutual', but there is the striking fact that o′ uses the compound πρόσταγμα, which in L is split into two clauses, one using only the simple πρᾶγμα, the other explaining the πρός preposition of the compound used in o′. Πρόσταγμα is more than 'business'; it is a 'decree', just as surely it is less than 'government', 'royal power'. If L's first two phrases interpret 'our command is common/openly declared', then L's last phrase, 'the sceptre is in your hand', could be taken as a substitute, but hardly an explanation of 'draw near' (πρόσελθε) in o′. The reverse would be that L's clear text was too long, too loaded, but became corrupt or unclear in the reduction process as preserved in o′. The reader must decide.

The sixth difference listed above shows o′ adding a note of drama with the second fainting, and furthering the scores of twos, pairs and dualities of Esther. In contrast, one can suggest that L does not want to cast Esther as too frail. To have her faint twice negates the position of strength she symbolizes and for which she prayed.

Plan and Complications continued (LXX 5.3-14)
At o′ 5.3 // L 5.13 the dialog begun in section D continues (note that the Göttingen LXX text follows the Hebrew versification and hence omits

5.1-2, which are included within D 1ff.). The king requests to know Esther's wish (the existence of some quest on Esther's part is obvious enough from her unannounced entry). Easily seen from the presentation being developed in this study is the fact that, a *crisis* now past, Esther continues to act on the *plan*. After the prayers (step 1) and her entry to the king (step 2), her first request becomes step 3 of the plan conceived in ch. 4. The reader expects her to ask for the lives of her people—after all, the king offers 'up to half my kingdom' (5.3b). In fine storytelling style the author creates suspense by delay. Esther invites the king and Aman to the celebration of her 'special day' (v. 4). Nevertheless the suspenseful pause is tastefully short: v. 5ab records the king's urgent response; v. 5c tersely reports compliance—the banquet is in progress. Dialog resumes in vv. 6-8. L reports compliance in 5.19 with a speech; o′ leaves the reader to assume. L closes with a conclusion lacking in o′.

The following structure returns to the overall sequence established prior to sections C and D.

o′ Text

III.   B.   3.   b. (*continued*)

3) 3rd step: dialog continued: king & Esther:		
2 invitations (1st delay = 1st invitation & drinkfest;		
2nd delay = 2nd invitation); king accepts		5.3-8
a) Speech: king's query/offer to Esther		3-5a
α Introductory quotation formula		3aα
β Speech: question/offer (2 + 2)		3aβ-b
αα What do you want?		3aβ
ββ What is your request?		3aγ
γγ up to half of empire		3bα
δδ it will be yours		3bβ
b) Speech: Esther's answer: 1st delay = 'invite'		4
α Introductory quotation formula		4aα
β Speech proper (7 pt)		4aββbc
αα Announcement: 'today is a		
notable day for me'	1	4aβ
ββ Protocol	2	4bα
γγ Answer = invitation		4bβc
α1 What: please come	3	4bβ(1-3)
β1 Who: king & Aman	4	4bβ(4-5)
γ1 Purpose: reception	5	4bβ(6-8)

δ1 'Amphitryone': I   6   4c(1-2)

ε1 When: today   7   4c(3)

c) Speech: king's response to Esther   5ab

  α Introductory quotation formula   5aα

  β Speech: command (to pages)   5aβb

    αα 'Hurry Aman (here)!'   5aβ

    ββ Purpose: do Esther's will   5b

d) Compliance statement: reception in progress   5c

  α both present themselves   5cα(1-3)

  β at reception   5cα(4-6)

  γ that Esther said/ordered   5cβ

e) Dialog resumed: speech: king's 2nd question

  & offer to Esther   6

  α Setting: at drinkfest (!)   6aα

  β Introductory quotation formula   6aβ

  γ Speech: question & offer (2)   6b

    αα What, Queen Esther?   6bα

    ββ Whatever you ask   6bβ

f) Speech: Esther's 2nd delay: 2nd invite   7-8

  α Introductory quotation formula   7a

  β Speech: 2nd invitation (8 pt) & promise   7b-8

    αα Announcement (2)   1   7b

    ββ Protocol (single)   2   8aα

    γγ Invitation proper   8aβγδbα

      α1 What: please come   3   8aβ(1)

      β1 Who: king & Aman   4   8aβ(2-5)

      γ1 When: tomorrow   5   8aγ

      δ1 Why: drinkfest   6   8aδ

      ε1 'Amphitryone': I   7   8bα(1-2)

      ζ1 Honorees: them   8   8bα(3)

    δδ Promise (3)   8bβ

      α1 Time: tomorrow   8bβ(1-2)

      β1 Promise: I will do   8bβ(3)

      γ1 Obj.: Circumstance: same 8bβ(4-5)

c. 2nd new complication: Aman offended by
Mordecai's indifference & so plots to hang
Mordecai immediately—next morning   9-14

1) Exposition: character, emotion   9a
   a) Aman leaves king   9aα
   b) Emotions (2): happy/rejoicing   9aβ
2) Complication (villain's viewpoint): 3rd offense
  by Mordecai against Haman   9b-13
   a) Act: Aman sees Mordecai/Jew at king's gate   9bα
   b) Reactions: Aman   9bβ-13
    α 1st: very angry   9bβ
    β 2nd: goes home   10a
    γ 3rd: calls home council   10b
     αα Act: calls   10b(1)
     ββ Objects: friends/Zeresh   10b(2-8)
     γγ Report of boast speech: 4
      signs (self praise)   11
      α1 Introduction: Aman tells   11aα
      β1 4 signs: his greatness   11aβbc
       α2 richness   11aβ(1-3)
       β2 glory king gave   11aβ(4-6)b
       γ2 to be first   11c(1-5)
       δ2 & to rule   11c(6-9)
   c) Dialog: Aman's complaint (self-pity)
    & Zeresh/friend's proposal
    (maximum vengeance)   12-14a
    α Aman's speech   12-13
     αα Introductory quotation formula   12aα
     ββ Speech proper   12aβ-13
      α1 2nd boast   12aβb
       α2 I alone invited   12aβ
       β2 with queen tomorrow   12b
      β1 Complaint   13
       α2 this pleases me not   13a
       β2 Reason: I see Mordecai   13b
    β Wife & friend-council speech:
    they propose ghoulish plan   14a
     αα Introductory quotation formula   14aα
     ββ Speech proper   14aβbc
      α1 make high hanging tree   14aβ
      β1 speak to king in morning   14bα

γ1 let Mordecai be hanged on it 14bβ

δ1 go to reception, be happy (2)   14c

3) Solution (for Aman): plan to hang Mordecai

accepted & implemented

(new complication for heroes)   14d

  a) Acceptance report   14dα

  b) Compliance report   14dβ

L Text

III. B. 3. b. (*continued*)

3) 3rd step: dialog continued: king & Esther:

2 invitations (1st delay = 1st invitation & drinkfest;

2nd delay = 2nd invitation); king accepts   5.13-20

  a) Speech: king's query/offer to Esther   13

    α Introductory quotation formula   13aα

    β Speech: question/command;

    promise/offer (2 + 2)   13aβbc

      αα What is it?   13aβ

      ββ Tell me   13bα

      γγ & I will do it   13bβ

      δδ up to half of empire   13c

  b) Speech: Esther's answer: 1st delay = 'invite'   14

    α Introductory quotation formula   14aα

    β Speech proper (7 pt)   14aβbc

      αα Announcement: 'today is a

      notable day for me'   1   14aβ

      ββ Protocol   2   14bα

      γγ Answer = invitation   14bβγδc

        α1 What: please enter   3   14bβ

        β1 Who: king & Aman   4   14bγ

        γ1 Purpose: drinkfest   5   14bδ

        δ1 'Amphitryone': I   6   14cα

        ε1 When: tomorrow   7   14cβ

  c) Speech: king's response to Esther   15

    α Introductory quotation formula   15aα

    β Speech: command (to pages)   15aβb

      αα 'Hurry Aman (here)!   15aβ

      ββ Purpose: do Esther's will   15b

a) The same told to Aman 20a
b) Reaction: he marvels 20b
c) Reaction: departing king rests 20c
c. 2nd new complication: Aman, still offended
by Mordecai, plots to hang him immediately
—next morning 21-24
1) Exposition: change of place; council 21ab
a) Aman goes home 21a
b) Calls home council 21b
α Act: gathers 21bα
β Object = new characters 21bβγδ
αα friends 21bβ
ββ sons 21bγ
γγ Zosara, wife 21bδ
[L has no counterpart to oʹ 5.11]
2) Complication (villain's viewpoint): dialog:
Aman's complaint (self-pity)/Zosara's proposal
(maximum vengeance) 21c-23
a) Aman's speech 21c-22
α Definition/Intro. quotation formula 21cα
αα Verbal def. of foll. speech 21cα(1-3)
ββ Form: λέγων ὡς 21cα(4-5)
β Speech proper 21cβ-22
αα Boast 21cβγd
α1 none invited 21cβ
β1 on queen's day 21cγ
γ1 except king & me only 21dα
δ1 I am called tomorrow 21dβ
ββ Complaint 22
α1 but this grieves me 22a
β1 when I see Mordecai, Jew 22b
γ1 & he will not worship me 22c
b) Wife & friend-council speech: they propose
ghoulish plan 23
αα Introductory quotation formula 23aα
ββ Speech proper 23aβ-h
α1 he is of Jewish race 23aβ
β1 since king agreed to
destroy Jews 23b

> γ1 & gods gave you 23cα
> δ1 death day for revenge 23cβ
> ε1 cut high tree 23d
> ζ1 let it be erected 23e
> η1 hang Mordecai on it 23f
> θ1 go early, speak to king 23g
> ι1 now go make merry with king 23h
>
> 3) Solution: plan to hang Mordecai accepted &
>   implemented (new complication for heroes) 24
>   a) Acceptance report 24a
>   b) Compliance report 24b

In Esther's speech in o′ 5.4 // L 5.14, there is a time difference:

1. o′ has her say that 'today is my great day', while L has her say, 'tomorrow is a special day for me';
2. o′ therefore has the first feast 'today', whereas L has the feast 'tomorrow'.

Both texts have the king fetching Aman immediately and the fact is stated that they both attended the feast. It appears that L already has the more believable story, or is trying to make it so, by having the feast on the next day. Readers would question how Esther could have arranged such a thing in such a short time, as the o′ text has it. However, the fact that the king immediately fetched Aman rather than just sending him word of the need to attend the feast is curious, and does not fit well the 'tomorrow' aspects of the L text.

In the king's speech in o′ 5.6 // L 5.17 and Esther's second invitation in o′ 5.7-8 // L 5.18, two differences may be noted:

1. in o′ the king restates his former offer, 'you shall have all your request', while in L he reassures Esther twice, reiterating his former 'as much as half my kingdom' along with o′'s reading above;
2. in Esther's invitation, o′ simply has 'if I have found favor in your eyes', whereas L expands with additional protocol, 'and if it pleases the king to grant my request'.

At o′ 5.9 // L 5.21 the subject changes to Aman, and readers are rewarded with an insight (albeit a black-and-white one by modern standards) into his thoughts and family and friends. Their 'Solution' (o′ 5.14d // L 5.24), as millions of faithful hearers know from EH, is a grisly counterpart to the earlier macabre 'final solution' to the Jewish question. The proposed solution for Aman's petty and overblown nastiness is: 'Hang Mordecai tomorrow so you can enjoy the banquet!' Narratively this sadistic proposal heightens tension and, unknown to the hero, creates a second *new complication*—a complication which catapults the story into its pivotal *crisis*.

The general flow of this section is the same in both texts. L tends to be more specific (expansive?—or is o´ vague by reduction?), but the same basic message comes through. On the other hand, the variations are so frequent and desultory that one has difficulty in tracing direct derivations, whether text-critically or by editorial revision. If a tentative assessment of the two texts so far may be allowed at this near halfway point, one could say that a core narrative lies behind both o´ and L, but each text has developed and diverged along different paths.

1. o´ assumes that Aman heard the invitation while at the first banquet with the king and Esther, while L has Aman being told that he was invited to the second banquet;

2. o´ has Aman 'very glad and merry' (ὑπερχαρὴς εὐφραινόμενος) upon receiving the invitation, while L has him 'astonished' (ἐθαύμασεν);

3. o´ notes that Aman saw Mordecai again, which enraged him, while L does not specifically note that Aman saw Mordecai again;

4. both texts have Aman calling friends and family together to celebrate (?) his achievements, but the o´ text has him more boastful in showing his wealth, position, and so on, while L has him only explaining the prestigious invitation to the queen's banquet;

5. in o´, all the things enumerated which show Aman's position of exultation are said to be worthless in light of Mordecai's defiance of him (the language indicates that until Mordecai is done away with, these glorious things will bring Aman no pleasure), whereas in L Mordecai's defiance (read fidelity to principle and Torah) is the single matter which distresses Aman.

Is the nuance of the first two points that o´ credits Aman with greater humanity and prominence, while L puts him down (having to be informed detracts from his outward control, and being astonished diminishes his inward personal control)? As for point 3, o´ may be giving readers who identify less with the story another reinforcement of a jealousy motif, whereas L, if it indeed is aimed at a Jewish audience, may feel that the racial antipathy already established is sufficient to 'carry' the narrative (see Chapter 5 of this study for other inner-biblical motives involved).

Some minor differences exist in the 'Wife and Friend-Council Speech' (o´ 5.14 // L 5.23):

1. in o´ the ghoulish plan is proposed by Zosara and Aman's friends, while in L only Zosara gives Aman the plan (a simpler contrast of the evil woman and Esther);
2. in o´ the plan is immediately outlined, while in L a description of Mordecai is given from a seemingly anti-Semitic perspective:
    a. he is from the race of the Jews;
    b. the king has given a decree to destroy the Jews;
    c. the gods have given a day of destruction for revenge;
3. the plan itself exhibits minor variants in the texts:
    a. the ξύλον ('tree') is fifty cubits high in the majority of MSS, but one text (a corrector of o´) adds ὑξηλόν ('lofty, high');
    b. o´ appears to have the gallows or tree erected and made ready, and Aman seeking permission to hang Mordecai in the morning, while L creates a delightful ambiguity with the order (1) gallows erection, (2) Mordecai's hanging, and (3) speaking to the king (thus Aman could hang/impale Mordecai and after the fact simply report);
    c. in o´ Zosara apparently tells Aman to go to the king's feast after the proposed hanging on the morrow, whereas in L she seems to tell him to go now and then speak to the king on the morrow.

Point 2 makes it appear again that L takes a more Jewish view than o´ in giving the reader the 'reasoning of the Gentiles' in order to show how poor and anti-Semitic it really is. Aman may appear just (and thus to the reader all the more unjust) on the grounds that the king (not the Almighty King) and the gods (not the One God) have approved his mischievous plans.

A ξύλον (noted in point 3a) is generally a cut piece of wood, hewn for a purpose. The word was used at times, however, for a living tree. It also often refers to implements made of wood used for punishment, like stocks or gallows. Of course, a cross (σταυρός) was also referred to as ξύλον.

The ambiguity noted in point 3c is resolved in L 6.7 by reporting that Aman came to the king so he could hang Mordecai. Both texts evoke the 'on the morrow' motif in Aman's speech, and in Zosara's 'rising early (tomorrow)'.

4. *Crisis Major/Pivot (LXX 6.1-5)*
In EG a second crisis is reached at 6.1. It has been called 'Crisis Major' not because it is more dramatic than Esther's entry to the king (it is not so), nor because of male importance (relative importance of the two heroes is still debated and does not affect the structure *per se*), but because here the complications cease and the whole plot turns.

This important plot turn may be called a *pivot*, especially here where various downturns in the heroes' fortunes are systematically reversed (see 'Reversals' in the microstructures). M. Fox,[51] though not the first[52] to notice that the structure of MT followed Aristotle's *peripateia*[53]—a step by step undoing of the progress, or regress of the principal character(s)—must be credited with the definitive study of this feature in EH. Showing repeated words, phrases or motifs on opposite sides of the pivot point, Fox successfully demonstrated that the author intended readers to conceive certain words and events as reversals. That insight has been checked here in EG and EH through the microstructures and has been found to be correct; it has also been used as a starting point to press further toward the macrostructure or narrative unity of these texts.

Thus a new unit begins with another location and charter: God acting, not to put man in a deep sleep (Gen. 2.21), nor to stupefy prophets and seers (Isa. 29.10), but the reverse. The Persian king becomes sleepless 'on that night'—again the opposite of a prophetic phrase used scores of times, 'on that day'. So much for the opening of this section. Where does it end? The two texts differ significantly here in length and content. The o′ text extends to v. 5 before a new character enters and dialog begins in earnest, ending in a clear reversal of fortune for Mordecai. L extends to v. 8 before the same changes take place. Those changes clearly signal a new unit.[54] Within o′ 6.1-5 // L 6.1-8, then, one finds a classic *crisis* in which the action must either terminate or deliver the heroes.

---

51. Fox, 'The Structure of Esther'.

52. As early as 1873, Schultz avers that Esther 'appears like a well-planned drama; developing scene after scene in rapid succession, and progressing by fascinating movements, to a consummation which we may compare to the tying of a knot. But when the *akme* is reached, the solution is also near at hand. There ensues a highly successful and impressive *peripetie*, a sudden turn of fortune, and all difficulties, though seemingly impossible, that stand in the way of a desirable conclusion, are continually and completely overcome as chapter succeeds chapter' (Schultz, 'The Book of Esther', p. 1). Schultz's description is difficult to improve upon, but he does not follow up to detail the peripety as Fox does.

53. Aristotle, *The Poetics* (trans. W.H. Fyfe; Cambridge, MA: Harvard University Press, 1932), 10-11.7.

54. This shift of report to dialog with the addition of another character may be used to highlight the imprecision of the term 'scene'. In terms of staging, the scene would remain the same; but in terms of focus, characters and plot progression, the scene has changed. This helps explain why recent Esther commentators—none of whom define 'scene'—diverge in describing Esther's 'scenes'.

Both texts report (differently) the action of God (ὁ κύριος in oʹ, ὁ δυνατός in L) on the king (an introduction) and the short event (called here a body) in which he discovers Mordecai's lack of reward and discusses it with his counsellors (again!). Some three-part reports have been seen in Esther (introduction, body, conclusion), but reports may have only two parts.

oʹ Text

4. CRISIS MAJOR/PIVOT (2nd Divine Intervention) Report		6.1-5
a. Introduction: 2nd intervention: Lord deprives king of sleep		1a
1). Intervention: Lord takes king's sleep		1aα
2). Time: that night		1aβ
b. Body: king discovers Mordecai's lack of reward regarding		
regicide plot (!)		1b-5
1) Command: indirect discourse		1b
a) Command proper: said to teacher		1bα
b) bring chronicles		1bβ(1-5)
c) to be read to him		1bα(6-7)
2) Act: discovers writing = Mordecai saved king		2aα
3) Description of royal record		2aβbc
a) Actor/hero: he (Mordecai)		2aβ(2)
b) Act: denounced/exposed to king		2aβ(1-4)
c) Object: 2 eunuchs		2bc
α Job description		2b
αα royal eunuchs		2bα
ββ guarding		2bβ
β Crime		2c
αα they sought/plotted		2cα
ββ against Artaxerxes		2cβ
4) Dialog: king & pages/council; flashback		3-5
a) Royal speech		3a
α Introductory quotation formula		3aα
β Speech: query: what honor?		3aβ
b) Page speech		3b
α Introductory quotation formula		3bα
β Speech: answer: nothing!		3bβ
c) Digression		4a
α while king inquired		4aα(1-6)
β re Mordecai's good deed		4aα(7-l)

L Text

Selected differences will be listed as before, with the double reminder that no attempt is made at completeness in these section-by-section summaries, and that the reader is encouraged to find and assess others.

1. o′ has the name of God as κύριος ('Lord'), while L has it as ὁ δυνατός ('Mighty One'—to avoid κύριος's connection with secular rulers?);

2. oʹ designates the books for which the king asks in his sleepless condition as 'books of daily events', while L has 'books of events';

3. oʹ is more compact at this point, as to the description of the chronicle concerning Mordecai (he is described as saving the life of Artaxerxes), while L is more personal (the king states that Mordecai saved 'my life', but the king is not named);

4. oʹ does not give a description of Mordecai, whereas L gives a royal speech regarding Mordecai's character:
    a. faithful;
    b. protector of the king's life;
    c. the very reason the king now sits on the throne;
    d. more righteous than the king, since the king did nothing;
    e. 'savior of affairs' (in the king's enquiring as to what should be done for Mordecai);

5. oʹ does not have the king enquiring of his servants what he should do for Mordecai, but they do dialog, while L has the king ask his servants for their opinions as to what should be done to honor Mordecai, and they are fearful, somehow being aware of Aman's plot against Mordecai (entirely lacking in oʹ)—or perhaps they know that Aman was somehow connected with the original regicide plot (A 18, stronger in L than in oʹ);

6. oʹ has Aman enter while the king is first discovering the fact that Mordecai had been overlooked for his kindness, whereas L has him enter the court in the morning, presumably sometime after the sleepless night;

7. L has 'and the king understood' (lacking in oʹ), apparently referring to the silence of the servants at his request for their opinion on how he should honor Mordecai;

8. though longer than either oʹ or MT, L seems to be farther from MT in the king's self-speech and praise of Mordecai, but closer to MT in the use of flashback to tell the reader why Haman/Aman has arrived.

From the standpoint of reader reponse, oʹ is more dramatic, having Aman enter during the very conversation of the king with his servants regarding Mordecai, with polished Greek of the infinitive in a prepositional phrase. The L text, however, though more pedestrian and Semitic-sounding (six occurrences of καί in 6.5-6, four of them in v. 6), is more believable and realistic, in that one can hardly conceive of Aman entering the court during a sleepless night of the king. Even if it were early morning, it seems too compacted in oʹ, a problem the L text overcomes by the omniscient author's καὶ ἐγένετο ὄρθρος—that is, having Aman enter after the events of the reading of the books and the discovery regarding Mordecai

The penultimate point above raises a particular difficulty. Exactly what the king understood is very vague in the text. If he understood that

Aman had plotted against Mordecai, the text gives no basis for his knowing about this, unless the servants said something. Is it to be subsumed under the divine intervention motif? Either way, the king acts unwittingly to initiate the peripetic reversal for Mordecai and to put Aman in precisely the pickle that the reader (and, by extension, God) wants him in. EG makes a restrained, but clear theological suggestion that 'the King' uses the king to establish His/his kingdom (cf. Dan. 4.17).

Regarding point 4, it may be commented that the underlying ethos in L's description of Mordecai's character is less that of Hellenism, more that of Jewish Torah righteousness and merit; that is, צדק and זכה.[55]

5. *Dénouement: Peripety (LXX 6.6–E–8.14)*

It is tempting to include all of ch. 6 in one unit, but based on the action which takes place (that is, the plot), the pivot point consists of no more than the Lord's action on the king and his resultant discovery of Mordecai's lack of reward. That was a pivot because the king then became ready to do something positive for the hero(es), but action directly involving the principals did not yet occur. Therefore it was not a *dénouement*, but only an intention.

That situation changes with o′ 6.6 // L 6.9. When Aman enters, the king—unbeknown to Aman, and therein lies rich irony and humor—is extracting the solution to Mordecai's reward from the one who hates Mordecai the most! So the change of characters, the change from report to dialog, and the action upon Mordecai which directly results from the dialog, mark this off as distinct from the *crisis/pivot*. A compliance report in fact details the first of a series of reversals which comprise the *dénouement* and carry on into the *conclusion*.

Thus the *dénouement* contains turnabouts for the heroes, but are the subunits to be determined solely by switches in fortune? Apparently not. The author sets the first reversal within a new cluster of characters (after the omniscient author allows the reader into the king's private chambers in o′ 6.1-4 // L 6.1-8). Within o′ 6.5-12 // L 6.9-19 the king and Aman, then Aman and Mordecai, are brought together in a logical cause–event sequence (Alter's 'narrative event'). The subsection is then closed by a report of the departure of protagonist and antagonist. Departure is a common device for completing a narrative element, a scene change or a

---

55. See the excellent and corrective (to the common Christian concept) discussion of merit and legalism in E.P. Sanders, *Paul and Palestinian Judaism* (Philadelphia: Fortress Press, 1977), pp. 183ff.

closure. This departure report and a new clustering of characters in o′ 6.13 // L 6.20-22 mark off the end of the first subsection and the beginning of the next. Thus the cluster of characters gives a clue to identifying the subunits of the *dénouement*: one or more reversals may take place while a certain group of players are present.

The second reversal comes in o′ 6.13 // L 6.20-22. In 5.14 Zosara proposed a solution for Aman's hateful frustration: hang Mordecai. In this next section, introduced by a new grouping, the proposal of Zosara (MT has Zeresh, possibly an Elamite goddess, the consort of Humman) 'reverses' into a prophecy of her own husband's doom (in o′). In L her words do not quite rise to prophecy, but to an inspired warning (does L not wish to attribute visionary power to a Gentile woman?). 'Inspired', because somehow Zosara knows what Aman does not: God is involved. Since the text itself makes a point over Zosara and associates offering a macabre solution for the troublesome Mordecai, the later prophecy or warning constitues a clear reversal.

The 'Plan' resumes at o′ 6.14 // L 6.23. The only problem here structurally involves the transition or opening. Does the 'while they were speaking' close the previous section, or open the new? By nature transitional phrases create this problem, and in direct proportion to their artistry—the 'smoother' the crossover, the harder it is to attribute the material to one side or the other. At first glance, the chapter divisions would seem to be correct: o′/MT v. 14 and L v. 23 close the section. This position can be buttressed by noting that Aman in a way departs from his house.

However, a closer examination tips the balance in favor of Maas's division (space plus indentation in BHS) and Murphy's structure (6.14 opens a new section). This determination can be supported by two factors: both Greek texts use a genitive absolute construction (though a different wording), and new characters (eunuchs, or 'one' in L) rush Aman to another place and simultaneously introduce him to the banquet and of course to a new cluster of characters. If the genitive absolute is used as a transition, it usually opens, not closes (it has already been shown to introduce major transitions in epistles). In the case of MT, עודם מדברים seems to depend on the *hiphil* perfect הויעו of 6.14aβ; then 7.1 follows with waw-conversive verbs, which would indicate connection with and dependence on 6.14.

After the transition, there is a brief exposition which resumes an original 'Plan'; of course the reader was not forewarned that Esther would ask for banquets, but they function as part of the duo's plan to approach the king to save the nation. The rest of the subunit presents two logically-connected reversals through dialog and narration. The unit closes in o' with the assuaging of the king's wrath (7.10); this is further confirmed by the time phrase opening 8.1. Thus the unit in o' is 6.14–7.10.

The unit differs in L. Structurally the opening is similar to o', though transition and exposition fall within one verse, L 6.23. One may be reminded that although both texts started in parallel with 6.1, L numbers verses more frequently in ch. 6, and has narrative pluses also, so that the verse numbers do not match between the two texts. Within the unit, L presents material not in found in o': the sealing of Aman's life (= his death) with the royal ring, possibly the ring Aman used to seal the decree of death. This plus in L adds another irony to the story. After this narrative statement, the king speaks to Esther in disbelief over Aman's dastardly plan (again not in o'); thus the king is a little more intelligent in L than he is in o'.

Where does the unit end? Mordecai actually appears in L 7.15, so it could be argued that a new unit begins there; the unit in question would then be 6.23–7.14. However, since Mordecai is mentioned in 7.14 within the king's dialog expressing disbelief and therefore a new character is narratively introduced, this verse has been chosen here as the opening for a new unit in L. Thus the text again develops action and narrative advancement by means of clustering different characters. So the unit becomes 6.23–7.13 for L.

A new unit follows with the king, Mordecai and Esther: 'Intercession for the People' (o' 8.1-14 // L 7.14-38). The reason for opening a unit at that point should already be clear. A brief glance at the microstructures will also make clear how much the two texts differ. How far do these differing subunits extend? In o' two reversals take place in rapid sequence, one for each hero; then the letter of license is inserted before the narrative section is completed. At the end of the letter, narrative information on its distribution resumes (vv. 13-15). The point of view then shifts to Mordecai and the celebration of the people (vv. 15-17)—a new section. Thus there are three parts within this section: the reversal of Mordecai's promotion (reversal number five), Esther's intercession (reversal number six), and the result of that intercession: a facsimile of the letter itself.

In the L text, 7.14 (a plus vis-à-vis o') serves as exposition for this cluster of characters (the same as in o') and for reversals 5-9, three more

than in o´. Reversal five parallels that of o´, but in L Mordecai asks that
'Aman's epistle' be taken away/annulled (ἀναιρέω).[56] A simple statement is all that prepares the reader for a decree, and that would not be
deduced from the words 'And the king commissioned him with the
affairs of the empire'. No more is heard of Mordecai in this passage.
Esther speaks next (reversal 6), seeking to execute her enemies and
Aman's sons (7.18-19). Immediately following is reversal seven: a battle
report, without benefit of narrative background or a decree of defense
(which one suspects only seems strange due to the general familiarity
with MT and LXX). Since an earlier decree of death is extant, this contrapositive decree—that is to say, its text—will constitute reversal eight.

o´ Text

5. DÉNOUEMENT = *Peripety/Reversal* of Fortune for Mordecai,
    Esther & People vs. Aman (in narratives, decree, reports etc.,
    to 8.17, & resumes in Epilog)   6.6–E–8.14
      a. King, Aman & Mordecai: reversal 1: Mordecai
         honored by Aman   6.6-12
            (Setting: understood that Aman enters)
           1) Dialog: king & Aman (complication for villain)   6-10
             a) Royal speech   6a
               α Introductory quotation formula   6aα
               β Speech proper   6aβγ
                 αα Question: What?   6aβ(1-2)
                 ββ Object, general: man   6aβ(3-4)
                 γγ Object, specific: I wish to honor 6aγ
             b) Digression: self-speech: Aman's thoughts 6bc
               α Introductory quotation formula (in self) 6bα
               β Self-speech proper   6bβc
                 αα Question: who?   6bβ(1)
                 ββ Object, general: honor   6bβ(2-l)
                 γγ Object, specific: me   6c

---

56. Apparently a late use; = ὡς ὅτι which picks up the ὅτι 'of contents' after
verbs of mental or sense perception, especially verbs of saying, indicating, etc., to
indicate the content of what is said, thought, etc. Probably also carries the 'subjective'
meaning 'as (of such content) that (in the author's mind/opinion) such and such'.

c) Vizier speech: Aman (as defense lawyer for self) 7-9
    α Introductory quotation formula   7a
    β Speech proper   7b-9
        αα Declaration (nominative absolute)   7b
        ββ Recommendations   8-9
            α1 servants bring   8aα(1-5)
            β1 royal linen robe   8aα(6-7)
            γ1 which king wears   8aβ
            δ1 & horse   8bα
            ε1 which king rides   8bβ
            ζ1 give to noble friend of king   9aα
            η1 let him dress   9aβ
            θ1 whom king loves   9bα
            ι1 let him mount   9bβ
            κ1 call out through city   9cα
            λ1 'Thus...honors'   9cβ
d) Royal speech   10
    α Introductory quotation formula   10aα
    β Speech proper   10aβbc
        αα Approval   10aβ
        ββ Order 1: do thus   10bα(1-2)
            α1 to Mordecai the Jew   10bα(3-6)
            β1 serving at gate   10bβ
            γ1 Order 2: omit nothing!   10c
2) Compliance: reversal 1: Mordecai honored,
Aman humiliated   11
    a) Act 1: takes robe/horse   11aα
    b) Act 2: clothes Mordecai (as slave)   11aβ
    c) Act 3: mounts him on horse   11bα
    d) Act 4: leads him in city   11bβ
    e) Act 5: crys, 'Thus...'   11c
3) Conclusion: Report of returns   12
    a) Return of protagonist: to court (calmly?
    no note of effect)   12a
    b) Return of antagonist & effect   12b
        α Aman hastens (?) home   12bα
        β Effects   12bβ
            αα mourning   12bβ(1)
            ββ head down/covered (?)   12bβ(2-3)

b. Aman, family & friends: debriefing dialog with Zosara;
    reversal 2: prophecy: Aman's doom   13
    1) Report: Aman   13a
        a) Act: Aman reports   13aα
        b) Object: what happened to him   13aβ
        c) Indirect Object: wife Zosara, friends   13aγ
    2) Speech/prophecy: friends, wife   13bcd
        a) Introductory quotation formula   13bα
        b) Speech proper   13bβcd
            α Condition: if Jew   13bβ
            β Fact: humbling began   13cα
            γ Result: positive & negative   13cβdα
                αα you will fall   13cβ
                ββ you will be unable   13dα
            δ Reason: Living God   13dβ

c. King, Esther & Aman: plan resumes: Esther's 2nd
    drinkfest & Aman's fall; reversal 3: request/response
    & accusation/exposure of Aman; reversal 4:
    execution   6.14–7.10
    1) Transition to drinkfest   14
        a) Time: while yet speaking   14aα
        b) Act: eunuchs arrive   14aβ
        c) Object: hurry Aman to Esther's drinkfest   14b
    2) Exposition: Royal escort & Esther's drinkfest begins   7.1
        a) Who: king & Aman enter   1a
        b) Purpose (2)   1b
            α to drink   1bα
            β with the queen   1bβ
    3) Reversal 3: royal dialog: request & response;
        description: Aman accused & exposed   2-8
        a) Speech: king to Esther   2
            α Introductory quotation formula   2a
                αα Address   2aα
                ββ Time (2nd day)   2aβ
            β Speech proper: triple questions/1 offer   2bcd
                αα Question 1: what?   2bα
                ββ Address: Ο Queen Esther   2bβ
                γγ Question 2: request?   2cα
                δδ Question 3: petition?   2cβ

α1 before king   6bβ(1-3)
β1 & queen   6bβ(4-6)
β King's reactions (2)   7a
  αα rises   7aα
  ββ (goes) to garden   7aβ
γ Aman's reaction   7b
  αα Act: beseeches queen 7bα
  ββ Reason: sees self 'in bad' 7bβ
δ Results: king, Aman, Esther   8
  αα Act 1: king returns 8aα
  ββ Act 2: Aman has fallen 8aβ(1-3)
    α1 Location: on couch 8aβ(4-6)
    β1 Purpose: beseech queen 8aβ(7-9)
  γγ King's speech   8b
    α1 Intro. quotation formula 8bα
    β1 Speech proper 8bβ
      α2 Question: So he forces?
      (unbelief) 8bβ(1)
      β2 Intensifiers 8bβ(2-9)
        α3 even my wife 8bβ(2-4)
        β3 in my house? 8bβ(6-9)
  δδ Act 3: Aman's reaction 8c
    α1 hearing (king's words) 8cα
    β1 he turned face aside 8cβ
4) Result: reversal 4: Aman executed at
counsel of Bougathan   9-10
  a) Servant speech: Bougathan 9abcd
    α Introductory quotation formula 9a
    αα Act: speaks/counsels 9aα(1-2)
    ββ Name: Bougathan 9aα(3)
    γγ Job: royal eunuch 9aβ
    β Speech: ironic solution 9bcd
      αα Exclamation, intensive & object 9bα
      ββ Description: tree & purpose 9bβcd
      α1 Aman prepared 9bβ
      β1 for Mordecai 9cα(1)
        α2 who spoke 9cα(2-3)
        β2 for king('s life) 9cβ

α1 Aman's evil   3bα(4-6)

  β1 what he did against Jews   3bβ

β Report: king's reaction & result   4

  αα extends gold sceptre   4a

  ββ Result: Esther rises to stand   4b

γ Esther's speech   5-6

  αα Introductory quotation formula   5aα

  ββ Speech proper   5aβ-6

    α1 Protocol (2)   5aβbα

      α2 if good to you   5aβ

      β2 if I found favor   5bα

    β1 Request   5bβc

      α2 (order) be sent   5bβ(1-2)

      β2 Purpose   5bβ(2-l)c

        α3 reverse letters   5bβ

        β3 sent by Aman 5bβ(5-8)

        γ3 to destroy   5cα

        δ3 in your empire   5cβ

    γ1 Reasons (2)   6

      α2 How watch evil?   6a

      β2 How can I be saved?   6b

b) King's response: speech/decree   7-12

  α Royal speech   7-8

    αα Introductory quotation formula   7aα

      α1 Formula proper   7aα(1-4)

      β1 Addressee: Esther   7aα(5-6)

    ββ Speech proper   7b-8

      α1 Protasis   7aβbcα

        α2 I gave   7aβ

        β2 I graced you   7bα

        γ2 I hanged (Aman)   7bβ

        δ2 for attack on Jews   7cα

      β1 Apodosis: what?   7cβ

      γ1 Permission/order (2)

      Mordecai/Esther's acts   8a

        α2 *you* write!   8aα

          α3 in my name   8aβ

          β3 as you like   8aγ

        β2 seal!   8bα

L Text

b) Digression: self-speech: Aman's thoughts   10
   α Intro. quotation formula (thought)   10aα
   β Self-speech proper   10aβb
      αα Question: who?   10aβ(1)
      ββ Object, general: honor   10aβ(2-5)
      γγ Object, specific: me   10b
c) Vizier speech: Aman (as defense lawyer for self) 11
   α Introductory quotation formula   11aα
   β Speech proper   11aβ-g
      αα Declaration (nominative absolute) 11aβ
      ββ Recommendations   11b-g
         α1 let be taken   11bα(1)
         β1 royal robe   11bα(2-3)
         γ1 & royal horse   11bβ
         δ1 which king rides   11bγ
         ε1 let one of nobles   11cα
         ζ1 of king's friends   11cβ
         η1 take these   11dα
         θ1 let him dress   11dβ
         ι1 mount him   11e
         κ1 lead through city   11f
         λ1 calling out   11gα
         μ1 'Thus...man who fears king 11gβ
         ν1 whom king honors'   11gγ
d) Royal speech   12
   α Introductory quotation formula   12aα
   β Speech proper   12aβbcd
      αα Order 1: run quick!   12aβ
      ββ Order 2: take   12bα(1-2)
         α1 horse & robe   12bα(3-6)
         β1 as you said   12bβ
      γγ Order 3: do! (all)   12cα(1-2)
         α1 to Mordecai the Jew   12cα(3-5)
         β1 sits at gate   12cβ
      δδ Order 4: omit nothing!   12d
e) Reaction: Aman suffers   13
   α When Aman knows   13aα
   β Object 1: he not honored   13aβ
   γ Object 2: Mordecai to be honored   13bα

α Introductory quotation formula: Esther 3aα
β Protocol (dual) 3aβγ
  αα if seems right… 3aβ
  ββ & decision good 3aγ
γ Requests (dual) 3b
  αα my people…for request 3bα
  ββ and nation for my life 3bβ
δ Reason & circumstances 4
  αα Reason & detail (2) 4ab
    α1 Reason: I & people sold 4aα
    β1 Further details (2) 4aβ
      α2 enslaved 4bα
      β2 children taken 4bβ
  ββ Disclaimer (2: Esther/Aman) 4cd
    α1 I didn't want to report 4cα
    β1 Reason 1: not to grieve
      my lord 4cβ
    γ1 Reason 2: for evildoer has
      suffered reversal (?) 4d
d) Result & speech: king 5
  α king angry 5aα
  β Introductory quotation formula 5aβ
  γ Speech proper (2) 5bc
    αα Who is it? 5bα
    ββ who dares humble royal sign 5bβ
    γγ so as not to fear you? 5c
e) Reactions & speech: Esther delays 6-7
  α Reaction: Esther 6aαβγ
    αα queen sees 6aα
    ββ it appears wrong to king 6aβ
    γγ & he hates evil 6aγ
  β Speech: Esther 6bcd
    αα Introductory quotation formula 6bα
    ββ Speech proper 6bβγcde
      α1 Do not be angry! 6bβ
      β1 O lord 6bγ
      γ1 Reason 6c
        α2 sufficient that 6cα
        β2 I find your mercy 6cβ

β3 a crime against

the kingdom? 11bγ

β2 Question 2 (= 2nd crime)

& 2 intensifiers 11c

α3 even my wife 11cα

β3 you force 11cβ

γ3 before me? 11cγ

γ2 Order (2 parts) 11d

α3 take him! 11dα

β3 no begging! 11dβ

δδ Conclusion: thus Aman led away 12aα

4) Result: reversal 4: Aman executed at

counsel of servant 12aβ-13

a) Servant speech: Agathas 12aβcd

α Introductory quotation formula 12aβ(1-2)

β Identity 12aβ(3)γ

αα Name: Agathas 12aβ(3)

ββ Job: a servant (of Aman or king?) 12aγ

γ Speech: ironic solution 12bcd

αα Exclamation & object 12bα

ββ Description: tree & purpose 12bβc

α1 in his court 12bβ

β1 50 cubits high 12bγ

γ1 Aman cut down 12cα

δ1 to hang Mordecai 12cβ

α2 who spoke good 12cγ(1-3)

β2 for king('s life) 12cγ(4-6)

γγ Inference: therefore 12dα(2)

δδ Counsel 12dα(1,3)β

α1 Petition: command 12dα(1)

β1 Address: O lord 12dα(3)

γ1 to hang him on it 12dβ

b) King's response: command & acts 13

α Speech 13ab

αα Introductory quotation formula 13a

ββ Command: Hang him! 13b

β Acts: official 13c

αα king removes ring 13cα

ββ seals his (Aman's) life 13cβ

Minor differences exist in the dialog between Aman and the king (o' 6.6-10 // L 6.9-13):

1. o' describes the robe of the king as 'fine linen', to which L has no parallel (this is consistent with L, which gives less specifics of the court, etc., as in the previous descriptions of the palace);
2. o' describes the man to be honored as one 'whom the king loves', to which L has no parallel;
3. o''s proclamation is 'thus shall it be (done) to every man whom the king wills (θέλει) to honor (δοξάζω)', whereas L has 'accordingly shall it be done for the man *who respects* (τιμάω) *the king*, whom the king wishes (βούλομαι) to honor (δοξάζω)' (emphasized English words find no parallel in o').

o' seems to leave this honor and the king's love to chance. In contrast, L evidences a Semitic type of antithetic parallelism with its concomitant reversal (a peripety-like, positive retributive justice), and also sounds a sermonic, didactic note applicable either in Diaspora or in subjugated Palestine.

When it comes to the royal speech of o′ 6.10 // L 6.12 and Aman's reaction to it (in L v. 13):

1. o′ has the king instruct Aman to carry out the plan, while L has the additional 'run quickly' to match the heightened irony of the moment;
2. o′ totally lacks any comment on Aman's reaction, whereas L has:
   a. heart utterly crushed;
   b. spirit changed to faintness.

It is difficult to conceive that any minority audience—Jewish or otherwise—could be brought to this emotional climax in seeing its archenemy fall into such an ironic trap, yet not be given a window into his thoughts of disgrace! Certainly L makes up for this narrative lack in o′ by giving the readers a look into Aman's thoughts (after the fact), similar to that of the self-speech given at the beginning of this unit. The hearers or readers 'deserve' to see the proud heart of their enemy crushed, and L gives them this privilege. Once again this stresses the humanity and psychology of L, as over against o′, which seems to operate on a flatter narrative plane. Does it also stress a certain Jewishness?

In the 'Compliance/Conclusion' (o′ 6.11-12 // L 6.14-19), L again takes the obvious opportunity to show the divine hand in peripety or reversal of fortune. A Jewish audience deserves this emphasis after the anti-Semitic aspects of the story so acutely outlined:

1. o′ gives a matter-of-fact description of the events, while L adds the comment (lacking in o′) that Aman did reverence to Mordecai 'precisely on that day he had determined to impale him' (v. 14b);
2. o′ gives no detailed description of Mordecai, while L, carrying on the humanistic, psychological note, relates (with a large textual plus) that:
   a. Aman ordered Mordecai to remove the sackcloth which he was wearing in mourning;
   b. Mordecai is described as fearful, apparently not sure what Aman intended to do (whip him, hurt him, put him in prison, execute him?);
   c. Mordecai is described as 'one who was dying';
3. o′ lacks any insight into the inner experience of Mordecai at this point, while L gives three insights into Mordecai:
   a. the curious statement 'and Mordecai thought he saw a portent' (a reference to prophetic powers?);
   b. 'his heart was toward the Lord';
   c. Mordecai became speechless;

4. o′ has Aman returning home after the event and Mordecai returning to the palace (the original place of mourning), while L has both returning to their homes;

5. o′ describes Aman as mourning with head covered, whereas L describes him as melancholy.

Despite the differences noted, both texts have Aman completing the assignment, taking Mordecai through the city (the streets of the city in o′) and proclaiming the prescribed call of honor. Both texts remain consistent within themselves in using the form of the announcement given earlier in the text.

Mordecai has been temporarily placed next to the king (a foreshadowing) and dressed in royal robes. This reverses his 'dishonor' of sackcloth and ashes in ch. 3; he has also temporarily thwarted Aman's gallows (of which he has not been told, but we readers know well). Yet tension stays high since technically and in fact he and his people remain under the coming death threat. Readers and Mordecai also know well that this honor will be vapid, cruelly ironic, if the decree of death is carried out.

The two texts take a different viewpoint in the 'Debriefing Dialog' of o′ 6.13 // L 6.20-22: in o′ Aman's wife and friends deliver a 'woe oracle' of defeat, or more likely destruction (note the ambivalent and Semitic-sounding πεσὼν πεσῇ, 'falling you will fall'), while L has them giving sage advice—advice which seems to leave room for repentance and escape from calamity.

The logic of o′ is this:

a. Mordecai is a Jew;
b. you have already been humbled before him;
c. you have planned to hurt all the Jews;
d. therefore you may likewise plan to be humbled (or destroyed) before all of them,
e. since God who lives is with them.

The logic of L is this:

a. calamity began when you spoke evil of Mordecai;
b. cease speaking evil against him and
c. calamity will cease,
d. for God must be controlling the situation in Mordecai's favor.

Both texts seem to draw on a form of *lex talionis*, and to emphasize God's role, but with different operative hermeneutics: o′ seems to assume, in line with the story's outcome, that the penalty is set. L, in line with many biblical prophetic appeals to repent in order to avoid the sentence of Yahweh, seems not to assume the story's conclusion. One may risk the suggestion that o''s adherence to the storyline perhaps reflects the color of Greek tragedy and blind fate, while L reflects the Judaic theology of repentance and Yahweh's willingness to relent (cf. Amos 5; Jeremiah 18).

The further difference may be noted that o' seals the oracle of woe against Aman with the immediate arrival of messengers to take him to the banquet (the reader now suspects, with this oracular foreshadowing, that Esther will succeed this time), whereas L (humanely, or ironically?) attributes remaining hope to Aman after receiving the advice from wife and friends, thus setting the audience up for more vicarious vengeance. L therefore notes that the arrival of the messengers to escort him to the banquet resulted in his being 'gladdened' and that he arrived in ample time for the drinkfest. In a real sense L has, once again, shown itself to be more literary. The o' text, in forewarning readers of Aman's fate, has reduced the sharpness of the next encounter. L, however, has 'greased the pig for the fire' by having Aman come to the feast with renewed gladness and hope.

When it comes to the 'Royal Dialog' in o' 6.2-8 // L 7.1-12, beginning with the king's speech to Esther (o' 7.2 // L 7.1) and her feelings (L 7.2), the following differences may be noted:

1. o' has the king begin the dialog immediately, while L has the dialog begin 'when the drinking was well advanced/going well' (alcohol could make a difference!);
2. in o' the king asks, 'what is your request/petition?', while in L he asks in addition, 'what is the danger?' (the text has given no clue as to how he knew this);
3. L has two compound sentences, lacking in o', describing Esther's inner feelings:
   a. she was anxious;
   b. she saw the adversary before her eyes;
   c. God gave her courage;
   d. because she called on Him.

This plus in L, rich in pathos, allusion and theology, constitutes a third *crisis* and intervention, of which there is no clue in o'. If L is later than o', the author could have added Esther's feelings and this crisis; but in that case it is less likely that L, as a late text presumably familiar with some form of o', would leave a dangling element such as that noted in point 2 above. It is easier to explain that phrase, 'what is the danger?',

as an element at least independent of o´, and possibly earlier than o´.
Another possibility, maintaining also that the phrase is original to L and
earlier than o´, is that it was deleted by o´ for cohesiveness, and that the
description of Easther's inner feelings was added independently by L at
a later date to increase the drama and the roles of both Esther and God.
The question of priority and possible confluence of texts will be explored in Chapter 4 of this study.

The differences in 'Esther's Response: Revelation' (7.3-4 in both
texts) are:

1. in o´ the request protocol is 'if I have found favor in your eyes', while in L
    the dual protocol is 'if it seems right to the king, and the decision is good in
    his heart' (note the parallelism, as if from a Semitic source);
2. in o´ Esther requests that the peoples' lives and her life be added to her
    request, while in L (it appears that) Esther requests the lives of the people or
    nation 'for my life' (= in exchange for?).
3. o´ gives no reason for Esther's not coming to the king earlier, whereas L
    gives such a reason, namely that Esther did not want to disturb the king (the
    difference now is: the villain has undergone a reversal, i.e. he is shown to be
    a villain).

There is a difficult dative and genitive combination in L, as noted at the
end of the second point above. It may mean 'give me the λαός [dative]
as my gift' and 'give me the nation of [genitive] my (very) life', meaning her life is bound with the corporate life of her nation. But with the
genitive/ablative form it is possible to think of verbs of buying and
selling used with the genitive and of an elliptical (ἀντὶ) τῆς ψυχῆς μου,
meaning 'in exchange for': Esther is willing to sacrifice her life for her
people in a greater way than Mordecai in his prayer. In narrative terms
one finds a possible plurisignation here—delightful ambiguity for more
than one meaning.

The two texts vary significantly in the '(Result and) Speech' of the
king (7.5 in both texts) and in what follows his speech:

1. o´ does not describe the king's attitude, while L says, 'the king was angry';
2. o´ has the simple question, 'Who has dared to do this thing?', while L
    expands the question into 'Who has dared to humble the sign of my
    kingdom by paying no heed to fear you?';
3. o´ does not give Esther's inner thoughts at this point, while L notes that she
    became aware that the king agreed a great wrong had been done and that 'he
    hated the evil';
4. The o´ text has Esther identify Aman immediately upon the king's question,
    while the L text prolongs her answer (specifically at this point it appears that

she will offer yet another banquet at which she will reveal the villain's name);

5. L continues with the king's persuasion of Esther to tell him who has acted so corruptly, adding an oath to grant her request, to which o′ has no parallel;

6. o′ has Esther merely answering the king's question, whereas L once again shows the inner feelings of Esther: before answering, she 'takes courage'.

L's plus under the second point above seems a little obscure, but Esther clearly receives honor here that is not hers in o′. Again the king has been given more credit in L, somewhat so under point 2, more so under point 3. Both the divine intervention and the human drama are played out more completely in L than in o′. For the second time Esther has called on God (only in L) and for the second time the deity has intervened to help her (also only in L), for a total of three times with 6.1. God has changed the heart of this Gentile king. What is more, for those who may have already faulted Esther for marrying a Gentile, to show him truly sympathetic to the Jews is to soften the transgression somewhat.

When Esther exposes the exterminator in o′ 7.6a // L 7.8, the difference is that in o′ she identifies him in a compact sentence (Aman is an adversary and wicked), whereas in L the description is somewhat expanded (Aman is your friend, a deceiver, a wicked man).

The reactions of the two men vary in the texts (o′ 7.6b-8 // L 7.9-12aα) by degree. L is more dramatic, as usual.

1. o′ summarizes regarding Aman, that he was troubled before the king and queen, while L reserves comment regarding him until after that of the king, and has Aman being terrified, falling at the feet of the queen;

2. o′ has the king getting up and going out to the garden, while L, more dramatic, has the king enraged, springing to his feet and walking about (it is not said that he leaves);

3. in o′, while the king is in the garden, Aman actually lies on the queen's bed to entreat her (a hint of seduction?), the text being more suggestive and faintly risqué, whereas in L Aman 'fell at the feet of Esther as she lay on her bed', the text being more restrained and possibly euphemistic;

4. in o′ the king returns from the garden, a flashback tells what Aman has done (slowing the action), and thus the king sees Aman in a compromising position (literally, 'had fallen on the/her couch') and accuses him of improper advances upon his consort, whereas in L Aman's emotion is revealed and the action follows quickly and uninterruptedly upon Aman's falling 'at the feet of Esther the queen still reclining...';

5. in o′ there is no command of the king to remove Aman at all, and the narrative never indicates what happens to Aman from the point of exposure until his hanging, whereas in L the king commands Aman to be removed and not to beg for mercy in the process.

Does the king need something more than Aman's plot against the Jews in order to substantiate his royal condemnation? No, the king's absence allows Aman to fall onto the second tine of a trident-like irony: he appears to breach protocol with regard to the king's wife! The first spearpoint was Aman's vanity and futility in proposing how he wished to be honored; now the irony rises even higher with o´ seeming to want the reader to see Aman taking liberties with Esther. The third shaft of irony involves the gallows.

o´ heightens the irony, humor and entertainment in professional story-telling style (in spite of some choppiness and wooden flatness in the characters), and, one must admit, has extra spiciness in sexual allusion. L, along with a literary smoothness, concerns itself with another pathos: the emotional satisfaction of readers/hearers. The epithets L heaps on Aman, and the verb ἐταράχθη ('was agitated/troubled', classically used of the bowels as well as of the mind, as against o´´'s cognitive ἑώρα... κακοῖς, 'saw...bad things'), the abject falling at Esther's feet, plus the king's prohibition against Aman's begging for mercy, all support the view that L's readers are acquainted with persecutors/oppressors, and would identify with this victory. Thus L here continues its tendency to help the reader see into the personae of the story's main players and find more pathos in the plot.

One might argue from this either that o´ is older and based upon oral tradition while L is literary, or that o´ is a wooden and wordy translation by a Greek scribe who neither did nor could enjoy the subtle nuances of a Semitic *Vorlage*. If the latter were true, then L would be a literary attempt to render into Greek what may have been a literary masterpiece in Semitic (in part, Torrey) or to improve the poorer o´ (Tov).

The two texts differ in their account of the 'Result: Reversal 4' (o´ 7.9-10 // L 7.12aβ-13):

1. o´ identifies the servant as Bugathan, a chamberlain, while L identifies him as Agathas, one of the king's servants;
2. o´ identifies the gallows built by Aman as 'in the premises of Aman', to which L has no parallel;
3. in o´ the servant (Bugathan) suggests to the king that Aman be hung on his own gallows, while in L the king comes to this conclusion on his own;
4. in o´ the execution of Aman follows immediately, whereas in L the king seals a royal command with his signet ring, and an ironic insertion in the text notes that Aman himself was therewith sealed.

Aman has been run through for the third time with his impalement (or crucifixion) on his own pole. It is difficult to judge which of the differing elements in this panel are prior to which; it is clear, however, that the king gets more credit in L (see point 3 above), and that L adds a final—and dual—note of irony (see point 4).

The section 'Intercession for the People' (o´ 8.1-14 // L 7.14-43) opens with a royal speech found only in L (7.14). The speech consists of the king wondering at the gall of Aman and being amazed that Aman over-looked the good Mordecai had done for the king and that he overlooked the family ties between Mordecai and Esther (but how did he know?).

'Reversal 5: The Elevation of Mordecai' (o´ 8.1-12 // L 7.15-17) has clear differences between o´ and L:

1. o´ immediately, on the execution of Aman, has the king giving all of Aman's possessions to Esther, while L has the king giving Aman's possessions to Mordecai;
2. in o´ the ring which the king gave to Aman is now given to Mordecai, while L has no mention of the ring (to avoid a note of magic?);
3. o´ gives a reason for the king calling Mordecai, namely that Esther had revealed her relationship to Mordecai, while L, assuming this to be common knowledge as the former narrative indicates, has no mention of this;
4. in o´ Esther appoints Mordecai over all that had been Aman's, while in L the king himself appoints Mordecai to oversee the affairs of the kingdom;
5. in o´ there is no mention of Mordecai requesting the revoking of Aman's letter, whereas in L this specific request is granted by the king.

Note that L emphasizes Mordecai and not Esther. L's extra crisis/inter-vention for Esther in 7.2 should be read in terms of encouraging prayer and/or the view that women are tender, in need of support (a view which is more Palestinian, less Hellenistic?).

When we come to 'Reversal 6' (from 8.3 in o´ and 7.18 in L), we may observe that, while the request of Esther exists in both texts, the o´ text is considerably longer than the L parallel. In fact, with the exception of the letter/decree, o´ and L diverge permanently from this point on.

1. The o´ text describes the posture of Esther's coming to the king as being prone at his feet, to which the L text has no parallel;
2. o´ has the king extending his scepter to Esther, to which again L has no parallel;
3. in o´ the basic request of Esther involves the reversal of Aman's letter and plot against the Jews, while in L her request is for the execution of Aman's sons, which is granted;
4. the L text notes that Esther smote enemies in great numbers according to the command of the king, but there is no equivalent in o´ at this point;
5. in o´, after Esther requests the reversal of Aman's letter and plot against the Jews, the king gives her authority to write whatever she wants and to seal it

with his ring, whereas in L Mordecai (who is pictured as someone more important) is given the right to write whatever he wants and to seal it with the king's ring, but this comes after the letter/decree.

Following the text of the royal letter (to be discussed in detail below), there are striking differences as well as important similarities between the two EG texts, and one may also note L's structural and content differences here from both o′ and the EH text. The reader, already aware that verse numbers in o′ and L no longer correspond (since L ends the book with ch. 7), must not be surprised that for the first time *whole sections of content do not match.* More obvious differences will be noted as usual in the discussion here in Chapter 2 of the present study, but overall assessment must await Chapter 4 on redaction.

There are a number of important differences with regard to the continuation of Reversal 6 (in o′ 8.13-14) as compared with L's 'Reversal 9' (in L 7.33-38):

1. o′ spells out details of publication throughout the empire, while L shows a minus;
2. o′ details the contents of the letter, while L again has a minus;
3. o′ has no specific parallel to L's letter from Mordecai.

o′'s and MT's spelling out of the data of publication and content serves to heighten suspense in storytelling fashion. Conversely, L speeds the action by its minus and by mentioning only Sousa. Either the short or the long form could derive from the other, theoretically, but the case is different with regard to the last point, which is a major divergence.

This major difference of Mordecai's letter appearing only in L must be discussed because it offers an otherwise unattested passage—a possible witness to an earlier form of Esther, if it can be momentarily assumed for the purpose of argument that it *could* represent the earliest form of Esther. L's text with the two writings, one from the king and a lesser one from Mordecai, shows signs of being prior to o′, since it is more difficult to explain an original Mordecai decree being watered down to two writings, the most important or dominant of which is now the king's. Within the narrative the king of course must do something, so the storyline or plot is a factor sufficient to generate a writing from the king.

An additional factor, it is submitted here, is the influence of the royal novella or *Königsnovelle*: the king or queen always acts at critical junctures because he or she is the central character[8].[57] Within the Esther story this influence means the king must either write or at least give permission to Mordecai/Esther to write. Both these factors militate against a royal writing being added *later* to an original Mordecai writing.

Further, if one begins with a longer royal letter and a shorter one from Mordecai (as in L), it is far easier to see how that royal letter could be co-opted by Mordecai (both Mordecai and Esther are told to write in o′ and MT 8.8), through a later development, than to explain the reverse. That is, how could an original writing from Mordecai evolve into a crucial document from a secondary character (the king), leaving the letter from Mordecai (as now in L) to play such a non-important role? A reader familiar with MT or o′ will recognize that the presence there of Esther's letter (ch. 9), which is non-existent in L, can also be better explained on this model.

Another indication of L's being earlier than o′ is the lack of a feast name in Mordecai's letter (a fact which would help explain why it is called the 'Day of Mordecai' in 2 Macc. 15.29). This feature is easier to explain as early and natural, rather than as a later, deliberate reduction from a particular name to no name. This crucial point requires additional explanation. An older form of the story would either have Mordecai's writing about a feast from the beginning, or it would be the first addition. That is, a rescue story could have stood alone, or it may have connected the festival concept (as a result of rescue) with the story from its inception. Based solely on the evidence of L, one would have to say that this unpolished, brief epistle of Mordecai, without even so much as a name for the feast, or a date for it (only the date of destruction is given), or any mention of the two-day problem, preserves the oldest (and in this case crudest) form or kernel which later redactors expanded.

Even if one could assume a well-known, well-developed feast behind this simple letter, so that the points just mentioned would not need to be specified, it is hard to explain that the feast is not named. Is it not easier to take the opposite stance, namely that the problem of differences among communities has not arisen, or is not critical, and that the name is not yet fixed and/or the feast part of the story is minor, much less important than the story?

That judgment of course is not proof, but one imagines that the presupposition that L is a late text obscured this otherwise clear possibility.

---

57. See my Chapter 4 for a description of this form and a defense of the thesis that it influenced Esther.

And once Mordecai's embedded letter is posited as early, it is possible to argue further that MT—with its greater stress on Mordecai's role (8.9) in dictating the letter of license (decree of defense), and its greater festival detail (MT ch. 9)—occupies the last position in the development of (at least this part of) Esther.

Although the king could be the one dictating his letter/decree in o´ 8.9, in view of the king's permission to Mordecai in 8.8 to write ἐκ τοῦ ὀνόματός μου, the 'whatever he ordered' of 8.9 is *likely* to mean Mordecai. But right here MT *specifies* Mordecai. Chronologically, then, o´ would hold the middle position between L and the final form of EH. If this order is correct, it means that o´ witnesses to a more important role for Mordecai than that attested in the earliest form (L), where the king clearly does the writing and towers over Mordecai in importance. Looking forward from this putatively early L, the normal historical processes would argue for less and less importance attaching to the king, but more and more to Mordecai.

The Royal Letter (LXX E 1-24)

In Hanhart this unit contains 424 words, including the narrative introduction, versus 465 in o´. Both texts consist of two parts, and while they 'narrativize' a good deal (not to mention the style of bombast, convolution and piling up of modifiers), some legal type language and formulas can be seen. No Semitic *Vorlage* can be posited.

As before with sections B, C and D, the decree of defense—not found in Hebrew and denominated 'E' in Hanhart—will stand outside the normal sequence of structure. As it appears here (note the different collation in the L text), it epexegetically details and validates the author's foregoing letter/decree resume—found variantly in Hebrew—with a purported archival copy of the *ipsissima verba*. Serving as a reversal (= reversal 6) and contrapositive to the decree of death in ch. 3, this decree of defense intrudes into the narrative of the fifth reversal after 8.12, before vv. 13-14. Although both 'decrees' are labeled *letters* in the text, the first *epistole* (section B) shows more affinity with decrees known from the Roman period. Contrastingly, this contrapositive 'decree' more closely follows the form of a Hellenistic letter. With some narrative license assumed in order to honor both genre and function, it is titled here as follows.

o´ Text of the Royal Letter (E 1-24)

I. LITERARY INTRODUCTION: Statement = Quotation Formula:	
'A copy of the letter (*epistole*) is appended'	1aα
II. LETTER PROPER	1aβ-24
A. OPENING	1aβbcd
1. Titulature	1aβbc
a. Title & addressor: Artaxerxes	1aβ
b. Addressees & areas	1bc
1) Addressees	1bα(1)c
a) rulers of provinces	1cα
b) those loyal . . .	1cβ
2) Areas	1bα(2-7)β
a) from India to Ethiopia	1bα(2-7)
b) (in) 127 provinces	1bβ
2. Salutation: χαίρειν	1d
B. BODY	2-24
1. Opening: Background/occasion = accusatory description	2-4
a. Background, general: . . . becoming proud	2
1) Subject: many (in office)	2aα
2) Reason	2aβb
a) benefactor's kindness	2aβ
b) honored too often	2bα
3) Act: become proud	2bβ
b. Background, specifics (3 acts)	3-4
1) Physical (2)	3
a) Act: seek to injure subjects	3a
b) Condition: unable to bear success	3b
c) Act 2: connive against benefactors	3c
2) Ethico-Theological: (1 act/2 descriptions)	4
a) killing off gratitude	4a
b) puffed up by . . . no-gooders	4bα
c) Object	4bβcαγ
α evil hating judgment	4cαγ
β of always	4bβ(5)
γ all-seeing God	4bβ(1-4,6)
d) Subject & act: they presume to escape	
(God & justice)	4cβ

L Text of the Royal Letter (7.22-32)

3) Accusation 1st: immediate purpose: plot to kill
   us & Jews   26ab
   a) Attitude: arrogance   26a
   b) Act: planned to remove   26aβε
   c) Objects, general   26aγδ
       α our government   26aγ
       β & life   26aδ
   d) Objects, specific   26bc
       α Mordecai, our constant savior   26bα
       β Esther, his blameless partner   26bβ
       γ & whole race (Jews)   26bγ
   e) Manner: intricate cunning   26cα
   f) Act 2: schemed to kill   26cβ
4) Accusation 2: ultimate purpose: a coup d'etat
   for our enemies   26de
   a) Manner (conspiracies)   26dα
   b) Act: imagined ... seize   26dβ(1-2)
   c) Object   26dβ(3-4)
       α us   26dβ(3)
       β while defenseless   26dβ(4)
   d) Purpose   26e
       α cause seizure (= betray)   26eαδ
       β Persians to Macedonians   26eβγ
d. Disclosure 3: verdict of royal fact-finding
   investigation: exoneration   27
   1) Transition: οὖν   27aα(2)
   2) Object   27aα(1,3-8)
       a) Status: betrayed (to extinction)   27aα(1,3-7)
       b) Name: Jews   27aα(8)
   3) Prosecutor: archvillain (Aman)   27aα(3-5)
   4) Subject/Act: we find (= king)   27aβ
   5) Findings proper (object completed)   27aγbc
       a) Acquital: not subversives   27aγ
       b) Exoneration (3)   27bc
           α living as citizens   27bα(3)
           β by just laws   27bα(1-2,4)
           γ being sons of   27bβ
               αα only God   27bγ(1-3)
               ββ & true   27bγ(4-5)

a) Agent: Jews of empire	30aβ
b) Object completed: to keep	30aγ
c) Date	30b
α 14th	30bα
β = Adar	30bβ
γ & 15th	30bγ
d) Object completed 2: to feast	30c
e) Motive	30d
α in these (days)	30dα
β Almighty made	30dβ
γ salvation & joy	30dγ
3) Royal approval	31
a) Time	31aαβ
α now	31aα
β & hereafter	31aβ
b) Subject/Act: they do well	31aδ
(with object understood: to regard it)	
d) Description	31aγb
α salvation, Persians	31aγε
β memorial	31bβ(1)
αα destruction	31bβ(2-3)
ββ for plotters	31bα
c. Penalty/threat for disobedience	32
1) Transition: δέ	32aα(2)
2) Description	32aα(1,3-6)β
a) Applicablty: city/province	32aα(1,3-6)
b) Non-compliance	32aβ
3) Penalty proper	32b
a) Means: by spear & fire	32bα
b) Extent: totally wiped out	32bβ
c) Manner: wrathfully	32bγ
4) Intensity	32c
a) for men, impassable	32cα
b) for birds/beasts	32cβ
c) Act: will lie	32cγ

Some differences are these:

1. o´'s introduction is an authorial statement certifying that what follows is an (official) copy, while L merely says 'And he wrote ... ' (7.22);

2. o´'s narrative progresses logically from request through letter preparation, but inserts the letter within the distribution phase, whereas in L a battle takes place—apparently in Sousa—before the decree is written;

3. in L Esther seeks and receives permission to kill the enemies (7.18-20), whereas o´ has this later;

4. the o´ letter also sits uneasily in its context (it can be removed and both seams and developmental logic hook up perfectly), while L's letter starts abruptly without a clear antecedent for 'he wrote' (but the publication data which follows clearly refers to the letter text with τάδε [v. 33aδ]).

5. L's narrative logic breaks down between vv. 16 and 17—Mordecai requests that Aman's decree be annulled and the king's answer is to give him the royal ring, but no explanation or specific follow-up appears—while o´ has none of this;

6. o´ has abundant detail leading up to the letter text, thus standing closer to MT, whereas L lacks these details and shows signs of a different closure.

The 'he' in L's 'And he wrote' (7.22—see the first difference listed above) could refer either to the king or to Mordecai. Since Mordecai specifically writes a few verses later, and the king is the last to speak in the near context (7.21), the weight of probability falls on the king. His authorship would be an opposite to both o´ 8.8, 10 and the explicit statement of the Hebrew, where scribes write everything Mordecai commands in the king's name (8.9-10). It is concluded, then, in light of the king's permission to write in o´ 8.8, that the two texts attribute the writing to different authors—Mordecai in o´, the king in L. This constitutes a major difference which cannot have been either accidental or due to a minor *lectio varia*; it must derive from a separate tradition or from significant editorial revision.

Is there similarity or difference, genre-wise, between the first and second letters/decrees—between what narratively may be called the 'decree of death' (section B) and the 'decree of defense' (section E)? In ch. 3 the passage is called *epistole* in both texts; since in the discussion of B it was demonstrated that the form there evidences more affinities with a Roman decree than with a Hellenistic letter, the passage here (E and parallel) must also be discussed.

The titulature of the opening serves equally well for either a letter or a decree; the salutation is χαίρειν, used only in letters, not decrees. It is not to be assumed that royal letters do not use this greeting; they do, as one example from c. 306 BCE will show: Προτανις Μελιδωρος. Βασιλευς Αντιγονος Ερεσιων τηι βουληι και τηι δημωι χαιρειν ('When Melidorus was prytanis: King Antigonus to the council and the people of Eresus, greeting').[58] Apart from salutations, letters manifest a content distinct from decrees: letters inform, ask questions, accompany emissaries, and so on. Where a decision or edict is concerned—naturally intended to stand permanently as law, and in many cases to be inscribed in stone—it is not introduced by an essentially ephemeral 'greeting'.

Furthermore, a non-narrative conciseness is the hallmark of decretal writing. In section E and parallel the 'background' of the Body contains vague, indirect and somewhat abstract generalities (which of course apply to the Aman problem and the Esther plot). In the second part of the Body the disclosures (a standard feature of letters) present so much confession on the king's part that one can hardly think of the imperious language of decree. Something similar can be said of his royal reassurances (also a feature of letters): they not only reassure for the future; they implicitly confess fault (see especially E 9). These features definitely do not show the standard stuff of decrees.

It is true that the usual letter close ἔρρωσο is lacking (as in section B). This feature can be explained as caused by the editorial process of embedding the letter in a narrative text where a farewell is superfluous— or, as White notes, speaking of 'legal texts that appear in letter form', 'the close is sometimes omitted'.[59] In sum, one must conclude that in this instance, distinct from section B, both texts are generically royal letters. Recognizing this as an important conclusion, the right will be reserved to refer to it, within the spirit of its narrative function, as a 'decree of defense'.

Clearly the internal structures of o´ and L very nearly resemble each other, while the structural placement of the two texts varies widely. The royal letter does not occur at the same place in the narrative, and the narrative itself differs notably.

Some aspects may be noted in relation to the battle in L (points 2 and 3 above): no other text has a battle before the letter, not even Jos; the king's permission to kill Aman's sons is extended without justifition to

58. This example (with dative iotas not yet subscript) comes from a collection (*OGIS*, 8) which 'is a body of precedent, decisions of special tribunals, decrees of the assembly, and royal ordinances' (Welles, *Royal Correspondence*, p. 13). Although this letter treats a city decision/decree, the lacuna and the letter greeting forbid us to classify it other than as letter.

59. White, *Light from Ancient Letters*, p. 200; the same point is made concerning embedded letters in his unpublished essay, 'Royal Correspondence in Pseudo-Aristeas and the Parallel Letters in Josephus and Eusebius', p. 7.

'And she smote a multitude of enemies' (v. 20); that smiting report and the prior permission stand in tension with what is granted in the royal letter: mere defense. Surely this is another sign that the 'decree of defense', or more accurately 'letter of license', derives from another source and that it was appended, or more correctly was inserted, at a later date.

With respect to point 5 above, it is difficult to see how an intentional rewriting for literary improvement (Tov) would leave the text this choppy. Esther's request scene also leaves questions. The narrative logic here is also not entirely lucid. It seems to indicate that the king's word is sufficient in the capital, but that a written form must be sent to the far-flung corners of the empire. Yet 7.21 specifically mentions the king approving Esther's killing in Sousa, and this 'came to pass'. Retrospectively, then, it appears that the 'multitude of enemies' smitten in v. 20 were not limited to Sousa after all. This in turn makes one think that these verses contain an old ending, or summary of the two battles: one in the outlying country, one in Sousa. The royal letter, if that older ending remains, has been inserted just before Mordecai's letter which in primitive terms tells the people to remain and to celebrate to God (7.33-38); of course the report of the decree's publication constitutes a separate item which could have been inserted at another time, or along with the decree.

6. *Triple Conclusion (LXX 8.15–9.19)*

One normally looks to the end of a book for its conclusion, although it will be argued here that 10.1-3 and parallel, now existing as a type of frame, was an ending before the dream and interpretation were appended to the book (cf. above on 1.1ff. and see also Chapter 4 below). However, a yet earlier *conclusion* may exist in the texts.

After reporting the distribution of the letter (and after L gives Mordecai's feast letter), both texts (o′ 8.15-17 // L 7.39-41) report Mordecai's triumph, joy in Sousa and joy among the people (probably intended to include the empire). These are clearly reversals, turning around Mordecai's debasement in sackcloth and ashes (4.1), this time permanently, and the same for the city of Sousa (cf. 3.15) and the people (3.2-3) respectively. Narratively, no further reversals are needed.

But there is more. It is also the end of any further complications and the plan of the heroes, not to mention the original complication. Thus these three reversals resolve—that is, conclude—the major segments of the narrative. If a query be raised regarding the (unresolved) decree of death, it may be answered by noting that this decree and the contrapositive letter (sections B and E and parallels), as the text stands, cancel each other out. The whole matter storywise could stay on legal hold—a political standoff—or, if some Persians disobeyed the letter, the Jews, now allowed to defend themselves, would presumably suffer some losses but would 'live to fight another day'.[60] This last applies entirely to o′ and partly to L. In the case of L, Esther carries out a pre-emptive strike which is reported as successful. All the more reason, now that many (if not all) enemies are dispatched, that the 'decrees' may simply stand and the narrative may close.

Thus these last three verses (8.15-17) wrap up everything back to 3.1. If a story existed without the frame of 1.1ff. and 10.1-3, then one has to say that 8.15-17 and parallel would have concluded that story. Likewise, even if Esther was created *de novo* with its present frame, 8.15-17 still counterbalances the *exposition* and thus functions in a concluding way, even though the frame would be a second conclusion. Therefore, because of their summary nature and the artistic balance lent to the whole, these verses are called a *conclusion* rather than an extension of dénouement.[61]

Now what does one do with o′ 9.1-19 and parallel? It is argued here (more discussion and demonstration below under 'Redaction') that this chapter serves as appendix to Esther, standing outside the narrative structure. Testifying to words and phrases not found elsewhere in Esther, and consisting of report style without tension or complication, this section in both texts can be classified as added conclusions. The term 'stylized' has been added to the battle reports because they do not conform in some respects to the paradigms as exemplified in 1 and 2 Kings. As the microstructure will show, festal etiologies are also present.

60. The phrase is Clines's, in *The Esther Scroll*, p. 27. Further support for his conclusion regarding 8.15-17 has just been presented above.

61. It is comforting to find that this result, obtained by a close structuring of the text, is supported by Clines's narrative analysis, though he terms vv. 15-17 'resolution' (*The Esther Scroll*, pp. 27ff.).

o´ Text

b. Epilog 1: dual victory reports: 1st, 13 Adar: field;

    2nd, 14th: Sousa   9.1-15

        1) 1st victory: dual stylized battle reports (?)   1-11a

            a) Stylized battle report, general   1-4

                α Transition: γάρ   1aα(2)

                β Date   1aα(1,3-5)βγ

                    αα month 12   1aα(1,3-5)

                    ββ day 13   1aβ

                    γγ identification: Adar   1aγ

                γ Confrontation: (2) decrees take effect

                  (= battle)   1b

                    αα Act: occurred   1bα(1)

                    ββ Subject: letters/decrees (re:

                    destruction & defense)   1bα(2-3)

                    γγ Description: written by king   1bβ

                δ Battle proper: allies & reasons   2-4

                    αα Time: that day   2aα

                    ββ Act: perished   2aβ

                    γγ Subject: enemies of Jews (1st)   2aγ

                    δδ Result: victory: none stood   2bγ

                    εε Reason: fearing them   2bβ

                    ζζ Allies   3-4

                        α1 List   3aαβγ

                            α2 satrap rulers   3aα

                            β2 governors (?)   3aβ

                            γ2 royal scribes (!)   3aγ

                        β1 Act: honored Jews (2nd)   3aδ

                        γ1 Reason: Mordecai   3b-4

                            α2 fear of Mor. on them   3b

                            β2 Further reason   4

                                α3 king's edict   4a

                              β3 orders Mordecai   4bα

                              γ3 be honored   4bβ

                                         [no v. 5]

            b) Battle report, specific: Sousa   6-11a

                α Place: Sousa   6aα

                β Subject: Jews (3rd)   6aβ(2-3)

                γ Act: kill   6aβ(1)

                δ Death toll: 500 + 10 sons   6b-9

L Text

γ1 10 sons	44cαβγ
α2 of Aman	44cβ(1)
β2 son of Amadatha	44cβ(2)
γ2 Bougaios	44cβ(3-4)
δ2 enemy of Jews	44cγ
γ Statement	44d
αα plundered (!)	44dα
ββ all that was theirs	44dβ
2) 3rd victory—through Esther's request—over enemies in empire: dialog/death toll	45-46
a) Dialog: king & Esther	45-46b
α Royal speech: king	45
αα Intro. quotation formula: to Est.	45aα
ββ Speech proper: question	45aβbc
α1 How fared	45aβc
β1 your people here	45bα
γ1 & in country?	45bβ
β Royal speech: Esther	46ab
αα Introductory quotation formula	46aα
ββ Speech proper: request	46aβb
α1 give	46aα(1)
β1 to Jews	46aα(2-3)
γ1 Object: whoever…	46bα
α2 to slay	46bβ(1)
β2 plunder	46bβ(2-3)
b) Notice: king approves	46c
c) Death toll	46d
α they kill	46dα
β 70,100 men	46dβ

There are slight differences in the description of Mordecai's clothing as well as in other minute details in the 'Narrative Conclusion' (o´ 8.15-17 // L 7.39-41):

1. o´ has Mordecai wearing a robe, a crown, and a diadem of fine purple linen, while L has royal garments and a headdress of linen edged with purple (no crown);

2. o´ describes the festival of the Jews as 'light and gladness', while L adds 'drinking' as well;

3. o´ indicates that wherever the letter went forth, it was accompanied with joy, gladness, feasting and mirth, whereas L has no equivalent here;

4. o′ indicates that many Gentiles became circumcised—that is, they became Jews—because they feared the Jews, whereas conversely L has the Jews practicing circumcision without opposition, for the people feared the Jews.

Here again L refuses to give the Gentile community anything which would identify them with the privilege of Jewishness. L could not have the result of Esther's victory be the circumcision of the Gentiles. Rather, the result is the freedom of the faithful to practice their religious festivals and rituals without Gentile opposition.

In the 'Dual Victory Reports' (o′ 9.1-15 // L 7.42-46), o′ is expanded in relation to L:

1. o′ gives the date on which the decree of the king arrived, as well as a summary of the enemies who perished, whereas L has no parallel here;
2. o′ indicates that the decree was carried out due to the order of the king to celebrate Mordecai in every province, while L indicates that the name of Aman and all who were opposed (to the Jews?) were mentioned throughout Susa;
3. o′ says 500 men were slain by the Jews in Susa, while L puts the number at 700;
4. the lists of names of those associated with Aman who were slain offers variations between o′ and L, with o′ listing ten persons (Pharsannes, Delphon, Phasga, Pharadatha, Barea, Sarbaca, Marmasima, Ruphaeus, Arsaeus and Zabuthaeus) and L five (Pharsan, Pharna, Gagaphardatha, Marmasaima and Izathouth), though both have 'the ten sons of Aman' (a sign of textual mixing?), and L lists the brother of Pharsan, which o′ does not;
5. o′ concludes the list with the statement 'and the number of them that perished in Sousa was rendered to the king' (= a report only?, or their land and possessions were granted to the treasury of the king?), for which L has no parallel.

After the account of the initial slaying, the texts record a dialog between the king and Esther and a granting of a further request (o′ 9.12-19 // L 7.45-46); they are not unified in the details, however:

1. In o′, Esther requests that the next day likewise be a day when Jews are allowed to treat their enemies as the ten sons of Aman were treated, while in L she requests that the Jews be allowed to plunder and slay whomever they desired;
2. in L the result is given only in brief as a death toll of 70,100 men, whereas in o′ the results are recorded as follows:
   a. the bodies of the ten sons of Aman were given for public exposure as a display of victory;
   b. the Jews in Sousa slew 300 men on the 14th of Adar;
   c. throughout the kingdom they destroyed 15,000 on the 13th of Adar (?);
   d. in each case, the Jews took no spoil.

The lack of any mention in L of hanging the bodies of Aman and sons out for display may be explained on the grounds that, for L, to introduce this into the text only brings another problem, namely the law forbidding a body to be displayed publicly after sunset (Deut. 21.18-23). With the other events in the narrative which already soil the reputation of Esther as orthodox, this one is best left out.

C. *Etiology of Purim (*Phrourai*) (LXX 9.20-31)*

The following section has long been recognized as different in vocabulary, style, content and tone. It documents facts about a festival without narrative tension. The microstructure is self-explanatory.

o´ *Text*

C. ETIOLOGY: History & Law of Phrourai Feast: How It Issues
    from Foregoing Narrative & Becomes Perpetual: 3 Steps: Mordecai's
    Decree (vv. 20-22); 'Canonizing' by Community Consent (23-28);
    Esther's Confirmatory/Regulatory Decree (29-31)   9.20-31
    1. Report: Mordecai's decree establishes a compromising
      2-day Purim, Adar 14-15   20-22
        a. Acts   20aα(1)bα(1-2)
          1) writes (words/decree)   20aα(1)
          2) sends (book?/letters?)   20bα(1-2)
        b. Author: Mordecai   20bα(2-3)
        c. Objects   20aα(4-8)
          1) 'these words' (cf. Exod. 20.1b)   20aα(4-6)
          2) (understood: book? letters?)   —
          3) in a book   20aα(7-8)
        d. Recipients   20bα(3-4)βγ
          1) Jews (1st)   20bα(3-4)
          2) in King Artaxerxes' kingdom   20bβ
          3) near & far   20bγ
        e. Purpose: to perpetuate   21-22bε
          1) Object 1 & dual complement   21aβγb
            a) these days   21aβ
            b) Complements   21aγb
              α Accusative: (as) holidays   21aγ
              β Infinitive   21b

αα keeping   21bα
ββ both 14 & 15   21bβ
γγ of Adar   21bγ
2) Reason   22a
  a) Causal conjunction: γάρ   22aα(2)
  b) Time: these days   22aα(1,3-5)
  c) Act: rested   22aβ(1)
  d) Subject: Jews (2nd)   22aβ(2-3)
  e) Object: from enemies   22aγ
3) Object 2   22b
  a) & (keeping) this month   22bα
  b) which gave reversal   22bβ
  c) = Adar   22bγ
  d) from grief to joy   22bδ
  e) pain to holiday   22bε
f. Manner   22c
  1) keeping all (of 2 days)   22cα
  2) (as) holidays   22cβ
    a) of weddings (!)   22cγ
    b) and merriment   22cδ
    c) sending out portions/gifts   22cε
     α to friends   22cζ
     β & poor (ones) 22cη

2. Compliance report: 'history' of compromise: step 1, old
'canonized' 1-day feast, + step 2, Mordecai's new 2-day feast;
reason/rehearsal; report: summary historicizing legislation   23-28
  a. Compliance proper   23
    1) Act: consented (= compromised)   23aα
    2) Subject: Jews (3rd)   23aβ
    3) Manner: as Mordecai wrote   23b
  b. Reason: rehearsal of story: origin & name
  etiology (Mordecai's decree? cult?)   24-26b
    1) Transition: πῶς (interrogative particle
    = catechetical: [remembering] how…?)   24aα(1)
    2) Rehearsal of narrative: pogrom plot: its
    intensity, means & reversal   24aα(2)-25
     a) Plot   24aα(2)-25a
      α Antagonist: names   24aα(2)βγ

αα Personal: Aman — 24aα(2)

ββ Family: Amadathos — 24aβ

γγ Race/symbol: the Macedonian — 24aγ

β Act: fought them — 24aδ

γ Intensity 1 — 24bαβ

αα Transition: καθώς — 24bα(1)

ββ he made (2) — 24bα(2)

α1 decree — 24bβ(1)

β1 & lot(s) — 24bβ(2-3)

δ Purpose: annihilate — 24bγ

ε Intensity 2 — 25a

αα Transition: ὡς — 25aα

ββ Acts (2) — 25aβγδ

α1 entered — 25aβ(1)

β1 to king — 25aβ(2-4)

γ1 asked to hang — 25aγ

δ1 Mordecai — 25aδ

b) Reversal — 25b

α Transition: as much as — 25bα

β Act: tried to harm — 25bββδ

γ Object: Jews (4th) — 25bγ

δ Reversal: came on him — 25c

c) Results (2) — 25d

α they hang him — 25dα

β & sons — 25dβ

3) Result: etiology — 26ab

a) Transition: διὰ τοῦτο — 26aα

b) Etiology proper — 26aβγb

α Naming — 26ab

αα they (Jews) call — 26aβ(1)

ββ these days — 26aβ(2-4)

γγ Phrourai — 26aβ(5)

β Reason — 26aγb

αα because of 'lots' — 26aγ

ββ because dialect — 26bα

γγ says 'Phrourai' — 26bβ

c. Report: further historicizing specification/legislation
of Phrourai compromise (from singular to plural?):
reasons, extent, manner & duration — 26c-28

1) Transition: διά (anacoluthon)	26cα(1)
2) Reasons	26cα(2-6)βde
a) words of this letter	26cα(2-6)
b) what they experienced	26cβ(1-3)
c) because of these things	26cβ(4-5)
d) what happened to them	26d
3) Acts (2)	27aαβ(1-2)
a) (Mordecai) fixed?/it was agreed?	27aα
b) made customary	27aβ(1-2)
4) Subject: Jews (5th)	27aβ(3-4)
a) for selves	27aβ(5-6)
b) & children	27aδ
5) Manner: not otherwise	27aε(1-3)
6) Act: carry out (= celebrate)	27aε(4)
7) Description	27b
a) Subject	27bαβ(1)
α these days	27bα
β = memorial	27bβ(1)
b) Act: being observed	27bβ(2)
c) Duration: every generation	27bγ
d) Extent	27bδ
α every city	27bδ(1-2)
β every country	27bδ(3-4)
γ every province	27bδ(5-6)
8) Vow (?)	28
a) Subject: 'These . . . Phrourai'	28aα
b) (understood: they said?)	—
c) Act: be celebrated	28aβ(1)
d) Duration: all time	28aβ(2-5)
e) Subject 2: remembrance	28bα
f) Act: never cease	28bβ(1-3)
g) Sphere: from descendants	28bβ(4-5)
3. Report: Esther's & Mordecai's confirmatory and regulatory	
decree: step 3: fasting added/formalized	29-31
a. Confirmation, dual	29
1) Act: writes	29aα(1-2)
2) Author: Esther	29aα(3)
3) Further identification	29aβ

a) Title: Queen	29aβ(1-2)
b) Family: Aminadab	29aβ(3-4)
4) Author: Mordecai the Jew (6th)	29aγ
5) Object (2)	29b
a) their 'history'	29bα
b) & confirmation	29bβ
α of epistle	29bγ
β of the Phrourai	29bδ
b. Regulation	30
1) Authors, dual	30aα
a) Mordecai	30aα(1-2)
b) Esther, Queen	30aα(3-6)
2) Act	30aβ
a) established (a fast?)	30aβ(1)
b) for selves	30aβ(2)
c) privately	30aβ(3-4)
3) Result:	30b
a) Time: then	30bα(1-2)
b) (they were) practicing	30bα(3)
c) Manner	30bβγ
α against health	30bβ
β against own counsel[62] (= that others feast)	30bγ
c. Authorization/verification	31
1) Authorization	31a
a) Authoress: Esther	31aα
b) Act: established, by this word = Esther book?	31aβ
c) (Object understood: it = fast/things = Phrourai?)	—
d) Duration: forever	31aγ
2) Verification	31b
a) (Author: unexpressed)	—
b) Act: was written	31bα
c) (Subject understood: it = fast/things = Phrourai?)	—
d) Purpose: memorial (or Locative: in chronicle?)	31bβ

---

62. Or '(were) practicing their own plan against their health'.

L Text

Both texts include the fact that a festival was consecrated and became perpetual for the Jewish nation. However, there are pointed differences which are best explained not as deriving from one or the other, but as reflections of divergent concerns in separate communities. o´ and MT show signs of detail, expansion and conflict resolution over festival differences, while L knows none of this. The two former texts seem to preserve later traditions than L (the other possibility, defended by

Tov,[63] is that L has been rewritten in a summarizing direction). Two quite different presentations of the festival are shown in o′ 9.20 // L 7.47; the festivals themselves even bear slightly different names in the two EG texts, with Jos supporting o′. The o′ text presents a history of compromise: Mordecai's solution resolved a then current difference regarding which festival days were observed. In L there is only Mordecai's letter; Esther's confirmatory letter is conspicuously absent, as is all mention of fasting.

This section also stands outside the narrative arc of tension, and follows the appended conclusions, but it is not another appendix with just one more bit of information. It functions to establish a specified feast celebration. Thus in o′ it is both history and law, whereas in L it is only law. Note too that o′ gives a summary of the fact of the holy day immediately following the account of the number slain by the Jews, while L gives the foundation for the festival only after the writing in the books by Mordecai is outlined.

Further, o′ specifies that Mordecai established the laws of the festival. In o′ it is represented as follows:

a. established as joyful days;
b. because the Jews obtained rest from their enemies;
c. a change from mourning to joy, from sorrow to a good day;
d. the festival is to be spent in good days of feasting and gladness, sending portions to friends and to the poor;
e. a summary of the whole plot, reversal etc. is given to substantiate the name *Phrourai*, since the lots which Aman used to discern the manner and time to kill the Jews turned against him: much expanded in comparison with L.

L represents it this way:

a. the days were to be kept for hymns and rejoicings in the place of pain and grief;
b. Mordecai sent portions to the poor (as an example of what others should do?);
c. for this reason the festival is called *Phourdaia*, explained as the falling out of the lots (in favor of the Jews).

D. *Frame Epilog (LXX 10.1-3)*

Our investigation has arrived at a (partial) reprise of the opening 'frame'. Missing in 10.1-3 and parallel are the specific mention of 127 provinces,

---

63. Tov, 'The "Lucianic" Text'.

Sousa, a date and a banquet. But items which are present substitute functionally for at least two of the lacking elements. Present, then, are the King, his PN (albeit different ones in each text—Jos supporting o΄), his kingdom/empire, its territorial extent ('over [L: the extremities of] land and sea'—thus the 127 provinces are included and surpassed), and his power ('he writes' [L may mean 'he controls'] or 'he writes over' [o΄ may mean 'he taxes']). This last action substitutes for the giving of a banquet in the opening frame. Only the date and mention of the capital—minor items—fail to find a reflex at the end. One can view the important addition of Mordecai as displacing these less significant details.

What then seems to be the point of this concluding frame? The king is portrayed as even more powerful now than when the story opened with a banquet so lavish as to be legendary! Whether the frame derives from an author or a later editor, its point is to stretch the royal grandeur to the maximum (note L's τὰ τέλη), then associate Mordecai with it—it is a propagandistic motive. As evidence one can cite the generally overlooked verb in o΄ 10.3 // L 7.52: διεδέχετο. As any classical lexicon will show, διαδέχομαι means either 'to receive one from another' (or 'relieve one another', thus, in Esther, 'vizier'), or more often 'to succeed (in office)'. Translators and commentators, not quite grasping the humorous and exemplary/didactic intention of this story, take the rationally safer 'became vizier' or 'acted for King Artaxerxes'.[64] In my view, the Greek translators/writers intend Mordecai to become, not vice-regent, but *rex*—in modern terms, a superhero.

Still the reader learns nothing of the king's personality or personal life. Of course one does not get inside Mordecai's personality either (although section F gives a brief glimpse), since that is not the author's style, but one learns more of him than of the king. One other purpose of this brief subunit must be noted: the appeal to check the royal records. Reflecting off the biblical historical books in an imitative, midrashic way, the author wants readers to know that confirmation is possible.

---

64. Cf. L.C.L. Brendan, *The Septuagint with Apocrypha: Greek and English* (London: Bagster, 1851; repr.; Grand Rapids: Zondervan, 1970); and see J.C. Dancy, *The Shorter Books* (Cambridge: Cambridge University Press, 1972), p. 166. Clines can be credited for breaking with tradition thus: 'was successor' (*The Esther Scroll*, p. 247).

o´ Text

D. FRAME EPILOG/RESUME: King 'Enshrined;' Extent & Richness of
Empire (shown by king in control of far-flung empire and vast wealth
through tax/corvee over land & isles); Epitome of Reign & Citation of
Record; King Artaxerxes Associates Mordecai (as vizier or successor?)
With His Royal Self in Unparalleled Magnitude; Praise of Mordecai's
Good Reputation Among the Jews   10.1-3

  1. Epilog   1
    a. Act: wrote   1aα(1-2)
    b. Subject: king   1aα(3-4)
    c. (Direct object understood: levy)   —
    d. Indirect object   1aβb
      1) over empire   1aβ
      2) Extent   1b
        a) of land   1bα
        b) & sea   1bβ
  2. Epitome formula: king   2ab
    a. King's attributes   2abα
      1) power   2aα
      2) bravery/virtue   2aβ
      3) richness   2bα
    b. His success: glorious empire   2bβ
  3. Citation formula: statement (reader can check)   2c
    a. Exclamation: behold!   2cα(1)
    b. Citation proper   2cα(2)βγ
      1) Statement: stands written   2cα(2)
      2) Place: in book/chronicle   2cβ(1-2)
      3) kings of Persia & Media   2cβ(3-6)
      4) Purpose: memorial   2cγ
  4. Epitome formula: Mordecai   3ab
    a. Subject: Mordecai   3aα
    b. Act: served (vizier)/succeeded (king)?   3aβ
    c. Object: King Artaxerxes   3aγ
    d. Further description   3b
      1) great in empire   3bα
      2) honored by the Jews (/th)   3bβ

5. Concluding praise: Mordecai   3c

    a. Subject (Mordecai)   —

    b. Manner: beloved   3cα

    c. Act: conducted his life   3cβ

    d. Sphere: among all his people   3cγ

L Text

D. **FRAME EPILOG/RESUME**: King 'Enshrined'; Extent & Richness of
Empire (shown by king in control of far-flung empire); King Writes
Epitome of Reign; Mordecai Magnifies Him & Writes in Records of Persia
& Media; Mordecai Succeeds (?) King Assueros; Praise of Mordecai's
Leadership of, Good Repute among, & Benefaction to the Jews   7.50-52

  1. Epilog: king   50

    a. Act: wrote   50aα(1-2)

    b. Subject: king   50aα(3-4)

    c. Extent: throughout land & sea   50aβ

    d. Objects: (= epitome formula) concerning   50b

      1) power   50bα

      2) richness   50bβ

      3) glory of his empire   50bγ

  2. Epilog: Mordecai   51-52

    a. Act: Mordecai magnifies   51aα

    b. (Object understood: king)   —

    c. Act 2: wrote (it)   51aβ

    d. Indirect object   51b

      1) in records of   51bα

      2) Persia & Media   51bβ

    e. Purpose: for a memorial   51c

    f. Act 3: Mordecai succeeds Assueros   52a

  3. Epitome formula: Mordecai   52bcde

    a. Mordecai's success   52bcd

      1) great in empire   52b

      2) beloved by all Jews   52c

    b. Mordecai's acts for his people   52de

      1) he led them   52d

      2) gave glory to his people   52e

4. *Concluding Sections (LXX F 1-11)*

Major sections now follow. Not a great deal needs to be said, but a discovery emerged from careful structuring. The dream interpretation (o´ F 1-6a // L 7.53-54) flows directly into sermonic speech (o´ F 6b-9 // L 7.55-58), possibly intended to represent Mordecai himself leading some type of congregational worship or doxology. One is reminded of the doxologies in Daniel after a dream is interpreted. This sermonic material constitutes either a subunit of the interpretation, or a whole new unit (i.e. unit V, with the 'Concluding Legislation' as a final unit VI). The latter alternative was chosen—in spite of the intimate connections between the identification of the symbols themselves and the homily developed out of them—since the form and function indicate another material unit. Thus both o´ and L have six major parts at the final text level.

Here however, as distinct from Daniel, the language is specific, development is greater, a reinterpretation takes place with κλῆρος (it is not just the lot one casts, but becomes the 'lot' or inheritance of God), and a congregational response occurs (again in different ways) in o´ and L. MS 93, an L witness, closes 7.59 with ἀμήν. These facts, coupled with a parallelistic type of repetition (see the structure analysis below) has prompted my suggestion that preserved here is an early haggadic homily with its opening quotation, or proem, usually called by its Aramaic name, *petiḥta*.[65] Sonne reports that Bacher discovered the purpose of this opening quotation in the Jewish homily, usually taken from the Hagiographa (the third section of the Hebrew scriptures):

> The underlying idea was to stress the unity of the three parts of Scripture: there is nothing in the Prophets and the Hagiographa that could not be found in the Pentateuch, that all three parts are but one and the same expressed in various forms, various modes of the same substance.[66]

Furthermore, Sonne quotes Mann's emphatic statement that the *petiḥta*

---

65. The Hebrew word is פְּתִיחָה. For a discussion of the two types of synagogue sermons, the proem and the *yelammedenu*, see J. Mann, *The Bible as Read and Preached in the Old Synagogue*, I, with Prolegomenon by B.Z. Wachholder (New York: Ktav, 2nd edn., 1970), *passim*, and see note 66 below; D. Patte, *Early Jewish Hermeneutic in Palestine* (SBLDS, 22; Missoula, MT: Scholars Press, 1975), pp. 43ff; cf. J.W. Bowker, 'Speeches in Acts: A Study in Proem and Yelammedenu Form', *NTS* 14 (1967), pp. 96-111.

66. J. Mann and I. Sonne, *The Bible as Read and Preached in the Old Synagogue*, II (Cincinnati: Hebrew Union College Press, 1966), p. xxxi.

and *haftorah*[67] could not easily be determined for this reason: 'the haftorah was not [always] used explicitly because it was tacitly employed throughout!'[68] In spite of some criticisms of Mann and Sonne,[69] and in spite of the difficulties in unveiling tacit connections between proem, *haftorah* and Torah/*seder* texts, no one can doubt the existence of the phenomenon, thanks to the scores of examples adduced by Mann.

If the understanding adopted here is correct, namely that two (different) proems and two (similar) kernel homilies are embedded in o′ and L, it will explain for the first time the apparently repetitious phrases in this section, and the as yet unexplained function of this closure to Esther (see Chapter 4 below).

One more detail must be accounted for in any classification of this striking passage. Both o′ and L include a response from the congregation, but one which is unique to each text. Since unit V contains both a homily and a congregational response, the unit in question may be classified as a report of a worship service. A homily exists in both texts, with a different content in each, and the additional difference of a responsory in o′ and a doxology in L; the latter unique elements also find unlike locations in each text. While the term 'homily' is chosen for brevity in both macrostructures, these important differences must not be overlooked.

Following the homily one finds a seven-part legislative command (o′ F 10 // L 7.59) which reconfirms the observance of the *Phouraia* or *Phrourai* Feast. This concluding part of EG is unit VI, 'Concluding Legislation', or more specifically 'Final 7-Part Command'. Although standing in the position of an appendix, this last verse clearly presents material central to a final redactor's concern: the Purim feast.

---

67. At some time during the development of Torah reading in the synagogue, a haftorah or 'completion'—passages from the Prophets section of the Hebrew Bible—was added; for an explanation, see K. Bland, 'Lectionary Cycle, Rabbinic', in *IDBSup*; pp. 537-38, and the bibliography there.

68. Mann and Sonne, *The Bible as Read and Preached*, II, p. 12.

69. J. Heinemann, among others, has criticized Mann's over-optimistic establishment of a single Torah (*seder*) reading cycle, and, among other items, his failure to distinguish between 'live' and literary sermons. See J. Heienemann, 'Profile of a Midrash: The Art of Composition in Leviticus Rabba', *JAAR* 39 (1971), pp. 141-50; and the even-handed treatment by B.Z. Wachholder in the introduction to Mann's first volume.

o´ Text

L Text

1. Act: made	55aα(1-2)
2. Subject: God	55aα(3-4)
3. Object	55aβb
a. signs	55aβ(1-2)
b. these wonders	55aβ(3-6)
c. Further detail	55b
1) which did not happen	55bα
2) among the nations	55bβ
B. HOMILY PROPER	55cd-57
1. His Sovereign (Exclusive) Election	55cd
a. Act: he made	55cα
b. Object: 2 lots	55cβ
1) 2 lots	55cβ
2) Description	55d
a) one for God's people	55dα
b) one for nations	55dβ
c. Intervention: 'Lord' of history	56-57
1) Setting: confrontation	56
a) Act: came	56aα
b) Subject: 2 lots	56aβ
c) Detail	56bc
α in hours & days	56bαγ
β at right time	56bβ
αα of the ruling	56cα(1)
ββ of Eternal One	56cα(2-3)
γγ among all nations	56cβ
2) Intervention/Mighty Act	57
a) Act: remembered	57aα
b) Subject: God	57aβ
c) Object: his people	57b
d) Act 2: justified	57cα
e) Object: his inheritance	57cβ
C. REPORT OF WORSHIP	58
1. Report of Responsa	58a
a. Subject: all the people	58aα(1-4)
b. Act: cried out	58aα(5)
c. Manner: with loud voice	58aβ
2. Responsory Quotation	58aγbcd

The two texts differ dramatically in the manner in which they conclude:

1. the o´ text has an extended section indicating how this festival is an eternal one for the Jewish people, how it is celebrated throughout the world, and that the Jewish nation was agreed upon its significance and manner of celebration, whereas the L text has no parallel;

2. o´ has Esther and Mordecai writing the whole matter together as confirming what was done, along with a confirming letter regarding the decree of the king, whereas again L has no parallel;

3. o´ has the king levy a tax upon his kingdom as a prelude to the statement that he was powerful and wealthy and a mighty king recorded in annals of the

Persians and the Medes, while in L the king simply writes about his power, glory, and wealth (both texts include the phrase 'land and sea' as a designation of the breadth of the king's power/influence);

4. o′ has Mordecai as the successor to Artaxerxes, while L has him as the successor to Xerxes.

As for the final dream interpretation (o′ F 1-5 // L 7.53-54), both texts agree in touting signs and wonders done in Israel which were not done in the nations, and they agree that two lots were made, one for Israel and another for the nations, but they differ in a number of respects:

1. o′ casts the dream interpretation in the first person, while L has it in the third person, with the narrator doing the interpreting;
2. o′ states, 'not one particular of them has failed', while L states, 'and it was accomplished';
3. for o′ the river is Esther and the two serpents are Mordecai ('I') and Aman, whereas for L the tiny spring is Esther, the two dragons are Aman and Mordecai ('myself'), the river is the nations which were against the Jews, and sun and light represent divine revelation;
4. o′ describes 'my nation' as Israel, those who cried to God and were delivered/rescued out of all these calamities, but L has no parallel;
5. L includes a covenant ceremony with the people blessing the Lord 'who has remembered the covenants with our fathers. Amen', but o′ has no parallel.

In regard to the first difference listed above, it may be noted that the first person in o′ is contrary to an analyst's expectation, based on the frequent reportorial (some might say more objective, historical or drier) style of o′ versus the socio-psychological tendencies (and they are only tendencies) in L. And in regard to the last difference, one may note that the L text seems more Judaic (as distinct from Hellenistic) once again; the covenant made with the fathers is twice mentioned, and thus the text draws on the corporate solidarity of the nation by basing the nation's existence upon the cumulative history of the patriarchs. This is no doubt a homiletical device to encourage the response of a Jewish audience to appreciate their heritage and respond properly to their election.

From a literary point of view the Esther narrative ends at o′ F 10 // L 7.59. But from a MSS standpoint there is a colophon (F 11 in Hanhart), which in printed texts appears to be a final verse. It consists of 34 words, describing the 'bringing in' of the (or a copy of the) *epistole/* letter of *Phrourai* by one Dositheus in the reign of Ptolemy and Cleopatra. This Dositheus, father of Ptolemy, claimed to be a Levite[70] and

_____

70. Bickermann argues that Λευίτης here is not a title, but a proper name. See

priest. A son of Ptolemy (probably the same as Dositheus' son), Lysimachus, who lived in Jerusalem, is said to have interpreted (translated) the letter. All of this seems to be lacking in L (and Old Latin), except that MS 19—one of the four witnesses to L—contains the colophon with three differences: there are no capital letters, ἔφθασαν stands for ἔφασαν, and τὸ φρουραι occurs instead of τὸν Φρουραι. Note that MS 19's φρουραι stands in contradistinction to L's φρουραι (7.49).

This festival name is important, as multiple (and pregnant) variant readings attest whenever the name occurs (a feast is enjoined even on the Persians in both texts of the letter of license, but it remains unnamed there). For example, at o´ 9.26 // L 7.49 one finds the following textual variants for o´'s Φρουραι: φρουριν, φρουριμ, φουρουρειμ, φουρειν, φουριμ and φουρ. The Hanhart apparatus documents other variants for L's Φουραια: φουρδια, φαραια and φουρμαια. Jos has yet another: φρουραιους (accusative; nominative *φρουραιος: 11.295).

The sheer mass of these divergent spellings may indicate more than a language root foreign to Greek. They may witness to 'original' translations in disparate communities. Additionally, some of these terms are pregnant because they clearly attest the Aramaic endings -*aia* and -*in*; this in turn points toward at least part of Esther being known in an Aramaic-speaking community, and possibly toward an Aramaic original for the earliest form of Esther. Others are so because they attest to two 'r's within the word, certainly not the easiest consonant cluster and syllable combination to pronounce and to preserve. But they nevertheless have been preserved and are extant, I would suggest, for three reasons: variants were created by the difficulty and foreignness of the original; variants also sprung up due to variant receptor languages/dialects within different communities which preserved the story/festival; and each community jealously guarded its characteristic vocable/pronunciation.

Further, the singular attestation of φουρδια in L MS 19 preserves what to J. Levy is significant for identifying the origin of the festival.[71] Using the clues cited here in conjunction with other data, Levy concluded that the feast in question was the old, year-end festival for departed (angel-like) spirits called *Farvardigan*. It is important to note that Levy's arguments have not been refuted, even though one does not

---

E.J. Bickermann, 'The Colophon of the Greek Book of Esther', *JBL* 63 (1944), pp. 339-42. The article is a treasury of data on colophons.

71. J. Levy, 'The Feast of the 14th Day of Adar', *HUCA* 14 (1939), pp. 127-51.

often find his explanation in Esther literature. For example, Moore,[72] while twice crediting Levy with putting a stop to all debate on *pur* (from Babylonian *puru*, meaning 'lot', and secondarily 'fate'; and probably connected in Jewish lore with Babylonian *purruru*, 'to exterminate'), does not mention Levy's choice of *Farvardigan* as the underlying feast even though he approvingly cites major points of Levy's article which argued for that very identification.[73]

One-page overviews of the EG structures (i.e. the macrostructures), arising from the detailed work presented above, may be consulted at the end of the next chapter of this study, together with the EH macrostructure for comparative purposes.

72. Moore, *Esther*, p. xlvii; idem, *Studies in the Book of Esther*, pp. xxxii xxxiii.
73. Moore, *Esther*, pp. xlviii-xlix. He does cautiously opine, however, that more recently 'a Persian origin for Purim has been gaining support among scholars' (p. xlviii).

Chapter 3

HEBREW ESTHER

It is time to look at EH/MT for purposes of comparison and for its own literary integrity and structural integration *per se*. After the somewhat diffuse style of EG (with Jos running closer to L in conciseness), EH will strike the reader as compact, polished, almost telegraphic.

With regard to structure, this study has reached conclusions which differ significantly from recent major works. The work of Dommershausen[1] offers a convenient point of comparison for the conclusions reached in this investigation. He selects style as the primary criterion for the determination of his *Gattungen* or genres. Secondarily, he says content should be brought in to subdivide and differentiate these genres further. In the approach taken here, structure is primary and aids in understanding both the content and its intention. His observations on stylistic features have been helpful in various places throughout for determining subunits, shifts in point of view, and so on. For reasons of his own 'systematization' of Esther material, Dommershausen does not follow the book's order when he lists the forms he discovered within Esther:

1.10-22	*Erzählung*	*Weisheitserzählung*
3.1-7	*Kurzerzählung*	*Anekdote*
3.8-15	*Erzählung mit Schilderung*	
4.4-17	*Erzählung*	
5.1-8	*Erzählung*	*Weisheitserzählung*
5.9-14	*Kurzerzählung*	*Anekdote mit Weisheitserzählung*
6.1-14	*Erzählung mit* (sic)	*Weisheitsspruch*
7.1-10	*Erzählung*	
8.1-8	*Erzählung mit Bericht*	
9.11-15	*Kurzerzählung*	
2.8-14	*Bericht*	
2.15-20	*Bericht*	
2.21-23	*Kurzbericht*	

1. Dommershausen, *Die Estherrolle*.

4.1-3	*Kurzberich*	
9.1-10	*Bericht mit Notiz*	
9.16-20	*Bericht*	
8.9-17	*Dekret mit Kurzbericht und Schilderung*	
9.20-28	*Dekret*	
9.29-32	*Dekret*	
2.5-7	*Notiz*	*Biographische Notiz*
10.1-3	*Notiz*	
1.1-9	*Schilderung*	*Schilderung mit Notiz*
2.1-4	*Rede*	*Dienerrede*

The left-hand column contains the stylistic forms as uncovered by his analysis; the right represents further refinements based on content. After determining that the narrative category dominates numerically (frequency is apparently the organizing principle in this unusual system), Dommershausen then asks after a *Rahmengattung* or macro-genre. Before an answer is given to that question, he introduces the matter of the *Sitz im Leben*. That in turn leads him immediately to the Purim feast as the answer. Working backward from that *Sitz* leads him consequently to discover, as answer for the first question, the genre of *Festlesung*, bearing with it the memory/reminder of rescue from a pogrom and the flavor of wisdom paranesis.[2] Although no thorough critique of Dommershausen will be given, a few problems in his conclusions must be mentioned.

First, it is not clear how numerical dominance of a certain element (does one call it 'style-genre'?) should be interpreted, or why it is so important. Not only does the author not explain that, but also the broad spectrum of topics that could be covered under the rubric of narrative leave one in doubt about the solidity of a conclusion regarding genre. Secondly, in the view taken here, not only should structure play a more determinative role in all of the above, but theoretic narrative considerations should also be allowed to integrate Dommershausen's 22 or 23 units into larger units where possible. Thirdly, how do these 23 parts lead one to think of a 'Festival Reading' or, in form-critical terms, a *hieros logos* or festal legend?

Two minor points concerning Dommershausen's interesting terms may be noted before proceeding to EH's microstructure. First, Dommershausen's use of the terms *Kurzbericht*, *Kurzerzählung* and *Schilderung* would serve as handy labels for varying lengths and types of literary forms if they could be rigorously defined.[3] Unfortunately, such

---

2. Dommershausen, *Die Estherrolle*, p. 156.
3. Dommershausen, *Die Estherrolle*, p. 154, where *Erzählung* and *Kurz-*

tight definitions were not forthcoming in the case of the two 'short' forms. In the two former terms, shortness seems to be the only criterion. Thus in the case of the *Kurzbericht*, Dommershausen seems to be using this term for what the Form Critical Project calls 'statement' or 'notice'. It is not clear until further study can be done whether the 'short narrative' is the same as the form-critical 'report'. Therefore, until more precision is forthcoming for 'short narrative' and 'short report', the two terms must be abandoned. The case is different with 'description', which already claims a venerable history within literary studies. Description, at the simplest level, can be recognized negatively by its conspicuous lack of action, and positively by the equally obvious stringing together or piling up of words or phrases which paint a picture.[4]

Therefore the next step will be to present the microstructure from a form-critical approach, using some of Dommershausen's and Murphy's insights in the area of sentence/paragraph composition, and delineation of form-critical units. The attempt will be made to improve on these and other authors' schemata in terms of narrative integration. Once that is accomplished, the macrostructures for all three texts—and a preliminary genre determination which such structures entail—can be shown. Then in Chapter 4 of this study the questions of genre (in greater detail), matrix or setting, intention and redaction can be pursued.

Only brief introductions to the microstructure units will be necessary, since much of what has been said regarding the delineation of pericopae in EG applies to EH as well. The first section, however, calls for some explanation.

1. *Frame Prolog (MT 1.1-4)*

In this case, as distinct from Ruth for example, the narrative-opening ויהי does not present a complete sentence: the next clauses continue refining the time period and the main action is presented by preterite עשה in v. 3.

---

erzählung are not distinguished in his discussion of *Gattungsbestimmung*, and *Kurzbericht* is not differentiated from *Bericht* beyond 'Bei geraftem Stil spricht man besser vom Kurzbericht'.

4.   See e.g. Holman and Harmon, *A Handbook to Literature*, p. 137: 'Description: One of the four types of composition (see Argumentation, Exposition, and Narration) that has as its purpose the picturing of a scene or setting. Though some-times used apart for its own sake...it is more often subordinated...especially to narration...' Shipley (*Dictionary of World Literature*, p. 93) calls it 'the Cinderella of prose fiction'.

Dommershausen would end the sentence here, but it is better to allow the dependent clause beginning with בהראתו (v. 4) to actually be dependent on the one and only preterite in v. 3. 1.1-4 thus forms a unit (with Murphy and most commentators); what kind of unit needs clarification.

What does this unit accomplish? It introduces an important—but not the central—character, the king, and a second group often overlooked: princes, servants (= officials), and so on. The king and counsellors—drawn from these and other groups, to be sure—play a repeating role in Esther. Beyond these characters this opening mentions the greatness of the kingdom, and the purpose of the king's 180-day banquet, namely to show his power and glory. It is argued here that precisely the same point is made in 10.1-3, only there it is greater power yet because the king's reach now extends not only over 127 provinces, but to the isles of the sea! Hyperbolic, perhaps, but it sets the stage for sweeping events. Four important items thus stand out in both opening and ending: the king, his vast kingdom, his power/glory, and—one crucial development—the counsellors of the prolog are replaced by Mordecai in the epilog.

Thus by virtue of content and intent, 1.1-4 in conjunction with 10.1-3 frame the entire EH story (see discussion *ad loc.* in EG). After 1.1-4 the greatest pogrom ever heard up to that time is planned and the situation appears hopeless; after 10.1-2aα the reverse occurs: Mordecai becomes associated with that incredible power of Medo-Persia and assurance appears not only for continued Jewish survival, but for peace, justice and betterment.

One may add that a narrative needs an exposition and that the seven-day banquet, introduced in 1.5ff., within which the first real narrative event occurs (Vashti's summons and refusal), serves that end quite well. As before, it may be noted that a minor *exposition, complication* and *conclusion* may occur in a preparatory or subsidiary manner within a larger or macro-section. These are minor or secondary in terms of the overall plot, which to be a plot must have some major complication, crisis/climax and conclusion. But these smaller clusters or subunits should be noted because they are important structural elements and they form smaller arcs of tension which carry reader interest forward.

I. FRAME PROLOG: King Introduced; Time, Extent & Richness of
    Kingdom (shown by 180-day feast)   1.1-4
       A. INTRODUCTION: Ahasuerus   1-2
            1. Opening time (general) & title of king   1a

2. *Rescue Novella Proper (MT 1.5–9.19)*

A. *Exposition (MT 1.5–2.23)*

Dommershausen tries to link 1.1-9 by means of a neat chiasm based on the root מלך, and thus there would be no frame, no subunit 1.1-4. His chiasm is printed so that it looks like a perfect X pattern beginning with '4× מלך', sporting '3× מלך' dead center, and ending with '2× מלך'.[5] In appearance this is an impressive argument for the unity of 1.1-9. But in order to achieve such an impressive pattern—one which would destroy the frame concept offered here—Dommershausen must leave out 1.6-7: of the three occurrences of מלך Dommershausen puts in the center, two are reused from two previous lines of the chiasm (v. 5) and the third is taken from the end of v. 7. This of course means his 'three-fold center' does not exist, so the product is vitiated. It is interesting to note that even though Dommershausen says vv. 1-9 present themselves 'as the first small unit', he still subdivides as 1.1-4 and 1.5-9, which actually supports the position taken in this study. The conclusion must be that two units exist, there is no chiasm, and they exhibit a *Leitwortstil* con-

5. Dommershausen, *Die Estherrolle*, p. 24.

nection (to use Dommershausen's term) with the root מלך.

For the material classed here as *Exposition*, Dommershausen divides EH ch. 1 into vv. 1-9 and 10-22 (with smaller subunits) and ch. 2 into vv. 1-4, 5-11, 12-20 and finally 21-23 (also with subunits); Murphy maintains four divisions: 1.1-9; 1.10-22; 2.1-20; 2.21-23.

Closer to the text, in my opinion, are the following observations. The seven-day feast opens a two-part exposition, related as cause to effect, and a marriage feast comes near the end (2.18), forming a near inclusio. The first feast sets the stage for the fall of Vashti, which is the first subunit (1.5-22); this causes the search for the new queen, which is itself only the second 'narrative event'. Verses 1-4, even if not *Frame*, only constitute a statement, an exposition, not a complication or narrative event.

Thus 1.5–2.20 should be included in *Exposition*, because new characters are being introduced, the smaller tensions or complications do not lead directly to the most important action and crisis of Esther, and the stage for that action and crisis is being set. True enough, one new character, Haman, is introduced in 3.1, but his presence is immediately linked with the central complication of the whole narrative: the pogrom. The introduction of Haman in this way serves to link *Exposition* and *Complication*.

Artistic skill can be noted here in several other ways, one of which is the use of minor complications or tensions that keep reader interest while setting the stage for the principal action. Another is the gradated and increasing importance of each subunit in the *Exposition* for understanding the narrative as a whole.[6] Just as the frame introduced several items which resurface at various later points in the narrative, so important motifs are introduced in this exposition.[7] The troublesome section 2.21-23, recognized as a subunit by all, explained differently by many along with the *crux interpretum* of v. 19, does not 'float' in isolation as it seems to in most commentaries, but clearly should be subsumed under *Expostion* because it gives basic information about the two main characters, and sets the stage for *Complication* and *Crisis*. See the microstructure for its interation within the larger schema.

Text-critically, if L preserves a text which at least in its 'core narrative' antedates MT, as will be argued later, then a case can be made to

---

6. Clines, *The Esther Scroll*, pp. 9-10, is incisive on this concatenation.
7. S.B. Berg, *The Book of Esther: Motifs, Themes and Structure* (SBLDS, 44; Ann Arbor: Edwards Brothers, 1979), pp. 31ff.

support the conjectural reading underlying the Luther and Jerusalem Bibles: הדתים ידעי, versus the MT's העתים ידעי.[8] Under this view, L could represent the oldest reading τοῖς σοφοῖς τοῖς εἰδόσι νόμον καὶ κρίσιν, which o´, more in line with the humanizing tendency in Greek storytelling, turns into the king speaking τοῖς φίλοις... and asking them to make 'a law and a judgment' (νόμον καὶ κρίσιν). Further, the MT would create the *lectio difficilior* by the phrase 'knowing the times' for the purpose of introducing a pejorative allusion to the Torah law which forbids dealing with 'diviners' (who cast lots [2 Kgs 17.17] in order to forecast the 'times'). One wonders if this phrase operated generically to cover all the forbidden categories of wizards, soothsayers, necromancers etc. of Lev. 19.26 and Deut. 18.10-14. Soothsayers, diviners and such were well known among Gentiles, who do not follow Torah.

II. NARRATIVE PROPER & 2 DUAL EPILOGS	1.5–9.19
A. EXPOSITION: New Feast & Vashti's Fall; Esther Made Queen	
& New Feast; Concluding Statement & Report	1.5–2.23
1. New Feast & Vashti's Fall; Statement	1.5-22
a. Exposition minor: setting/description/	
statement: dual 7-day drinkfests	5-9
1) Setting: old & 1st new feasts	5
a) Time: set when 180 days end	5aα
b) Act: king hosts drinkfest	5aβ
c) Recipients: Susaites great & small	5aβ
d) Duration: 7 days	5aβ12-13
e) Place: king's acropolis	5b
2) Description: luxury in decor, ballroom, furniture,	
service & drinking	6-8
a) Decor	6aαβ
α (white) linen awnings	6aα(1)
β blue hangings	6aα(2-3)
γ hung with cords (2 kinds)	6aβ
αα of fine linen	6aβ(3)
ββ & purple	6aβ(4)
b) Ballroom	6aγ
α silver rings (rods?)	6aγ(1-3)
β marble pillars	6aγ(4-5)

---

8.   D. Barthelemy *et al.* (eds.), *Preliminary and Interim Report on the Hebrew Old Testament Text Project* (Stuttgart: United Bible Societies, 1976), II, p. 547.

c) Furniture: beds/recliners	6bα
α of gold	6bα(2)
β & silver	6bα(3)
d) Ballroom: mosaic floor	6bβ
α of porphyry (?)	6bβ(3)
β marble	6bβ(4)
γ mother of pearl (?)	6bβ(5)
δ (valuable) stone	6bβ(6)
e) Service for drinking	7a
α gold goblets	7aα
β cups of various kinds	7aβ
f) Drinking described	7b-8
α Quality: royal wine	7b(1-2)
β Quantity: abundant	7b(3-5)
γ Manner: by special decree	8
αα Content: 'no constraint'	8a
ββ Further description	8b
α1 king set (law)	8bα
β1 let officials allow	8bβ
γ1 as each desires	8bγ
3) Statement: expansion: introduction of Queen Vashti & women's drinkfest	9
a) Transition (גם)	9aα
b) Introduction: subject: Queen Vashti	9aα
c) Action: hosted women's drinkfest	9aβ
d) Place: Ahasuerus' palace	9b
b. Complication minor: king calls; Vashti disobeys	10-12
1) Time and setting	10a
a) Time: day 7	10aα
b) Setting: king 'high'	10aβ
2) Action: king orders 7 eunuchs	10b
a) Statement: 'tells/orders'	10bα(1)
b) Names	10bα(2-8)
α Mehuman	10bα(2)
β Biztha	10bα(3)
γ Harbona	10bα(4)
δ Bigtha	10bα(5)
ε Abagtha	10bα(6)

ζ Zethar   10bα(7)

η Karkas   10bα(8)

c) Class: 7 eunuchs   10bβ

d) Position: serve king's presence   10bγδ

3) Object: to bring Queen Vashti   11a

4) Purpose: to display her beauty   11bα

5) Statement: she is beautiful   11bβ

6) Reaction: Vashti refuses his word   12a

7) Result (2 synonyms): king is vexed/angry   12b

c. Plan minor: 'what to do?': absentia trial   13-20

1) King calls council of wise men   13-15

a) Summons proper   13

b) 7 Perso–Median princes convene   14

c) Royal speech: question/accusation   15

2) Counsellor speech: Memucan's answer   16-20

a) Introductory quotation formula   16aα

b) Speech proper   16aβ-20

α Effects: Vashti's 'crime'   16aβ-18

αα not on king only   16aβ

ββ also on princes & people   16bα

γγ in all provinces of king   16bγ

δδ Reasons: 2 dangers   17

α1 word will spread   17aα

β1 wives dishonor husbands   17aβ

εε Result   18

α1 ladies will talk   18aα

β1 of what queen did   18aβ

γ1 disrespect/anger empire-wide   18b

β Proposed plan/antidote   19-20

αα protocol of politeness   19aα

ββ king publish royal decree   19aβ

γγ as Perso–Median laws   19aγ(1-4)

δδ so it cannot be altered   19aγ(5-6)

εε Vashti must be banished   19bαβ

ζζ royalty given to a better woman   19bγ

ηη Manner   20a

α1 let decree be heard   20aα

β1 which he will issue   20aβ

α Transition: 'when turn came'   12aα

β Time: after 12 months   12aβ

γ Manner   12aγb

    αα Introduction   12aγ

    ββ 6 months myrrh oil   12bα

    γγ 6 months with perfumes   12bβ

    δδ & feminine cosmetics   12bγ

b) Entry to king: manner & result   13-14

    α Introduction   13a

    β virgin asks for anything   13b

    γ evening: go; morning: return   14aα

    δ to 2nd harem, to Shaasgaz & concubines   14aβ

    ε Result: not again unless king calls by name 14b

5) Execution completed: Esther's turn   15-16

    α Flashback 4: Esther's biography   15aα

    β Time: her turn arrives   15aβ

    γ Manner: asks only what Hegai suggests   15aγ

    δ Result: she finds favor (חן)   15b

    ε Entry to Xerxes & date   16

      αα Entry: Esther is taken   16aα

      ββ Date: month 10, year 7 of king   16aβb

d. Resolution minor & digressions: successes of Esther

& Mordecai   17-23

1) Resolution proper (2 parts): coronation

& celebration   17-18

    a) Coronation   17

    α Reasons: (dual)   17a

      αα king loves her   17aα

      ββ she finds more (2)…   17aβ(1,4-6)

        α1 grace (חן)   17aβ(2)

        β1 & favor (חסד)   17aβ(3)

    β Result: Esther crowned   17bα

    γ Summary: Esther replaces Vashti   17bβ

    b) Celebration: feast/holiday/gifts   18

    α great Esther drinkfest   18a

      αα Act: king makes drinkfest   18aα

      ββ Recipients: (?)   18aβγ

        α1 for princes   18aβ(1-2)

        β1 for employees   18aβ(3)

γγ Estherfest (for marriage)	18aγ
β holiday declared	18bα
γ gifts given	18bβ
2) Digression 1: secrets kept by Esther, still obedient to Mordecai	19-20
a) Circumstance of harem, & Mordecai's service at king's gate	19
b) Esther keeps 2 secrets	20
α her relationship to Mordecai	20a(1-4)
β her ethnic background	20a(5-6)
γ per command of Mordecai	20aβ
δ Esther stays obedient to him	20b
3) Digression 2: report: Mordecai thwarts regicide	21-23
a) Setting: time & location	21a
b) Body: regicide plot	21b-22
α 2 eunuchs become angry	2.21bα
β they plot to kill king	21bβ
γ Mordecai learns, tells Esther	22a
δ Esther tells king, in Mordecai's name	22b
ε investigation & conviction	23aα
c) Conclusion: incident recorded	23b

One may add an approving and a corrective note to the textual remark in HOTTP on 1.22 (ומדבר כלשון עמו) which reads, 'This expression may be an idiomatic expression—or a usual formula of royal decrees, which is ironically used in this context'. The irony of an imperial highness having to legislate male dominance throughout the empire, within a culture already male-oriented, surely strikes a humorous note. However, the following comment that the phrase 'that every man be lord in his house' cannot be the content of the decree leaves most of the irony out, and leaves no content (or content summary) of the decree. The contents of the 'decree of death' and 'letter of license' are both summarized in EH; it is unlikely the reader would be left to total speculation in this instance. The o′ text phraseology gives no help text critically, but makes clear that the intent is to cause women, from poor to rich, to honor their husbands, and fully allows for the irony in MT. L, on the other hand, denies textual derivation from either MT or o′, and rationalizes that the decree will benefit 'all kingdoms', and 'all wives will give honor and glory to their husbands' in such a way as to leave two alternatives: either L gives a serious lecture on political and social stability, or heightens the irony by stretching the point *ad absurdum*.

B. *Complication (MT 3.1–5.14)*

This is a skillfully constructed unit with an exposition, a minor complication for the antagonist, and his plan to solve the complication. His plan of course constitutes the major complication of the narrative: a planned holocaust of all Jews. One could agree with Murphy and Dommershausen in finding two subunits in ch. 3, vv. 1-7 and 8-15,[9] if scenic factors were the principal ones. Chosen here as more basic is the narrative structural factor of the antagonist's plan, the *Complication* itself. It is true that the 'scene' changes in v. 8, but the development of Haman's plan has already begun and carries through into the throne room. Scenes, sometimes clear, sometimes fuzzy or amorphous, have been laid aside for presentation of the more consistent skeletal organization; this does not imply that the investigation of scenes and their interrelations with structure should not be investigated separately.

B. COMPLICATION: King Promotes Haman (who provokes crisis)	
& Approves Pogrom, Empire-Wide	3.1-15
1. Exposition: Haman's Promotion & Results	1-2a
a. Transition: passage of time	1aα
b. Promotion proper and Haman's biography	1aβb
1) Promotion (1st verb)	1aβ
2) Haman's biography: Agagite (Amalekite)	1aβ
3) Promotion (2nd verb)	1aβ
4) Promotion (3rd verb): above princes	1b
c. Result: servants all bow to Haman	2aα
d. Reason: so king commanded	2aβ
2. Complication: Confrontation of Hero/Villain	2b-5
a. Mordecai's 1st refusal (2 acts)	2b
1) to bow	2b(1-3)
2) to worship	2b(4-5)
b. First reaction of coworkers (speech)	3
1) Quote formula & introduction of workers	3a
2) Appeal-speech proper	3b
3) Frequency of their reaction (daily)	4aα

---

9. Murphy, *Wisdom Literature*, pp. 161-62; Dommershausen, *Die Estherrolle*, pp. 58ff.

          c. Mordecai's 2nd refusal (resoluteness)   4aβ
          d. Second reaction of workers (report)   4b
                1) Action: they inform Haman   4bα
                2) Purpose: see if Mordecai's words prevail   4bβ
                3) Reason: Mordecai reveals he is a Jew   4bγ
          e. Haman's reactions: confirmation & anger   5
                1) 1st: sees Mordecai disobey (sensual)   5a
                2) 2nd: his anger (emotional reaction)   5b
   3. Plan (of villain): Haman Plots Pogrom Empire-Wide:
   Conception, Preparation, Proposal, Approval
   & Initial Execution   6-15a
          a. *Conception*: 'final solution': more reactions & reason 6
                1) 3rd reaction (rational) & reason   6a
                      a) disdains killing only Mordecai   6aα
                      b) Reason: Mor.'s 'Jewish connection' revealed 6aβ
                2) 4th reaction (volitional): kill all in Xerxes' land 6β
          b. *Preparation*: *purim* ('lots') cast to find pagan/polytheistic
                propitious pogrom point   7
                1) Date: 1st month Nisan, king's 12th year   7a
                2) Act: casting *pur* ('lot') before Haman   7bα
                3) Manner: day by day, month by month   7bβ(1-4)
                4) Duration: (1st) to 12th month Adar   7bβ(5-9)
          c. *Proposal*: plan presented by prosecutor   8-9
                1) Introductory quotation formula, to Xerxes   8aα
                2) Speech proper: plan proper   8aβ-9
                      a) Accusations & conclusion: 8aβb
                            α a scattered people   8aβ
                            β with different laws   8bα
                            γ they do not obey king   8bβ
                            δ therefore not worthy   8bγ
                      b) Prosecutorial request   9a
                            α Protocol form   9aα
                            β Request proper: kill all   9aβ
                      c) Incentive/result: money   9b
          d. *Royal Approval*: king's reactions   10-11
                1) Report of act: he transfers ring(= power) to Haman 10
                      a) king removes royal seal   10a
                      b) gives it to Haman   10b

2) Royal speech (dual judgments)	11
a) introductory quotation formula	11aα
b) money is given to you	11aβ
c) do as you desire	11b
e. *Execution* of plan begins	12-15a
1) Preparation of decree	12
a) Action: royal scribes called	12aα(1-3)
b) Time: 1st month, 13th day	12aα(4-9)
c) Object: (decree) written	12aβ(1)
d) Author: Haman in control	12aβ(2-5)
e) Recipients: satraps, governors, princes	12aβ(6-l)
f) Manner: individual script & language	12aγδ
g) Validation: king's name & royal seal	12b
2) Publication: by couriers	13aα(1-4)
3) Area: to all provinces of kingdom	13aα(5-8)
4) Contents	13aβb
a) Action: to destroy, kill, annihilate	13aβ(1-3)
b) Object: all Jews	13aβ(4-11)
c) Duration: one day	13aβ(12-13)
d) Date: 13th of 12th month, Adar	13aγ
e) Reward: take booty	13b
[Greek has facsimile decree here]	
5) Distribution (dual)	14a
a) copies to be issued in every province	14aα
b) & proclaimed to all peoples	14aβ
6) Purpose: be ready 11 months ahead	14b
7) Compliance report	15a
a) at king's word, couriers go	15aα
b) decree published in Shushan	15aβ
f. *Reactions*: (dual) king/Haman versus people	15b
a) king and Haman drink/rejoice	15bα
b) Shushan in confusion	15bβ

It is interesting to note that L 3.7—precisely the point at which the MT is unclear and may have lost a line or more through homoteleuton[10]— appears not after v. 6, but after vv. 9, 11, 10 (*sic*), but it also remains ambiguous as to whether lots were cast throughout the year to Adar 13, or were cast for some shorter period and gave the answer 'Adar 13'.

10. Barthelemy *et al.* (eds.), *Preliminary and Interim Report*, II, pp. 548-49.

C. Plan and New Complication (MT 4.1–5.14)
At this point the heroes try to avoid the complication with a plan of their own—a step familiar in folktales and real life. More narrative skill surfaces here with the verbal exchanges which, with a certain see-saw effect, build tension until the point of (temporary) rest in the action, called here 'Result'. But as Van Seters has noted with the Abraham tale, the heroes may run into a new complication before their plan can be executed, or perhaps because of executing it; this in turn may lead to an impasse or crisis point which will determine their fate.[11]

C. PLAN AND NEW COMPLICATION: Mordecai Proposes to
    Thwart Death through Esther; They Begin Executing Plan: Entry
    Scene (Esther Succeeds); 1st Invitation/1st Drinkfest + 2nd
    Invitation; Haman Plots Mordecai's Death Next Morning   4.1–5.14
      1. Problem Discovered & Plan Proposed: Introduction;
        Four Mediated Exchanges Between Mordecai & Esther   4.1-17
          a. Exposition: Mordecai & people learn of plot
            & lament bitterly   1-3
            1) Report: Mordecai learns & reacts   1-2
              a) Setting: he finds out   1aα
              b) Body: 2 reactions   1aβ-2a
                α Lament described   1aβγ
                  αα rips clothes   1aβ
                  ββ dress: sackcloth/ashes   1aγ
                β Itinerary (2)   1b-2a
                  αα Departure: to city   1bα
                  ββ Travel mode: crying   1bβ
                    α1 cries a cry/yell   1bβ(1-2)
                    β1 Further details   1bβ(3-4)
                    α2 great   1bβ(3)
                    β2 bitter   1bβ(4)
                  γγ Arrival: king's gate   2a
                γ Digression: law of the gate   2b
             2) Description/statement: people learn and lament   3
               a) Place: where word & decree reach   3aαβ
               b) Act: Jews (learn)   3aγ(3)
               c) Reaction: 6 lament signs   3aγ(1-2)δb
                  α Emotional signs (4)   3aγ(1-2)δ

11. Van Seters, *Abraham in History and Tradition*, pp. 169ff.

αα great mourning   3aγ(1-2)

ββ fasting   3aδ(1)

γγ weeping   3aδ(2)

δδ lamenting   3aδ(3)

β Physical signs (2) spread for many   3b

αα sackcloth   3bα(1)

ββ & ashes spread for many   3bα(2)

γγ Action proper   3bβ

b. Development: 3 exchanges on plan: problem reaches

Esther; plan proposed by Mordecai; rejection by Esther   4-14

1) Problem reaches Esther (partial disclosure): statement:

1st exchange (3rd person; no discourse)   4

a) maids & eunuchs enter/tell Esther (2+2)   4aα

b) queen's distress   4aβ

c) she sends to Mordecai (2 purposes)   4b

α to clothe Mordecai   4bα

β to remove his sackcloth   4bβ(6-8)

d) he refuses   4bβ(9-10)

2) Problem further described (full disclosure) &

plan proposed: report: 2nd exchange through

Hatach (indirect discourse)   5-9

a) Act 1: Esther calls Hatach   5aα(1-3)

b) Job description   5aα(4-8)

α a royal eunuch   5aα(4-5)

β appointed to wait on her   5aα(6-8)

c) Act 2: sends him to Mordecai   5aβ

d) Purpose: to learn what & why   5b

e) Compliance report: Hatach obeys   6

α he goes to Mordecai   6a

β in street at king's gate   6b

f) Report of conversation   7-8

α Mordecai tells Hatach all   7a

β tells Haman's transaction   7b

αα Amount: exact   7bβ(1-2)

ββ Currency: silver   7bβ(3)

γγ Agent: Haman   7bβ(4-6)

δδ Action: payment   7bβ(7)

εε Beneficiary: king   7bβ(8-10)

ζζ Purpose: kill Jews   7bβ(11-12)

γ Proof: gives decree copy   8aα

δ Object: show/tell Esther   8aβ

ε Plan proposed   8b

αα Command: order Esther   8bα

ββ Purpose: go to king, ask, seek

mercy for her people   8bβ

g) Compliance: Hatach goes/tells Esther   9

3) Refusal of plan (Esther) & rebuttal (Mordecai):

report: 3rd exchange (2 speeches)   10-14

a) Introductions & Esther's refusal speech   10-12

α Intro. quote formula: Esther to Hatach   10a

β Command: sends to Mordecai (ellipse)   10b

γ Speech proper   11

αα General conditions   11a

α1 common knowledge   11aα

β1 entry to king = death   11aβγ

γ1 exception (sceptre)   11aδ

α2 Act: king offers   11aδ(1-8)

β2 Result: one lives   11aδ(9)

ββ Specific condition   11b

α1 no call for me   11bα

β1 30 days now   11bβ

δ Compliance: he tells Mordecai   12

b) Introductions & Mordecai's rebuttal

speech to Esther by Hatach   13-14

α Intro. quote formula: Mor. (to Hatach)   13aα

β Command: send to Esther (ellipse)   13aβ

γ Speech proper   13b-14

αα Prohibition   13b

ββ Reasons: positive and negative   14a

α1 if you are silent   14aα

β1 rescue arise from elsewhere   14aβ

γ1 you & family perish   14aγ

γγ Motive clause: who knows?   14b

c. Result: Esther agrees to plan & orders preparation:

report: 4th 'exchange' (Esther's speech &

Mordecai's compliance)   15-17

1) Introductions & Esther's acceptance speech   15-16

12. עבר; RSV 'went away'; possibly 'crossed over (the moat around the acropolis)'; later tradition 'transgressed (the Sabbath by fasting)'.

D. *Crisis/Pivot (MT 6.1-5)*

The reader is referred to the discussion of the parallel section in EG for justification of the terminology used here. In EH there is no explicit divine intervention to resolve the crisis; there is only coincidence. Few readers of the period of early Judaism would miss the inference, however.

2) Speech proper	5aβ
a) Exclamation: 'behold!'	5aβ(1)
b) Answer proper	5aβ(2-4)
α Haman (is)	5aβ(2)
β standing in court	5aβ(3-4)
f. Royal speech	5b
1) Introductory quotation formula	5b(1-2)
2) Speech/command: 'let him enter!'	5b(3)

E. Dénouement: Peripety (MT 6.6–8.14)

As the king begins to dialog with Haman, the reader knows that things are looking up for Mordecai. Two new structuring principles combine here for maximum effect. By altering the grouping of characters, the author presents fresh opportunities for plot reversals, peripety. The amassing of certain characters comes first, then one or more reversals of fortune for the protagonists (from negative events in chs. 3–5 to positive ones in chs. 6–8 and beyond). Those observations cover the material through to 8.14.

E. DÉNOUEMENT: *Peripety = 7 Reversals* of Fortune for Mordecai,	
Esther, People vs. Haman: (in narratives, reports, etc. to 9.19,	
resuming in 10.2aβ)	6.6–8.14
1. King, Haman and Mordecai: Reversal 1	6.6-12
a. Setting: compliance: Haman enters	6aα
b. Dialog: king/Haman (= complication for villain)	6aβ-10
1) Royal speech	6aβγδε
a) Introductory quotation formula	6aβ
b) Speech proper	6aγδε
α Question: 'what?'	6aγ
β Object, general: man	6aδ
γ Object, specific: king wants to honor	6aε
2) Digression: self-speech: Haman's thoughts	6b
a) Introductory quotation formula (in mind)	6bα
b) Self-speech proper:	6bβ
α Question: 'who?'	6bβ(1)
β Object, general: honor	6bβ(2-5)
γ Object, specific: me	6bβ(6-7)
3) Vizier speech: Haman (as defense lawyer for self)	7-9
a) Introductory quotation formula	7a

α1 of Haman	3bβ(4)
β1 the Agagite	3bβ(5)
ββ & plot	3bγ
α1 which he hatched	3bδ(1-2)
β1 against Jews	3bδ(3-4)
b) Report: king's reaction & result	4
α extends gold sceptre	4a
β Result: Esther rises & stands	4b
c) Esther's speech	5-6
α Introductory quotation formula	5aα(1)
β Speech proper	5aα(2-9)-6
αα Protocol: (4)	5aα(2-9)
α1 if good to king	5aα(2-5)
β1 if I found favor	5aα(6-9)
γ1 (if) right to king	5aβ
δ1 (if) I am pleasing	5aγ
ββ Requests	5b
α1 What: let be written	5bα(1)
β1 Purpose (2)	5bα(2-4)βγδε
α2 reverse letters	5bα(2-4)
β2 & plot of	5bβ(1)
α3 Haman (son...)	5bβ(2-5)
β3 he wrote	5bγ
γ3 to destroy Jews	5bδ
δ3 empire-wide	5bε
γγ Reasons: (2)	6
α1 how watch evil?	6a
β1 how watch destruction?	6b
2) Reversal 7: king's response: speech/decree	7-14
a) Royal speech	7-8
α Introductory quotation formula	7a
αα Formula proper	7aα(1-3)
ββ Addressees	7aα(4-5)β
α1 to Esther, the queen	7aα(4-5)
β1 to Mordecai, the Jew	7aβ
β Speech proper	7b-8
αα Exclamation	7bα(1)
ββ Rehearsal (2): king's acts	7bα(2-5)βγ
α1 Haman's house given	7bα(2-5)

β1 he is hung	7bβ
γ1 Reason: plot re Jews	7bγ
γγ Permission (2): Mor./Esther's acts	8a
δδ Result (reason?)	8b
b) Preparation of decree: Mordecai	9-10
α Act: scribes called	9aα(1-3)
β Time, general	9aα(4-5)
γ Date, specific	9aα(6-10)β
αα 3rd month, Sivan	9aα(6-10)
ββ 23rd day.(70 days after 1st decree)	9aβ
δ Subject: (decree) written	9aγ1
ε Author: Mordecai in control	9aγ(2-5)
ζ Recipients: Jews/sat's/gov's/princes	9aγ(6-7)δ
η Area	9aεζ
αα India to Cush	9aε
ββ 127 provinces	9aζ
θ Manner: (2) individual script & language	9aηθ
ι Recipients (!)	9b
αα to Jews	9bα
ββ in their script	9bβ(1)
γγ in their language	9bβ(2)
c) Validation (3)	10a
α Act: written	10aα
β Authority: king's name	10aβ
γ Evidence: royal seal	10aγ
d) Publication	10b
α writing sent out	10bα
β by mounted couriers	10bβ
γ riding swift horses	10bγ(1-2)
δ of king's best (?)	10bγ(3)
ε bred from royal stud (?)	10bδ
e) Contents of decree letters	11-12
α Introduction: 'pronoun of contents'	11aα(1)
β Act, general: allows	11aα(2)
γ Author: king	11aα(3)
δ Subject	11aα(4)β
αα Jews	11aα(1)
ββ in each city	11aβ

ε Act, specified[13]	11aγ
αα to gather (defense?)	11aγ(1)
ββ to stand (defense?)	11aγ(2-4)
γγ to attack	11aδεζ
α1 destroy	11aδ(1)
β1 annihilate	11aδ(2)
γ1 kill	11aδ(3)
α2 armed force	11aε(1-3)
β2 any opposers	11aε(4-7)
γ2 children	11aζ(1)
δ2 women	11aζ(2)
δδ to plunder	11b
ζ Time	12aα
η Area: all provinces	12aβ
θ Date	12b
αα 13th day, 12th month	12bα
ββ name: Adar	12bβ
[Greek has facsimile decree here]	
f) Distribution	13
α copy of decree	13aα
β to be given	13aβ(1)
αα How: (as) law	13aβ(2)
ββ Where: each province	13aβ(3-5)
γ (to be) proclaimed to all	13aγ
δ to be ready	13bα(1,3)
αα Who: Jews (= subject)	13bα(2)
ββ When: for this day	13bα(4-5)
ε to avenge selves on enemies	13bβ
g) Compliance	14
α Manner	14a
αα couriers	14aα(1)
ββ mounted on swift horses	14aα(2-3)
γγ the king's best (?)	14aα(4)
δδ ride out in haste	14aβ(1-2)
εε urged/pressed	14aβ(3-5)

13. An alternative scheme for ε Act, specified: αα defense (11aγ), consisting of α1 gather (11aγ[1]) and β1 stand for lives (11aγ[2-4]); ββ attack (11aεζ), consisting of α1 Acts: 3 verbs (kill) (11aδ) and β1 Objects: 4 (11aεζ); γγ plunder (11b).

β Area (all empire understood above): Susa   14b
                    αα decree published   14bα
                    ββ in Susa acropolis   14bβ

An interesting text-critical point surfaces in 6.13b, where MT has חכמיו ('his wise men'), referring to the same group in v. 13a which are called there אהביו ('his friends'). o´ has 'friends' (φίλοι) in both cases, but L has only one reference to Haman's associates and it supports MT: σοφοί. As HOTTP points out,[14] 'wise men' of MT is a B-level reading (i.e., next to the highest probability), and they are his friends in any case, but 'the expression is ironical: the wise friends of Haman!'

Tov[15] does not comment on these readings, but if one applied his theory here (that is, that L is rewriting, smoothing out, o´ in the direction of a Hebrew *Vorlage* that differed from MT), one *can* explain L's support of MT. But, based on the simple and terse account and rather choppy, sudden introduction of wise men in L (Aman explains to his wife, then his wife and the wise men answer), one can also explain these readings in this way: L preserves an old Semitic reading which captures both the (older) social importance of wise men and the irony (not at all beyond the capability of an original author poking fun at the dominant culture); o´, influenced more by Hellenistic culture, chooses the then culturally important 'friends' idea and perhaps misses both the former importance of wise men and the irony (not hard to do, especially if the translator has only written words to go by); o´ also smooths out the narrative by bringing Aman home to both wife and *friends*, so that when wife and *friends* respond, o´ has two references and they are consistent. EH, in its proto-MT form, honors both a Semitic 'wise men' and a Greek tradition of 'friends' by using both—one of each.

F. *Triple Conclusion (MT 8.15–9.19)*

It has been argued above (see the parallel section in EG) that the straightforward, pointed statements and reversals of 8.15-17 cover more ground than may appear at first glance. As in the book of Ruth (parallel to a certain extent) and in Hellenistic romances (to the full extent), the end of the story restores the heroes to their rightful—usually high or noble—station in life, after a series of defeats, injustices or twists of fate. In all texts, Jos included (11.284-285), these concluding, over-arching

14. Barthelemy *et al.* (eds.), *Preliminary and Interim Report*, II, pp. 549-50.
15. Tov, 'The "Lucianic" Text', *passim*.

2

reversals occur at this point. These final reversals bring the arc of tension, or the 'falling action', to a necessary and sufficient closure. The fact
that the book itself does not conclude here is a problem for this study's
next Chapter on redaction. It has been argued in Chapter 2 of the study
that 8.15-17 gives a satisfactory closure to the narrative proper. The
material that follows thus stands as additional conclusions or epilogs.

22

F. TRIPLE CONCLUSION: 3 Final Reversals (8-10) & Final	
Results (2); Epilog 1: Dual Victory Reports: Epilog 2: Dual	
Etiologies	8.15–9.19
1. Narrative Conclusion: 3 Reversals; 2 Results	8.15-17
a. Final reversals (8-10): Mordecai's triumph;	
1st celebrations: Shushan's joy; people's joy	15-16
1) Reversal 8: Mordecai's triumph (3)	15a
a) Setting: Mordecai leaves king	15aα
b) Reversal proper: description	15aβγδ
α dressed, royal blue/white	15aβ
β large gold crown	15aγ
γ cloak: fine linen & purple	15aδ
2) Reversal 9: joy in Shushan (2)	15b
a) Setting: Shushan	15bα
b) Reversal proper: description	15bβ
α rejoicing	15bβ(1)
β gladness	15bβ(2)
3) Reversal 10: joy of people (4)	16
a) Subject: Jews	16aα
b) Reversal proper: description	16aβb
α light	16aβ(1-3)
β gladness	16aβ(4)
γ joy	16bα
δ honor	16bβ
b. Results (2): description of Jews (4); reaction of Gentiles	17
1) Jews	17a
a) Description of extent	17aαβ
α every province & city (2)	17aα
β where command & decree came	17aβ
b) Further description: personal	17aγδ
α gladness	17aγ(1)
β joy to Jews	17aγ(2-3)

16. 'The Jews' are explicitly mentioned seven times in this passage (9.1-10): vv. 1bβ, 1bδ, 2aα, 3aε, 5aα, 6b and 10aγ, with several more explicit mentions in the following passages.

17. Note that MT v. 11 (followed by *setumah*) functions as inclusio with v. 1 (= two time phrases).

β 75,000	16aε
e) Booty: statement: not taken	16b
f) Date	17a
α day 13	17aα
β month Adar	17aβ
2) Etiology proper: celebration/feast	17b
a) Rest	17bα
b) Date: day 14	17bβ
c) Feast	17bγδ
α Act: they made it	17bγ
β Object: day	17bδ(1-3)
αα drinkfest	17bδ(2)
ββ & joy	17bδ(3)
b. Etiology 2: 2-day battle (13th–14th) & feast (15th)	18-19
1) Battle report: Shushan	18a
a) Confrontation	18aαβ(1)
α Jews	18aα(1)
β in Shushan	18aα(2-3)
γ Act: organize (as troops)	18aβ(1)
b) Dates	18aβ(2-4)γ
α on day 13	18aβ(2-4)
β & on day 14	18aγ
2) Etiology proper: celebration, 15th Adar	18b
a) Rest (victory implied)	18bα
b) Date: day 15	18bβ
c) Act: they made it	18bγ
d) Object: day	18bδ(1-3)
α drinkfest	18bδ(2)
β & joy	18bδ(3)
3) Etiological restatement: why the 14th	19
a) Transition: inference	19aα(1-2)
b) Jews, rural areas	19aα(3-4)
α who dwell	19aβ(1)
β in country (= unwalled towns?)	19aβ(2-3)
c) Act: they make/celebrate	19aγ
d) Object: 14th Adar	19aδ
α joy & drinkfest	19aε(1-2)
β a holiday	19aε(3-4)
e) Specification: gift exchange	19b

3. *Etiology of Purim (MT 9.20-32)*

At this point the narrative tension ceases, the style and subject change, the vocabulary differs, familiar terms become reinterpreted or possibly are misunderstood—the reader is in new territory. Again, remarks at the same location under EG apply here also, although o′ is much closer to the Hebrew, a fact which poses a difficulty for Tov's theory of L being a rewrite of o′ in the direction of a non-MT *Vorlage*. Of course, this problem could be overcome by positing more than one stage in L's development—something Tov does not propose. The theme of Purim dominates and repeats so much in this section that many students of Esther have missed the structural, narrative and stylistic differences between chs. 1–8 and ch. 9.

III. ETIOLOGY: HISTORY & LAW OF PURIM: How Feast of Purim Issues
    from Foregoing Narrative & Becomes Perpetual: 3 Steps: 'Canonizing' by
    Community Consent (vv. 23-28) + Dual Regulatory Decrees of Mordecai
    (vv. 20-22) & Esther (vv. 29-32)   9.20-32
      A. REPORT: Mordecai's Decree Establishes a Compromising 2-Day
          Purim, Adar 14th–15th   9.20-22
            1. Author: Mordecai   20aα(2)
            2. Acts (2)   20aα(1)bα(1)
               a. writes (words/decree)   20aα(1)
               b. sends (writings/letters)   20bα(1)
             3. Objects   20aβbα(2)
               a. 'these words' (cf. Exod. 20.1b)   20aβ
               b. letters   20bα(2)
             4. Recipients   20bα(3-5)bβγ
               a. all Jews (1st mention)   20bα(3-5)
               b. in all provinces of King Ahasuerus   20bβ
               c. near & far   20bγ
             5. Purpose   21
               a. to enjoin them (to)   21aα
               b. continue celebrating   21aβ
               c. Objects   21aγδ
                 1) both 14th Adar   21aγ
                 2) & 15th   21aδ
               d. Duration: from year to year   21b
            6. Mode (comparative)   22a

4. *Frame Epilog (MT 10.1-3)*

Returning to a prominent but not central figure in the story, this frame or epilog once again talks about the king. Most readers will not have come to either like or dislike this hapless figure, around whom so much takes place and upon whom so much—both good and bad—depends. This is because the plot uses the bumbling monarch more as foil than character, and does not encourage readers to become emotionally involved with him.

The two apparent oddities inherent in that description of the king need explanation. Speaking of tales, novellas and historical romances, one may observe that Esther's king, like all good kings, is stupid.[18] This explains why he makes such a good foil for our heroes, why we do not detest him even when he 'embroils himself' (cf. the language of the letter/decree of license) in Haman's cruel plot, and why—if we will but enter into the spirit of the story—he provides not a few laughs. While this much is clear, one is left with the problem of why the king is here at all, or why he is so central if he is merely a foil: the story opens and closes with him, and he figures in the central *crisis*, not to mention other places where he could be dispensed with. This second unusual phenomenon usually escapes discussion, but will find explanation under the chapter on redaction. For now it only requires the repetition of the observation that Mordecai receives great power and honor at the very end of EH by being associated with King Ahasuerus' legendary greatness. This is true for all Esther texts in spite of the fact that the king and the irresistible might of Persia are gently lampooned or spoofed. No doubt this humorous, ironic aspect helped sell the story to downtrodden Diaspora Jews.

IV. FRAME EPILOG/CONCLUDING RESUME: King 'Enshrined'; Extent
 & Richness of Kingdom (shown by king in control of far-flung empire and
 vast wealth through tax/corvee over land & isles); Reversal 10: King Aha-
 suerus Associates Mordecai (as vizier) With His Royal Self in Unparalleled
 Magnitude; Documentation in Medo-Persian Annals; Praise of Mordecai's
 Good Deeds   10.1-3

---

18. One wonders, with Sanders, if this common concept parallels the popular, modern view which nearly equates God with 'luck' or 'fate'.

A. EPILOG: King's Last Act = Greatness	1
1. Act: levied	1αa
2. Subject: King Ahasuerus	1aβ
3. Object: tax/corvee labor?	1bα1
4. Extent	1bα(2-3)β
a. (all) the land	1bα(2-3)
b. isles of the sea	1bβ
B. EPITOME FORMULAS: King & Mordecai	2a
1. King	2aα
a. all acts	2aα(1-2)
b. of power	2aα(3)
c. & greatness	2aα(4)
2. Mordecai	2aβ
a. precise account	2aβ(1)
b. of greatness	2aβ(2)
c of Mordecai	2aβ(3)
d. to which king raised him	2aγ
C. CITATION FORMULA: Query (may not reader check?)	2b
1. Are they not written…?	2bα
2. in the Annals	2bβ
3. of the Kings of Medo–Persia?	2bγ
D. CONCLUDING EPITOME: Reversal 10: Mordecai as Vizier;	
Praise of Mordecai's Good Deeds	3
1. Transition: כִּ	3aα
2. Subject: Mordecai the Jew	3aβ
3. Status: Dual (vizier & benefactor)	3aγδ
a. 2nd to King Ahasuerus	3aγ
b. great among Jews (10th mention)	3aδ
c. pleasing to bulk of brethren	3aε
4. Last Acts	3b
a. speaking good to (benefiting) his people	3bα
b. speaking peace to his kinsfolk	3bβ

With the background now laid, it will be helpful to see the overall macrostructure of EH on one page. For purposes of comparison, the macrostructures of L and o′ are also now presented here, and in that order. While the least amount of differences between the three texts show up at the macro-level, and of course the greatest contrasts appear in the microstructures, the reader is asked to note both what is said and not said within the macro-presentations. Under such a view, sufficient variation exists to justify distinguishing different *Sitzen im Leben* and intentions for the three texts.

The Macrostructure of Hebrew Esther

I. *Frame Prolog*: Ahasuerus' greatness (territorial control & 180-day drinkfest)   1.1-4

II. *Rescue Novella Proper* and 2 Dual Epilogs   1.5–9.19

    A. *Exposition*: 7-day drinkfest/Vashti falls; Esther made queen; Mordecai saves king   1.5–2.23

    B. *Complication*: king approves Haman's empire-wide Jewish pogrom; report of royal death decree   3.1–5.14

    C. *Plan and New Complication*: heroes execute 2-step plan: entry episode; delays = 2 invitations/drinkfests; new complication: Haman plots to hang Mordecai   4.1–5.14

    D. *Crisis/Pivot*: the coincidentally sleepless king discovers Mordecai's lack of reward; counsellors   6.1-5

    E. *Dénouement*: *Peripety* = 7 reversals of fortune for Mordecai, Esther, people vs. Haman (resumes in 10.2aβ); report of royal defense letter   6.6–8.14

    F. *Triple Conclusion*: narrative end = 3 final reversals and 2 final results; 2 dual epilogs: 2 victory reports; 2 feast etiologies   8.15–9.19

III. *Etiology: History and Law of Purim*: compromise: Mordecai and community combine 2 separate days into 2-day feast: 3 steps: Mordecai's decree; 'canonizing' by community consent; Esther's confirmatory/regulatory decree   9.20-32

IV. *Frame Epilog*: documenting resume: King Ahaseurus' and Mordecai's greatness enshrined (control/taxes); Mordecai becomes vizier, great among Jews, benefactor   10.1-3

The Macrostructure of Greek Esther L

I.   *Mordecai's Dream*: 2 dragons/war; we cry; a spring; rivers devour the honored   A 1-10

II. *First Fulfillment of Dream* (Partial): reports: Mordecai saves King Assueros; Aman, given to serve Mordecai, seeks to hurt him/people   A 11-18

III. *Second Fulfillment of Dream* (Complete): rescue novella; etiology: Mordecai's letter (= law?)   1.1–7.52

    A.   *Frame Prolog*: King Assueros' greatness (territorial control and 180-day drinkfest)   1.1

    B.   *Novella Proper*   1.2–7.46

       1. *Exposition*: 7-day deliverance drinkfest/Ouastin falls; Esther made queen   1.2–2.18

       2. *Complication*: king approves Aman's empire-wide Jewish pogrom; text of royal death decree   3.1-18

       3. *Plan and 2 New Complications*: heroes execute 3-step plan: 2 prayers; entry episode (crisis minor/divine intervention); delays = 2 invitations/banquets; 2nd new complication: Aman plots to hang Mordecai   4.1–5.24

       4. *Crisis Major/Pivot*: 2nd intervention: Mighty One removes sleep from king who then discovers Mordecai's lack of reward; self-speech/counsellors   6.1-8

       5. *Dénouement*: Peripety = 9 reversals of fortune for Mordecai, Esther, people vs. Aman (resumes, 7.51-52), including a 3rd crisis/intervention; 2 texts: royal defense letter and Mordecai's letter   6.9–7.38

       6. *Dual Conclusion*: narrative end = 3 final reversals & 2 final results; dual epilog: 2 victory reports   7.39-46

    C.   *Etiology (?) of Phouraia*: report: Mordecai's letter (= law?) and gifts; etiology proper   7.47-49

    D.   *Frame Epilog*: documenting resume: King Assueros' and Mordecai's greatness enshrined (control/decrees); Mordecai becomes king(?)/beloved, benefactor of Jews   7.50-52

IV. *Mordecai's Dream Interpreted*: Mordecai/Aman and pogrom/Esther   7.53-54

V.   *Homily/Doxology* (God's mighty acts/covenant)   7.55-58

VI. *Final 7-Part Command*: observe 2-day *Phouraia* feast   7.59

The Macrostructure of Greek Esther oʹ

I. *Mordecai's Dream*: 2 dragons/battles; they (people) cry; a spring;
the humble devour the honored   A 1-11

II. *First Fulfillment of Dream* (Partial): Reports: Mordecai saves King
Artaxerxes; Aman seeks to hurt Mordecai/people   A 12-17

III. *Second Fulfillment of Dream* (Complete): Rescue Novella; etiology:
history and law   1.1–10.3

   A. *Frame Prolog*: King Artaxerxes' greatness (territorial control
and 180-day reception)   1.1-3

   B. *Novella Proper*   1.4–9.19

      1. *Exposition*: 7-day marriage drinkfest/Astin falls; Esther
made queen; Mordecai saves king again   1.4–2.23

      2. *Complication*: king approves Aman's empire-wide
Jewish pogrom; text of royal death decree   3.1-15 + B 1-7

      3. *Plan and 2 New Complications*: heroes execute 3-step plan:
2 prayers; entry episode (crisis minor/divine intervention);
delays = 2 invitations/banquets; 2nd new complication:
Aman plots to hang Mordecai   4.1–C/D–5.14

      4. *Crisis Major/Pivot*: 2nd intervention: Lord removes
sleep from king who then discovers Mordecai's lack of
reward; counsellors   6.1-5

      5. *Dénouement: Peripety* = 7 reversals of fortune for Mordecai,
Esther, people vs. Aman (resumes in 10.3); text of
royal defense letter   6.6–E–8.14

      6. *Triple Conclusion*: narrative end = 3 final reversals
and 2 final results; 2 dual epilogs: 2 victory reports; 2
feast etiologies   8.15–9.19

   C. *Etiology*: History and Law of *Phrourai*: Mordecai combines
communities' separate days into 2-day feast compromise:
3 steps: Mordecai's decree 'canonizing' by community consent;
Esther's confirmatory/regulatory decree   9.20-31

   D. *Frame Epilog*: documenting resume: King Artaxerxes' and
Mordecai's greatness enshrined (control/taxes); Mordecai
becomes king(?)/honored, beloved by Jews   10.1-3

IV. *Mordecai's Dream Interpreted*: Mordecai/Aman and pogrom/Esther   F 1-6a

V. *Homily/Responsory* (God's mighty acts)   F 6b-9

VI. *Final 7 Part Commund. observe 2-day Phrourai*   F 10
[Colophon: Data and Verification of Translation (F 11)]

Chapter 4

REDACTION, SOURCES AND TEXT HISTORY

The study undertaken here, to locate layers in the text prior to the final form, is not intended to be exhaustive. Rather it is exploratory and intended to capitalize on the results of the previous structure analysis as informed by narratology. Now that the structural blocks of o′, L and MT have been identified, they can be compared, contrasted and examined for tensions between the units. Jos, except for a few comparative references, must await a separate study.

1. *The Frame*

1.1. *A Final Frame?*

Not counting the titular superscriptions, o′ opens with a 299-word section, compared with L's (normally shorter!) 309. Neither EH nor Jos have section A (dream and regicide plot), nor its concluding complement, section F (dream interpretation and homily).

To begin, the focus will include only the dream in o′ A 1-10 // L A 1-8, plus its interpretation, o′ F 1-6aδ // L 7.53-55. Afterwards, the closing verses of sections A and F (in both EG texts) concerning Mordecai's discovery of the regicide plot, plus the homiletic and legal material following the dream interpretation (the final verses of both texts) can be discussed. The dream comprises 160 words in o′ and 130 in L; the interpretation takes 82 words in o′ but only 52 in L. For simplicity of discussion A will now refer to the dream in o′ and L, while F will stand for the dream interpretation in both texts, unless greater precision is needed.

One notices that A is complete in the sense of being self-contained, but not in the sense of being self-explanatory. Necessary for its understanding are the Esther novella (not sufficient of itself) and the decoding in F.

The dream interpretation constitutes a complementing frame, quite necessary for understanding the dream. In fact the two sections exist in an interdependent relationship akin to prolog and epilog; but the interdependency of A and F surpasses that of most prolog/epilog units. That is, A does not merely set the stage, and F does not just carry forward, or update a timeline. Rather, A transports what follows into the transcendant realm of divine revelation; moreover, both A and F are narratively necessary for each other; they both must exist for the reader to grasp the meaning of either section. The symbols in A are not interpreted within A, nor are they even hinted at in the Esther narrative (what does Queen Esther have to do with springs or water in the story?). Thus without F the symbols of A not only dangle, they remain opaque, not to say mysterious.

Correspondingly F makes little or no sense without A. One does not find a new stage set nor an orienting repetition of section A in this passage; various mood-setting items—crys, darkness, tumult on earth, etc.—are not mentioned in F at all. Therefore A is assumed, and an attempt is made in F to interpret A. Thus before judgments are announced about the success of F's *pesher*-like attempt to elucidate A, tensions or problems in these two sections, and whether they were written by the same hand, it can be concluded that the two sections function together at the final level of the text.

In further support of that contention it must be observed that such a dream report and its interpretation could have been included elsewhere within the narrative. The second chapter (or Jos's parallel material) in all Esther texts employs the technique of flashback and/or digression. If the flashback technique were not chosen to insert the dream, the execution of the heroes' plan could have been interrupted or suspended, as it is between Esther's two drinkfests (there to allow character development [Aman] and plot tension [the new complication: preparations to hang Mordecai]). During that suspension the reader could have been introduced to Mordecai's (prophetic) dream. As for the interpretation, it could follow the dream, spreading throughout the narrative in piecemeal fashion, element by element, as the fulfillment progressed. Or, to pick another possible insertion spot for the whole 'epilog', it could appear in its entirety after the letter of defense, just before the legislation regarding Phrouraia/Purim. Mordecai's prophetic power would then immediately fortify his (a redactor's?) commands concerning the new feast in ch. 9.

Such hypothetical collocations of course are not the case. But realizing those possibilities should highlight this fact: the rest of Esther stands without either a word or hint of Mordecai's dream and/or prophetic gifts, or a reference to the symbols or their meaning. The fact that the interpretation mentions κλῆροι hardly constitutes an exception. Lots are not mentioned in the dream; they occur only in the interpretation. As for the text of Esther they do occur at 3.7 in o´ and EH, but not in L; thus 'casting lots' in 3.7 may be a later gloss.[1] Finally, the interpretation uses 'lot' in the sense of 'inheritance', different from that of the narrative. This realization helps one to crystalize a preliminary conclusion: placed as they are at the final text level, dream and interpretation constitute a later, framing addition to an earlier body of narrative and legislation: 1.1–(+ B, C, D, E)–10.3.

Corroborating evidence for this supplemental editorial activity can be garnered from the observation that A immediately precedes another frame which intends to dramatize the extent and power of the king, who somewhat oddly figures prominently throughout the narrative (see the discussion above [especially in Chapter 3, on EH 1.1-4 and 10.1-3] and below [regarding its literary history and genre]). The unusual prominence or presence of the king (although he often serves as comic foil or antihero) helps one to know that his legendary greatness and 180-day banquet at the opening, along with his sprawling world control at the end, is all integral to the narrative. As S. Berg has shown,[2] both the banquet/drinkfest and the kingship motifs are important (her term is 'dominant') in Esther; as will be defended in this study, the power of the king and the consequent regal or near-regal status of Mordecai and Esther is critical to the narrator and his or her audience.

1.2. *An Earlier Frame?*
For purposes of easy distinction, the frame of 1.1ff. + 10.1-3, which has been argued for in both EG and EH (Chapters 2 and 3), will be called the 'king frame', as distinct from the 'dream frame' above.

Given the integral nature of the king's role in the story, and the smooth grammatical flow and narrative development of the first chapter (in all texts), it is difficult to claim that the king frame originally stood outside, but next to, the present dream interpretation frame; that is, that

---

1.   With Moore, *Esther*, pp. 37-38, who says, 'The verse was undoubtedly added by a later editor for whom the liturgical and cultic aspects of the story were of primary importance'.
2.   Berg, *The Book of Esther, passim.*

the two frames somehow switched places. Nor is it likely that the king frame was inserted after the dream, in its current position. If it were, one could reasonably expect to find one or more of the following: the fuller and proper introduction of the king (date and data) moved up to the verses on the regicide plot; some reference or relation regarding Mordecai's prophetic powers and their effect on the king (as with Joseph and Daniel); and some tension or lack of smoothness between the king frame and the narrative.

On the contrary, what one does find is this, addressing points in reverse order: there is no tension between the king frame and the narrative (although discreet units have been argued for on the basis of grammar, content and function); no link or relation regarding Mordecai and the king comes forth; abruptness remains between the end of section A and 1.1; and one finds the strange feature that a major introduction of the king appears in 1.1ff. after he has already been mentioned, without background or ceremony, in the latter verses of A, and conversely, Mordecai's introduction occurs twice (A 1-3; 2.5-6)[3] in o′ and L (with less repetition in L).

On balance the conclusion must be: A and F are later (editorial) supplements added to the king frame. This does not mean *ipso facto* that they were added to the present EH, the MT. The MT could theoretically be a reduction from an earlier Semitic *Urtext* which contained Mordecai's dream and interpretation.

1.3. *The Genre and Intent of the Dream*

It has been mentioned in discussing the frame of EH (Chapter 3) that treatments of frame composition and functions are not easily come by. The well-known 'frame narrative' of secular literature—a story begins, then is interrupted in order to tell another, or many, stories (a cyclical framed tale[4]; cf. the storyteller Scheherazade in *Arabian Nights*)—constitutes an artistic device and functions perhaps to heighten suspense, certainly to please aesthetic taste and to entertain. Other types are possible: frames could consist of simple statement, more lengthy prose introduction and conclusion (not interrupted story), quotations of poetry, slogans, mottos or other quotations (as repeated), newspaper clippings, photographs, and so on.

---

3. o′ 2.5-6 // L 2.5, minus v. 6.

4. Cf. Holman and Harmon (eds.), *A Handbook of Literature*, s.v. 'Framework-Story'; Shipley (ed.), *Dictionary of World Literature*, s.v. 'Frame'.

Since discussion of frame types in the standard handbooks is sparse, one offers here some possible examples from the potentially numerous frame functions for purposes of comparison. Frames can be historicizing (as Jos's introduction and conclusion is for Esther, 11.184, 296), doctrinally orienting (cf. the epilogist which Fox[5] discusses in connection with a 'frame narrative' in Qohelet [1.2, 7.27 and 12.8ff.] and the prose frame in Job), disclaiming, fictionalizing, 'humorizing', mood-setting, focusing, hortatory and educative, among other functions.

The question arises as to what purpose the dream frame serves—as placed here, not in other possible contexts mentioned above—and what effect it has on the now included Esther narrative and legislation, bounded already with a king frame.

The microstructure has shown that the dream itself is framed by a third-person report, beginning and end. A recognized authority on dreams in the ancient world, A.L. Oppenheim, says this:

> The typical dream-report of our source-material appears within a strictly conventionalized 'frame', the pattern of which can be reconstructed from evidence that is surprisingly uniform from the Sumer of the third millennium up to Ptolemaic Egypt and from Mesopotamia westward to Greece. The 'frame' consists of an introduction which tells about the dreamer, the locality and other circumstances. The actual report of the dream content follows and is succeeded by the final part of the 'frame' which describes the end of the dream and often includes a section referring to the reaction of the dreaming person, or, also, to the actual fulfillment of the prediction or promise contained in the dream.[6]

J.J. Collins[7] shows that the visions of Amos and Zechariah lack the above documented frame, but apocalyptic dream visions characteristically have it, Daniel being the chief biblical example. Mordecai's dream conforms to the long-lasting ancient Near Eastern model Oppenheim describes, and shows affinity to Danielic dreams.

Is the dream symbolic? The dream itself contains a curious mix of mythic motifs—dragons, a spring becoming a river, light—with this-worldly concerns: every nation prepares to fight the righteous nation, fear, preparing for death—clearly a symbolic dream as opposed to a

5.   M.V. Fox, 'Frame-Narrative and Composition in the Book of Qohelet', *HUCA* 48 (1977), *passim*.

6.   Oppenheim, *The Interpretation of Dreams in the Ancient Near East*, p. 187. See I. Mendelsohn, 'Dream', in *IDB*, I, pp. 868-69.

7.   J.J. Collins, *Daniel, with an Introduction to Apocalyptic Literature* (FOTL, 20; Grand Rapids: Eerdmans, 1984), pp. 6-7.

simple one in which a message is conveyed in plain language.[8] Speaking of the symbols which occur in such dreams, Collins mentions two forms: mythic–realistic and allegoric.[9] He explains the two categories using biblical and non-biblical examples:

> The symbolism of these visions is usually allegorical, i.e. the object seen stands for something else: four beasts represent four kings, a lion and an eagle represent the messiah and Rome. In some cases, however, the symbols are mythic–realistic. In 4 Ezra the man from the sea is identified rather than interpreted. Similarly, in Dan. 7 the divine throne does not stand for something else but has its own reality. Both[kinds] can be found in a single vision (e.g. Dan. 7).[10]

The dream under discussion qualifies as symbolic, but is it apocalyptic? It could not be classified 'apocalyptic eschatology' as defined by Hanson,[11] since it is not clear that it specifically applies to the end time, nor is special spirit activity documented, nor is an angel mediator involved. Yet it has the *ex eventu* prophecy usually associated with the revelatory content of the 'historical' apocalypses, and the interpretation follows a *pesher* style of explanation element by element. Also found in L's interpretation is the mention, if not the details, of epiphany (7.54fβ), which is frequently associated with this type of apocalypse. Lacking are such elements as would cast this dream into the second type of apocalypse, the otherworldly journey (vision of the abode of the dead, lists of revealed things, judgment scene, etc.). Yet again the interpretation in both o′ and L mentions 'judging' or 'judgment' of God, albeit in different ways, thus implying some influence from the apocalyptic arena.

Granting that the dream is symbolic, that it fits the dream report genre of the Near East, and that the interpretation applies it to the entire Esther story, what can be said relative to apocalyptic? A decided apocalyptic tinge does shine through in the dream/interpretation, though not in any of the Esther texts outside of A and F. Certain mythic motifs evoke apocalyptic images: every nation pitted against the righteous nation, apparently in a fight to the death; the permanent division of the two lots, as F interprets them, implies the permanent separation of Jews and Gen-

---

8. Mendelsohn, 'Dream', p. 868.

9. Collins, *Daniel*, p. 6.

10. Collins, *Daniel*, p. 6.

11. P.D. Hanson, *The Dawn of Apocalyptic: The Historical and Sociological Roots of Jewish Apocalyptic Eschatology* (Philadelphia: Fortress Press, 1983), pp. 429ff.

tiles, with God's favor unalterably resting on the former (cf. Ezekiel 37–39 for a similar duality specifically set in the end time). The 'hour, time and day of judgment before God and all the nations/Gentiles' may be recognized as at least moving toward apocalyptic eschatology (Hanson).

Furthermore the content seems to show influence from motifs originating outside of the usual biblical currents, at least in the matter of the dragons (o′ A 5 // L A 4) and especially in the direct identification of Mordecai with the dragon symbol (o′ F 4 // L 7.54). So outside, non-biblical elements may be admitted, although the precise source, whether Babylon, Persia, Egypt, Greece or Rome, cannot be investigated here. Yet biblical motifs also arise. The darkness reminds one of darkness and chaos in the creation account. There too waters are much or great, and light breaking forth begins to bring order; of course the waters of Genesis become divided whereas these waters devour the honored ones. The spring which becomes 'a great river' may remind the reader of the primeval river which 'flowed out of Eden to water the garden' (Gen. 2.10), and from there apparently watered the whole earth in its four branches. Or perhaps Ezekiel's river, connected with an eschatologically restored temple (Ezek. 47.1ff.) and its possible prototype in Ps. 46.4 are closer to home: 'There is a river whose streams gladden the city of God.'

What then can be concluded about its relation to the wider biblical context? The dream purports to carry a level of prophetic import for the future—akin to the dream of Joseph in Gen. 37.5-11 and the dream of Pharaoh which Joseph interprets in ch. 41. This is not to claim that language or motifs from Joseph's dreams/interpretations are utilized in Esther A and F. It is to suggest that a reader familiar with Israel's traditions could easily connect the similar contexts of the wise (Jewish) courtier in a foreign court, if not also the biblical motifs just mentioned. It should be remembered that the recorded dreams of antiquity were vouchsafed, not to commoners, but to prophets, priests and royalty. Through this medium, it was believed, the gods made known their intentions[12] (then as now the comman man could have nightmares [!], but these were attributed to sorcerers and evil spirits). If it is objected that Joseph and Mordecai do not qualify for any of these three classes, the answer has to be twofold: both these heroes end up as a fourth category, near royalty—viziers of vast empires and great benefactors of their people (10.3 in o′ and EH, and especially the parallel but stronger

---

12. Mendelsohn, 'Dream', p. 868.

7.52 in L); secondly Blenkinsopp has documented the tendency during post-exilic times to make prophets of earlier Old Testament heroes, even including Abraham and Moses.[13]

So the *genre* of A is symbolic dream vision; of F, dream interpretation. The two units contain language and motifs showing influence from non-Israelite sources, apocalyptic and (earlier) biblical traditions.

The *intention* will be the normal one of the form: to transmit revelation. Its function is twofold: to establish the dreamer as one with whom God deals and communicates, and to enclose the rest of Esther as a frame.

So far only the A-and-F unit has been discussed; exposition of this unit's effect within its literary context or matrix must be postponed until other matters can be addressed. For now, one can pursue a second (possible) intention of A and F, opening the question of the presence or lack of the divine name in Esther. The Rabbis explained the non-occurence of 'Yahweh', or any other divine name, in EH by citing Deut. 31.16-18 ('they will forsake me and break my covenant...and I will hide my face from them').[14] In spite of other attempted explanations, the non-occurence of God's name in EH continues to be a problem for interpreters. Does the dream frame intend to supply that lack? The answer depends on the position one takes regarding the common assumption that EH represents the earlier version, and that the EGs in one way or another translate it, or are later corrections toward MT. Based on that assumption these and other sections appear to supply the lacking piety, the lacking reference to God.

All well and good if the story was originally secular, but reasons for an original secular story are rarely discussed, and a satisfactory explanation of how a non-religious Esther arose, in terms of form criticism or canonical criticism, has yet to be given.

Even if one posits two or three literary sources[15] (a Mordecai source blended with a separate Esther source at minimum, possibly combined with a written record of Jewish persecutions and elements from Ezra–

13. J. Blenkinsopp, *Prophecy and Canon: A Contribution to the Study of Jewish Origins* (Notre Dame: University of Notre Dame Press, 1977), p. 3 and *passim*.

14. J.H. Hertz (ed.), *The Pentateuch and Haftorahs* (London: Soncino Press, 2nd edn, 1963), p. 808.

15. H. Bardtke, *Das Buch Esther* (KAT, 27/5; Gütersloh: Gerd Mohn, 1963), pp. 248-52; H. Cazelles, 'Note sur la composition du rouleau d'Esther', in H. Gross and F. Mussner (eds.), *Lex Tua Veritas* (Trier: Paulinus Verlag, 1961), pp. 17-29.

Nehemiah to form the extant narrative), or if one stops at the next higher redactional layer and posits one source (a wise courtier plot with hero and heroine), either option could theoretically have contained references to the providential deliverance of God. If it did not contain such, possibly the dream interpretation intended to add the divine element—an element perceived by a religious community to be lacking. But it is possible, until demonstrated otherwise, that the dream frame was added to a narrative already religious in nature. And since this study does not make either assumption, the question of a particular 'spiritualizing' intention must remain open.

One may leave behind the intention of the form in the strict form-critical sense, and ask after two possibilities of authorial intention. The question of Mordecai's role vis-à-vis Esther herself in the dream frame is also difficult. Since Mordecai has the dream, and hence the contact with God, it would be easy to conclude that patriarchy dominates here, and that this addition intends to offset Esther's importance.

That would be to overlook, however, the fact that she is interpreted to be the instrument of salvation—the water that engulfs the honored ones. If this frame were inserted to raise Mordecai's stock, one would expect some hint of Mordecai's role in helping the little spring to become the (saving) river (o'). However, in the case of L, where Esther is the little spring, but has no further part in saving the people, it would be possible to argue that Mordecai is intentionally stressed at the expense of Esther, as Elkanah dominates (vis-à-vis Hannah) more in the LXX of 1 Samuel 1–2 than in the MT.

Another possible authorial intention involves the relationship of God to his people in the two interpretations; a nuanced analysis here may be able to discern a difference of intentions between o' and L in F. The o' text mentions the Jews once (F 5) and Israel twice (F 6, 10). L also logs three mentions, but here it is Jews twice (7.54ef) and Israel once (v. 59). The net effect is equal.

Not so with regard to the divine names, although the references to God eventuate in the same number, nine, if one credits L's unusual verbal noun κυριεύσις ('ruling, judging') as an allusion to Κύριος, the Lord (7.56c), which probably is intentional. One must add to the nine mentions the double direct address, namely vocative κύριε and Εὐλογητὸς εἶ in 7.58bαβ (contrasted with the third person ἐμνήσθη ὁ θεὸς κτλ. in F 9); add to that L's ἐπιφανεία and 'covenants of our fathers' (7.54fβ, 58bγ) neither of which are mentioned in o' (although o''s 'the

Lord saved his people' stands in place of the epiphany). Adding it all up, one feels that L is both more intense in its spiritual feeling and more orthodox or conservative in the praxis it reflects.

1.4. *The Interrelation of o′ and L in Sections A and F*
Some of the principal differences between o′ and L in the dream and interpretation have been noted at the end of each microstructure; it remains now to assess those differences so that something may be concluded concerning the interrelationship of o′ and L in these passages, the theory that L represents a rewriting of o′, the function of A and F at the final level of the text, and a preliminary model for the relationship between o′ and L in the whole book of Esther.

1.4.1. *Introductory Remarks.* If one postulates a direct linkage between the two texts, one normally begins elementally with the natural tendency of texts to progress from shorter to longer, from simple to more complex, from textual (as distinct from narrative) tensions to greater smoothness, and from gaps and indeterminacy to stated reasons, explanations, etc.—in brief, to greater determinacy. In the case of EG, then (Jos aside), taking A and F together, that progression would normally be judged to go from L to o′, given L's brevity plus its simplicity of language and definitions, given the tensions within L itself, which o′ largely but not totally smoothes out, and given o′'s overall greater determinacy. That general conclusion will now be defended in what follows.

One notes that the dream reports in A are closer to each other than are the interpretations in F; thus the dreams proper offer few touchstones for comparison beyond the general rules of thumb stated in the previous paragraph. One could argue for the priority of either text on the basis of section A alone. For example, accepting the near certainty of a Semitic *Vorlage* behind both texts,[16] one could argue that the

---

16. R.A. Martin's specific investigation of translation Greek in Esther, 'Syntax Criticism of the LXX Additions to the Book of Esther', *JBL* 94 (1975), pp. 65-72 (based on his pioneering methodological study, *Syntactical Evidence of Semitic Sources in Greek Documents* [Missoula, MT: University of Montana Press, 1974]), has both supported Moore and also caused him to refine his early statements about the language underlying the six non-canonical sections of EG. Martin concludes that sections B and E are clearly Greek compositions with no underlying Semitic original, while A, C and D are clearly translations from some Semitic base; 'F appears to be either original Greek or a very free translation of a Semitic *Vorlage*' ('Syntax Criticism', pp. 65, 69). His criteria are cautious, even understated, so his results are

additional Greek month name in L (A 1aγ), as well as the 'we' pronoun (possibly liturgical, in A 6dα), plus L's greater word length in the regicide plot (L's 179 versus o''s 139), all show a later form of the text. On the other hand, o''s clear declaration that Mordecai had seen 'what God had intended to do' (A 11a—a statement that removes the suspense which L maintains), plus its greater number of words for the dream itself (160 versus L's 130, although L has 10 more words than o' as a grand total for both parts of A), and o''s greater clarity in connecting the people's cry with God's answer (A 9bα) and in 'the humble ones' (10bα—versus 'rivers' in L), can be seen as later developments in the trajectory.

Section F, taken in conjunction with A, gives more material for tracing some developmental relationships between both texts. L has the spring becoming a river in A 7, then the rivers (plural!) are exalted and devour the 'honored ones' (i.e. enemies in high places, as one gleans from the following Esther narrative). The only tension is the unexplained change from a single river to plural ones. Yet in F's interpretation the spring does not become a river; rather, in L 7.54 the spring = Esther, but the river (singular once again!) = the nations gathered to destroy the Jews. Compare other differences referred to at the end of the microstructure. All of this goes to say that L's dream manifests some slippage in the river symbology, and its interpretation shows significant tension with the dream it intends to interpret.

On the other hand, one can read o' with less puzzlement overall. Even here, however, o' evidences some disjunction between F and A. Besides the non-mention of the cries, darkness, thunder, earthquake, and so on (not interpreted in o' or L), o' has the special problem of F 3aβ, the dangling phrase 'there was light and sun and much water' which is left uninterpreted. One can add o''s mention of Esther's marriage to the king (F 3b) which has no referent in the dream. From here on, however, o' concurs with the dream material and does not change the imagery as L does. To repeat, o' reads more consistently and smoothly than L.

On balance, in my opinion, the general assumptions (as listed above), combined with the specifics, weigh heavily against the theory that L is a rewrite of o'—at least in A and F. Moreover, one is left with the difficulties of explaining the presence of different elements in both texts,

---

to be accepted. Martin does not separately analyze the L text. My judgment is that L's parallel to section F has an even higher probability of being translation Greek than does o', which itself seems to reflect a Semitic original.

neither of which seem to derive from the other. But before drawing further conclusions, it will be helpful to move on to the second point under the relationship of A and F to Esther; this segment will discuss a bold explanation of how o′ and L interrelate.

1.4.2. *The Theory that L Represents a Rewriting of o′*. E. Tov has put forward the theory[17] that L is an intentional rewrite of o′ in the direction of a pre-Masoretic Semitic *Vorlage*. Only the briefest treatment of his detailed yet generalizing 25-page article can be offered, but all his examples were studied in depth by this author, so the attempt is made here to show a balance of both positive and negative aspects of his theory, and to draw conclusions from a broader base than is spelled out here.

Before proceeding to an evaluation of Tov's theory, it is well to provide a brief summary of his position without comment. Based on the clear structure and concrete statements of his presentation, one finds a skillful, succinct overview of the history of L and probable reasons for its neglect,[18] followed by four major assertions in this order: (1) L is based on o′ and is (therefore) a rewrite of the same; (2) underlying L's short 'additions' to MT there was a *Vorlage* differing from MT; (3) the 'apocryphal additions' have generally been studied in isolation from the canonical portions, but these 'additions' must be analyzed in conjunction with each other; and (4) the canonic and apocryphal sections form one unit, so they can and should be characterized as a whole.[19]

The first assertion, that L is a rewrite, is supported by three lines of evidence: L's dependence on o′ as shown by common readings that could not arise independently; L's errors/corruptions which show the same dependence; and a mention of support from two other specialist studies. The second assertion, regarding a different Hebrew *Vorlage*, finds evidence of Semitic influence in 'the short additions to MT' through Tov's retroversions and through examples of L's 'more literal renderings of MT than the LXX'.[20] The third assertion, that L's canonical and 'Addition' sections should be regarded as one organic unit, finds corroboration in that L's canonical sections refer to the 'Additions'; o′ still shows redundancy in content as a result of the 'Additions', but

17. Tov, 'The "Lucianic" Text'.
18. Tov, 'The "Lucianic" Text', pp. 1-3.
19. Tov, 'The "Lucianic" Text', pp. 4, 7, 10-11 and 14ff. respectively.
20. Tov, 'The "Lucianic" Text', pp. 7-9 and 9-10 respectively.

L has eliminated repetition by omitting canonical passages; and the 'Additions' share vocabulary with the canonical parts. Therefore, even though Tov states (or admits?) that L differs from MT with regard to large additions, large omissions, and other changes in content,[21] he accepts the entire L text as is for his analysis. The fourth assertion consists not of supporting arguments, but of nine descriptions which attempt to 'characterize L as a whole'.[22]

1.4.3. *An Evaluation of the Theory.* I will first make some general remarks, before responding to the four major assertions (regrettably most of Tov's examples cannot be commented upon), and finally giving my assessment. From here on, the abbreviations and terminology as established in my study will be followed instead of Tov's terms, for example 'section' instead of 'Addition', and 'plus' for 'addition' when the reference is to words and phrases not found in one tradition or another; o′ for LXX, and so forth.

Under the introduction Tov notes that 'the L text differs greatly from MT in omissions, additions and content'. And later he says, 'L differs from MT not only with regard to the large (as well as to some minor) additions, but also with regard to large omissions, inversions and changes in content'.[23] My more detailed microstructures lead me to agree with that opinion. All such variations must be taken into account. The question remains whether, on the one hand, Tov's selected examples explain how these texts 'differ greatly' within his postulate of intentional rewriting, or whether, on the other hand, Tov's admitted 'impossibility of conciliating the literal and free elements in L',[24] and the welter of variations as displayed in the microstructures, demand a more encompassing model.

Tov correctly places quotation marks around the term 'Lucianic', pointing out that though the Esther L comes from MSS which represent a Lucianic type, the 'Lucianic' text of Esther and the known Lucianic text of other books 'have little in common in either vocabulary or translation technique'.[25]

He also judiciously uses the phrase 'so-called Additions', states more

---

21. Tov, 'The "Lucianic" Text', p. 11.
22. Tov, 'The "Lucianic" Text', pp. 14ff.
23. Tov, 'The "Lucianic" Text', p. 11.
24. Tov, 'The "Lucianic" Text', p. 15.
25. Tov, 'The "Lucianic" Text', pp. 1-2.

than once that L's *Vorlage* may have been Aramaic,[26] and elsewhere employs 'Semitic' rather than 'Hebrew', thus leaving open the question of the original language of Esther. However, he seems to tacitly assume the priority of MT throughout his entire discussion. From a redaction-critical and text history point of view, that assumption obscures possible alternates, and at times more accurate explanations.

Now to my specific comments upon Tov's four major assertions.

(1) In my judgment, the first assertion is the one most in need of demonstration and Tov's supporting arguments fall short of conviction. His support is threefold: (a) four examples (1.20; 9.3 [twice]; 10.3) show '*dependence* in important renderings which could not have developed independently'; (b) errors in L (three examples) show derivation from o´; (c) citations of the names, but not the data from Jacob (1890) and Hanhart, lead Tov to conclude that L depends on o´.[27]

Analyzing in reverse order, one notes regarding (c) that his conclusion unfortunately relegates an important perspective (the complexity of this o´-to-L relationship) to a footnote. Secondly one asks, how strongly does Hanhart support the theory of rewriting? Hanhart's language is cautious; more importantly, Hanhart's examples of L's errors[28] come from sections C and E, where an early L text could have been dependent on a later o´, or where contamination could have taken place. To generalize from these few examples, even if one accepts Tov's taking of the whole L as 'organic', is a slippery proposition, especially when Tov himself admits the Semitic background of section C, but a Greek one for section E. Two proveniences thus granted, mixing of texts is just as likely as, if not more likely than, rewriting. On the page previous to the one cited by Tov, Hanhart says that L is 'not a recension of o´, but a new formation of the EG tradition, which in large part rests on o´'.[29] While this may be read as tending to support Tov, it does not of itself address all necessary issues nor the issue of rewriting, does not disprove what is offered here, and may also be read as partly supportive of this author's position.

26. Tov, 'The "Lucianic" Text', pp. 4, 10, 11.

27. Tov, 'The "Lucianic" Text', pp. 6-7.

28. Hanhart, *Esther*, p. 88.

29. Hanhart, *Esther*, p. 87; Tov, 'The "Lucianic" Text', p. 6, cites Hanhart, p. 88, where he cites apparent misreadings such as L's τραπεζῶν αὐτῶν ἅμα for o´'s τράπεζαν Αμαν. One can accept Hanhart's examples as secondary developments/ misreadings in L without generalizing about the entire texts.

Concerning (b), the second pillar of Tov's threefold support, one example of L's 'error' will suffice to show that other explanations can be offered for each of his examples. Admitting that the *hiphil* participle מתיהדים of 8.17 (incorrectly cited as 8.10) is a crux, Tov says both EG texts understood the verb as it could be simply taken, viz. Gentiles *became Jews* because they feared Mordecai; o′ translators chose a special verb, περιτέμνω ('to be circumcised'), to indicate this conversion. But Tov avers that L—following o′ with the same verb—makes no sense in saying that *Jews* became circumcised. On this basis Tov concludes that L is clearly erroneous and secondary to o′.

But from another perspective, o′ clearly has the element which is most fanciful and difficult to believe. Why should Persians go that far to show their support? Could we really expect a Persian monarch to remain at ease while his subjects in large numbers line up so radically with the vizier? On the opposite side, can we seriously maintain that deported Jews, Jews under severe pressure to assimilate and accomodate to the dominant culture, would never go lax on this difficult point? One thinks not, remembering the story in Joshua 5, and the various necessary cultic, covenant and ethical renewals in Israel's history.

The point is that L, whether early or late, does not necessarily demonstrate error here, but a different understanding of the story. If L is late, it may be changing o′ to encourage Jews to take on the 'yoke of Torah'. If L is early, it may present the sober way of telling this story, while o′—further removed in time and ethnic community—may be dramatizing and hyperbolizing for greater effect, or may be trying to foment proselytizing.

Following the reasoning that Jews themselves might need the kind of renewal L supports, one may note that the עמי־הארץ of MT (which Tov assumes is the root reading, but by his admission elsewhere would acknowledge may not have been what o′ or L translated) could refer to the Jewish 'people of the land', the countryfolk, often criticized by the urban religious population for lack of dedication to religio-cultural principles.

Finally, with regard to (a), Tov's first support for the dependence of L on o′, one must say that the four examples which constitute his first pillar for L as a rewrite do not succeed in showing that the dependence could not be the other way around. I agree here that the Greek readings he cites would not arise independently and yet be so closely alike. But how do we establish that L comes last? Tov's examples only show L's posteriority if the other arguments show conclusive evidence; they do not, in either an absolute or an exclusive way.

(2) The situation changes with Tov's second assertion: two lines of evidence converge to show that L worked off a 'Hebrew' (I would prefer 'Semitic') 'and/or Greek *Vorlage* which differed from MT'.[30] First it is to be noted that this second major proposition can stand whether the first one does or not. Secondly, one may agree with the two categories of examples that Tov adduces: by eight sample retroversions in areas where L has short pluses to MT, and by six examples of L exhibiting more literal translations of MT than o'.[31] In both these lines of evidence his examples show reasonable distribution throughout Esther.

(3) Tov wishes to combine the apocryphal sections with the canonical portions of L and then study the text *as a whole*—a procedure not to be faulted at the initial level. Here he makes a generalizing characterization (before those under his fourth assertion) that L differs from MT in both large and small additions, and in large omissions, inversions and changes in content. Noting that an original Semitic language of some sections (A, C, D and F) points to 'a fate closely connected with that of the canonical sections', Tov suggests that those sections of Greek provenance (B and E) could have been composed by the translator himself.

I can agree with Tov that the editorial seams in 1.1; 4.11 (L v. 15); and 5.1 give evidence of the 'organic unity' of L, though I must add: unity at the final level of the text. But Tov has to admit that o' makes similar seams in these verses, and in 2.20 and 4.8. No derivation can therefore be established from the mention of editorial seams vis-à-vis the two EG texts (perhaps a detailed comparison of the seams would yield evidence).

His second support under the 'organic unit' division, that L omits redundant material which o' contains, could be used to claim that L intends to improve o'. Instead Tov attributes L's cleaner text to the Hebrew or Aramaic *Urtext*![32] I have already argued in Chapters 2 and 3 that if L was trying to clean up o', he either did a poor job in numerous places, or else L is prior to o'.

Here Tov lists three examples, all 'omissions'. However, one of the three (5.1-2) is also an omission, or better a minus, in o'—in both EGs

---

30. Tov, 'The "Lucianic" Text', p. 7.
31. Tov, 'The "Lucianic" Text', pp. 7-9 and 9-10 respectively.
32. Tov, 'The "Lucianic" Text', p. 12.

the narrative 'event' or transformation is covered differently and expansively in section D, so it is not repeated as part of ch. 5. The narrative directness of MT could be original as commonly assumed, but since section D derives from a Semitic original, portrays a divine intervention, and highlights Esther herself, MT 5.1-2 could be a precis of section D, intending to highlight Mordecai and/or to keep the story theologically more neutral. I do not argue that such must be the case, only that such a possibility must be considered.

The first example is the minus in 2.6 in L, which as a plus in o' seems to be a repeat of the genealogy of Mordecai already given in o' A 2-3 // L A 1bβ-2. Tov may be correct here in attributing the minus to a Semitic *Vorlage* unlike MT; thus L indeed may be whole or organic. However, if one allows a redactional process as this study does, one can accept that an original narrative/rescue novella contained a genealogy, and that L deleted it by transposing it to the dream frame when the frame was added to the novella.

But Tov does not mention that o' may also be organic, since o' can, under a redactional view, be explained as faithfully copying/combining two traditions—the dream frame and the novella—each with a genealogy. That such a combinatory process took place, when one MS could not be chosen over another, has been demonstrated elsewhere in both Massoretic and Septuagintal studies.

The third example under organic unity is 2.21-23, a minus in L. o' understands the story not as an insipid repetition, but as a discovery of a second regicide plot. The suspicion arises that o''s second discovery betrays later expansion. But discussion here would take us too far afield, since Tov does not claim more for L's minus than 'omitted [by L] probably because the matter had already been mentioned' in section A. In my view, the balance of evidence with 2.21-23 and with the other examples under 'organic unity' tips toward L's earliness and o''s lateness, not the reverse.

(4) At this fourth level Tov characterizes L as a whole (his 'canonical and non-canonical parts') in nine different ways. His many technical insights—and a few points I would take issue with—neither establish nor diminish his case regarding L as a rewrite. Therefore for the purpose of this study the nine points may remain undiscussed. This fourth part is describing L, not arguing for its dependence on o'; of course Tov assumes a rewriting approach throughout, yet must concede, 'Again, no

consistency should be expected'.[33] Another interesting observation of Tov's is that L seems 'more interested in the first two thirds than in the last third of the biblical story';[34] I agree solidly here and find that this may be utilized to show the priority of L. L preserves a story that at one time was more important than the subsequent history and legislation of the *Phouraia* or Purim feast.

After the preceeding comments regarding Tov's four major assertions, it can be said that one wishes Tov had looked at other options, or kept his options open longer, rather than open his article with the most risky and tenuous alternative. In this writer's opinion, there are sufficient differences in sections A and F, and throughout EG (as notes and comments to the microstructures have shown), to call into question the concept that one of these texts derives *directly* from the other—in either direction.

Even disregarding for a moment the need for a redactional study (which Tov does not discuss), and even disregarding the two different language sources behind the sections (which Tov does admit, correctly), variant readings, retroversions and careful comparisons of words and phrases alone do not suffice to prove that either o′ or L copied each other wholesale, or even relied on each other throughout.

If one were to take into account the interesting pluses and minuses of OL (which overall is closer to L than o′) and the notably different vocabulary and content of Jos, the total differences between o′, L, OL and Jos would also be simply too great to link any of these together in a straight manuscript tree; that is, in direct parent-to-offspring relationships.

So much for the 'negative' part of this study's redactional contribution—the discovery that text variants and direct derivations among L and o′ do not account for enough of the evidence. The 'positive' part can now be gradually introduced.

1.5. *The Relation of A and F to Esther*

Up to now the discussion has proceded as if either o′ or L derived directly from the other. And a comparison of the two has been both fair and necessary, since we have no other Greek texts except Jos. However, the tensions between dream and interpretation at least open the possibility that A and F were not written of a piece. Based on the

---

33. Tov, 'The "Lucianic" Text', p. 19.
34. Tov, 'The "Lucianic" Text', p. 16.

evidence adduced so far, it is possible to offer a judgment here about the probable priority of one text to another at the level of A and F, the function of the A-and-F unit, and at least one step in their prehistory.

1.5.1. *Priority.* Regarding priority, one has to go with the historic tendency of growth toward both size and smoothness in the absence of compelling reasons to the contrary. Hard as it may be to imagine some redactor leaving the 'loose fit' of L's interpretation as far as the narrative goes, not to say the seeming mistake of mixed rivers with regard to the dream itself, it is harder to imagine a text such as o′—apparently in widespread use—falling into such shortened and choppy form when so many better texts would militate toward its being corrected. Even harder to accept is the idea that L at this spot has intentionally rewritten o′ in the fashion now extant. Both the greater consistency of o′'s interpretation and its larger volume of words would *prima facie* indicate a progression precisely the opposite of the historically-assumed earliness of o′ and lateness of L: rather, o′ has improved on L. The o′ text improves and smooths out the kinks, either from a Semitic *Vorlage* and/or from a text close to L, or even from L itself.

1.5.2. *Genre, Intention, Function, Matrix.* A fresh suggestion can now be offered regarding the genre of the two EG texts. Since the Esther story is directly implied as the fulfillment of the dream in o′ A 11, and directly stated to be its fulfillment in L A 9, two results ensue. First, the dream/interpretation becomes a prophetic deliverance dream, one given to a community or communities with this intent: encouragement during a time of foreign oppression or life-threatening crisis. Secondly, the dream vision functions to embue Mordecai with prophetic power. So whatever is later determined about the genre and intention of other EG materials, the outer dream frame propheticizes the book.

Although Esther does not capitalize on Mordecai's prophetic or interpretive power in order to bring Mordecai into close proximity to the king, the fusion of the wise courtier motif with a prophetic dreamer no doubt echoes the Joseph narrative, and thus functions to provide a link with inspired Torah.

Its relation to Daniel, which has the other biblical dreams most like Mordecai's, of course depends on how the respective works are dated. Mordecai's divine gift, thanks to the dream frame, coupled with his status as viceregent (or regent!) of the Persian empire, thanks to the king frame, both enhance his ability to initiate a feast not found in Torah.

As for the matrix, the dream would originate within religious circles, either a priestly/levitical one where dream interpretation was practiced, or perhaps in a 'school' of tradents or scribes where prophetic traditions were preserved. Its position as a frame could arise in the same groups, possibly in a Sadducean one where the nobility and regal stature of Mordecai and Esther would be especially prized, and at a time when festival standardization was gaining ground.

Since the symbols and their interpretations evince only loose connections with the narrative, one can say, more strongly than Moore[35] tentatively suggests, that the dream and interpretation had an independent existence from the Esther narrative. Whether Mordecai or some other person originally starred in the dream-interpretation sequence cannot be known with certainty, but it is probable that he did.

1.5.3. *Prehistory.* Because of different preferences or pressures within separate groups, variants in the interpretation arose. Then at some later time the still Semitic A-and-F unit was split and attached to the Esther narrative as envelope or frame, partly because Esther was also perceived as a deliverance or salvation story, and partly for the 'promotional' reasons mentioned earlier. Some competing variants would still exist apart from the now attached version, and would thus be available as alternate choices to a Greek translator. In addition, the early translator(s) may have had difficulty in understanding the Semitic original,[36] and would therefore have introduced variants into the MS tradition, but the function of transposing the deliverance story into a prophetic narrative would remain the same. Thus A and F is an editorial supplement to Esther, the original of which circulated independently and was closest to L.

1.5.4. *Alternative Models and a Generative Matrix.* In light of the above, one may consider other alternatives for the developmental history of o´ and L, such as different parent manuscripts (*Vorlagen*) existing behind o´ and L, understood as a simple and direct parent–offspring relation, or a more complex matrix of variant traditions which could be drawn into different *Vorlagen*—a 'narrative pool', so to speak—or possible mixing

---

35. Moore, *Daniel, Esther and Jeremiah: The Additions*, p. 249.

36. E. Tov, 'Did the Septuagint Translators Always Understand their Hebrew Text?', in A. Pietersma and C. Cox (eds.), *De Septuaginta* (Mississauga: Benben, 1984), pp. 53-70.

of the two text traditions at least once before assuming the final form known today, or some combination of the above.

It is suggested here that each surviving text, o', L and EH (Jos and OL also), has collected different traditional elements which existed within a larger matrix, probably comprised by several communities. This is to posit something larger as a first step than two discrete *Vorlagen*, which themselves may have existed within the matrix or 'narrative pool' being suggested here.

It would seem easier to explain both similarities and differences of EG by the hypothesis of a core narrative (oral or written) which collects variants, embellishments, and so on in divergent directions through its/ their life within separate communities. Such growth can be postulated within the period of 'original texts', the first phase or Period I of four in the development of biblical texts.[37] The four phases or periods, as distinct from the local text theory, were identified independently by both the Hebrew University Bible Project (begun in 1948) and the United Bible Societies' Hebrew Old Testament Text Project (launched in 1969). Remarking on the absence of collusion between the two Projects, and minor differences in nomenclature and dates aside, Sanders notes that

> Both projects arrived at the same general conclusions, based on the new, hard evidence available, about the shape and contours of the history of transmission of the text, [which fact] provides conviction in itself...Period I, both projects agree, falls outside the province of text criticism *in sensu stricto*. We have no autographs of any biblical book so that whatever one can say about *Urtexte* has to be said in terms of a history of the formation of texts... The text critic deals with apographs of texts and versions, not autographs.[38]

The aforementioned period of formation encompasses, in the case of Esther, converging and diverging developments which finally coalesce into the known surviving documents through the dominance of textuality. This first appearance of texts occurs in Period II. Since actual texts do not exist from Period I (except as implied or contained within surviving apographs), literary analyses serve as the operational tools for this level of investigation.

Further progress can be made in reconstructing the prehistory of the books of Esther. In my opinion, a critical element in this reconstruction has, ironically, been suggested elsewhere (but for the Song of Deborah,

37. Barthelemy *et al.* (eds.), *Preliminary and Interim Report*, I, pp. vi-vii.
38. Sanders, 'The Hermeneutics of Text Criticism and Translation', pp. 3-4.

not Esther) by Tov himself.[39] A preliminary model would show L, in its so-called canonical part, as preserving the earliest surviving Greek form of a now lost Semitic *Urtext*, which existed in at least two variant forms: eastern ('Persian') and western ('Palestinian'). The later o′ text translates either another Semitic text, or writes down oral tradition with reference to L. This concept goes some distance in explaining the rough simplicity of L, the difference between the two EGs, and their similarities. Under this model, L's and o′'s similarities derive from similar but variant originals, and possibly from mixing or mutual contact among themselves (notice the high correspondence between o′ and L in sections B and E, for example). Careful text-critical work remains to be done here.

Further sketching can be done regarding the non-canonical sections, but futher reconstruction will be best served by first completing the analysis of each part of Esther as uncovered in the microstructures.

1.6. *The Rest of F (o′ F 6bff. // L 7.55ff.)*

Niditch[40] has defined symbolic visions as a literary tradition, a prophetic genre with three distinguishable stages of development. Her third or 'baroque' stage (Daniel 7–8 and briefly-treated post-biblical examples from *2 Baruch* 36–43; 53–76; *4 Ezra* 11.1–12.39; 13.1-53) comes closest to the Esther example, with a move toward narrativity, conscious borrowing in an 'anthological style' and poetic interludes. But neither these nor the dreams in Daniel 2 and 3 with *doxologies* are exact parallels to the interpretation and the sermon-like material which follows it in F 6bff. and parallel.

One looks to the detailed and erudite FOTL volume on Daniel by J.J. Collins for an explanation as to why a doxology follows the dreams of chs. 2–4, but only a definition of the unit is offered.[41] Nothing is said about how doxologies function in this context, which conceivably could illumine the different but related material which follows the dream interpretation of F 1-6a.

One presumes that a doxology, which may variously include benedictions, affirmations, declarations of thanks and supporting reasons, intends

39. E. Tov, 'The Textual History of the Song of Deborah in the A Text of the LXX', *VT* 28 (1978), pp. 224-32.

40. S. Niditch, *The Symbolic Vision in Biblical Tradition* (Chico, CA: Scholars Press, 1983).

41. Collins, *Daniel*, pp. 51, 108.

to show a human response to what is considered a special revelation. If that response arises in the cultus, it can be presumed to be gratitude (sometimes programmed) on the congregation's part. In a literary context it may function also to emphasize that the dream/revelation comes from a divine source and hence deserves thanks and praise in addition to special notice. That surmise, however, leaves open the dual question of genre and function regarding the closing verses of EG, which are neither dream interpretation nor doxology (except for L 7.58).

The point of view shifts in o´ F 6bα and the subject changes to the Lord. No doxology occurs, but the material following that shift seems sermonic, perhaps even poetic. Thus the new suggestion has been made in the microstructure that the texts preserve—again in differing ways—an opening 'sermon text' or *petiḥta* (o´ 6bα // L 7.55ab), and building from it, a homily of recital (o´ F 6c-9 // L 7.55cd-57).

The recital in each text is structured differently, but both rehearse the mighty acts of God in terms of intervention(s) and exclusive election. Both texts quote worshippers: o´ has a responsory after the opening *petiḥta*; L offers a more intense doxological form as a close. The conclusion to the homily in L 7.58 is a quotation—apparently from a worship service—of a doxology in the second person; that is, a quotation of direct address, even down to the 'Amen'.

What *form* is this unit? In spite of the contrasting organizations in o´ and L, the decision here is that both texts generically represent a *petiḥta* and homily in reduced summary form (cf. the speeches of the prophets and in Acts) plus a quoted congregational response. The quotation of both speaker and congregation may be classified as a report of a worship service (for brevity and distinction the macrostructure says Homily/Responsory (o´) and Homily/Doxology (L).

As for *setting* and *intention*, a *petiḥta*/homily would originate in the synagogue if the text was generated in the Diaspora, which seems to be the case (no reference to Temple or Jerusalem, but multiple references to 'in' or 'among' the nations, etc.). In general the homily intends to show what lessons should be drawn from the Esther novella. In particular, the intention as it stands at the text close must have arisen in the cultus, as Esther was read officially, either on a sabbath or, more likely, on the feast of *Phrourai* or Purim. Thus the homily works in tandem with the last verse which can now be examined.

1.7. *The conclusion (o′ F 10 // L 7.59)*

In connection with the homily, the final verses present concluding legislation regarding *Phrourai* or Purim. o′ F 10 // L 7.59 enjoin, directly as from an authority, the observance of both the 14th and 15th as celebrative days. This edict issues from a religious authority, possibly a body of elders, to a community of worshippers. The multipartite command turns all foregoing chapters into what heretofore has been called a *hieros logos* or festal legend.[42] The verse itself is a seven-member ceremonial edict.

Important as this edict becomes at the final level of the text, it stands at the very end without roots or traces at the beginning of, or at key places throughout, the 'arc of tension' (that is, in the narrative proper). Thus an earlier narrative intention has been superseded by editorial supplements, of which this verse was probably the last.

Yet a festival has been enjoined already at the end of the strictly narrative portion, namely in section E (last vv. of the Letter of License; see the allusion in o′ 8.17 // L 7.40b), and several times (!) in ch. 9.17-19, 20ff., 26, 27-32. Therefore this final command serves both as a reminder and, in conjunction with the homily, as a genre/intention determinative. This final reminder (now almost tired in o′) would have been seen by the cult authorities, but probably only heard by the listening and feast-participating congregation (assuming the above interpretation of the homily). Even so, this final reminder is determinative for the whole book.

What is the *genre*? It is concluded here that the term 'festal etiology' improves on the older terms 'festal legend' (because it avoids confusion with the legend genre) and '*hieros logos*' (since the feast does not originate in, nor find sanction from, a divine or sacerdotal source, although the dream frame—with mention of God—lends a certain element of sanctity to EG).

But this final verse is only one of several evident redactional layers; other layers would imply other intentions and perhaps other genres. Without the evidence of EG, some commentators have focused on the admitted festival intention, failing to see the redactional clues to earlier intentions which are not absent from EH. The discussion must now proceed to those clues and earlier layers. A final determination of genre and

---

42. Cf. G. Botterweck, 'Die Gattung des Buches Esther im Spektrum neuerer Publikationen', *BibLeb* 5 (1964), pp. 274-92, who surveys an almost bewildering array of Esther genres.

a discussion of Esther possibly being multigeneric will be best postponed until other units of Esther can be covered.

The specific genre of the narrative portion has not been discussed yet, but the structure analysis has clearly demarcated the complications and reversals which are the property of narrative. That an integral narrative exists may be assumed for purposes of this immediate discussion of closure.

Proceeding toward the narrative core from EG's final verse, one finds the *petiḥta*/homily, or report of a worship service. The present literary context of this report or quotation reveals its principal intention: to place the entire book of Esther in a new setting. The homily and the congregational response transport any previous uses of Esther into the cultus. The apparent 'tack-on' unmistakably shows how the Esther narrative is to be used, namely that it must be read or quoted from on the holiday, and clues in the sermon indicate how one is to preach from it during the celebration of *Phrourai* or Purim. One could use the motifs of the homily as a sermon guide at future festivals.

Already shown is the next retrogressive step in the text: the semi-apocalyptic dream frame intends to cast an already complete story and festal etiology into the prophetic realm. Thus EG ends up being a propheticized festal etiology, intending not just to explain the feast, but to perpetuate it and to provide some direction for its homiletic presentation. Thus while most etiologies emphasize an explanation for some name or place, the EG etiology both explains and legislates for the future. The documents under study are complex indeed. It may be noted that both final forms, o' and L, document the festival use of Esther in terms much stronger than those of EH.

1.8. *The Rest of A: Discovery of a Regicide Plot*

At last the analysis can return to the rest of A, namely o' A 11-17 // L A 9-18. Although L's dream is 30 words shorter than o''s, the regicide plot in L requires 179 words versus 139 in o'. This difference alerts the analyst to compare structure, length and content closely. Both texts have only two parts: a short narrative and a report. Both texts introduce the deity at the same spot, but under different names (cf. the microstructure, Chapter 2). L leaves Mordecai with both more perplexity and struggle to understand than does o' and directly hooks the discovery of the regicide plot with the meaning of the dream. One understands the same connection from o', but only by implication; o' is simply more subtle in that it leaves a little more to the reader's deduction.

Conversely in A 14, o´ uses a stronger verb which leaves less to the imagination: the king tortures them. (Note the two verbs in A 13 for Mordecai's investigation: possibly a manifestation of a Semitic root which could be translated either way.) This time L spells out Mordecai's good will, so that it will not be missed (A 13a), but o´ leaves it to deduction.

Both texts show Mordecai receiving some reward, which contradicts the crucial pivot point in ch. 6 where the plot turns on Mordecai not having a reward. But the special twist in L again leaves less to the imagination; in fact it strengthens the motive for the antagonist's hatred (A 18bβ, 'because they were killed'), which is found less directly in o´ (it is due to the matter of the eunuchs), and adds a motive that the reader would never deduce: the king gives Aman to Mordecai (v. 17).

Overall the two texts show the same structure, and the greater length in L can be accounted for in the area of greater narrative specificity as detailed above. One could argue from this higher explicitness that the L text is closer to an 'original' (possibly oral) story, even though there are a few tiny indications of more literary Greek in L than in o´. That case will not be pressed here. What is most important is the collocation of this unit in both texts just after the dream and before the introduction of the king.

This passage could be placed elsewhere, as indeed it is in EH and Jos; it does not show after the dream in those texts. Of course the dream does not show either. This fact gives the clue as to why it is here, once in L but twice in o´, since it is repeated in 2.21ff.: it goes with the dream. Why? It is necessary at this spot, not primarily to present the reason for Aman's hatred (which also could be explained later), nor to bridge into the great feast of the king (which it does not achieve), but to make explicit that the already-known Esther plot actually is a fulfillment of a prophetic dream.

It must be noted that the contradiction with the pivot in ch. 6 is not so sharp in L as might at first appear. Mordecai is given two items: an appointment or office, and Aman himself (as aide, or slave?), both of which can be explained as merely administrative moves which bring the two characters together, but do not reward Mordecai personally. The king's fear of other coups may have motivated his placement of Mordecai and Aman both in the position of guards; the distraction of fear also may have caused the omission of personal reward. The personal element may be, but certainly does not have to be, the meaning implied in αὐτῷ in 6.4dβ. L does not repeat or have a similar pericope at 2.21 as o′ does (parallel to, but differing from, EH).

However, the contradiction is sharper and more difficult to explain in o′, where the king ἔδοκεν αὐτῷ δόματα περὶ τούτων (A 16b). This tension with ch. 6 suggests a source analysis, which *might* discover that two different stories were fused into the extant EG. That possibility cannot be pursued here. What does remain appears as a flat contradiction.

One possibility is that two different incidents are narrated in the two passages. This is supported by Mordecai's telling it to Esther in v. 22, which he cannot do in A because Esther is not yet queen, nor even in the story line. Conveniently, no eunuch names are forthcoming in ch. 2, so they can be understood as different from those in A.

Other possibilities are that either a scribe did not notice the contradiction (this is hard to accept), or that it was so important to show dream fulfillment taking place in Esther that a story element which already contained 'gifts'/rewards from the king had to be inserted here. In view of Esther's position in this (second?) episode, the lack of names, and the mention of writing once again, the decision favors an original regicide plot unit standing originally in ch. 2. This unit was altered slightly— almost duplicated—in order to appear as two separate instances. The one, with personal names for dramatic and historical effect, was placed at the end of A for the purpose of linking the dream fulfillment to the narrative.

This step would occur logically at the same time the dream first framed EG. The other remains at 2.21, minus names and plus Esther, leaving Mordecai without reward so that the reader will wonder why, and will see the plot connection in ch. 6.

Additional evidence that A and F (now meaning dream, interpretation, regicide plot and the homilies plus concluding legislation) constitutes a later redaction level, can also be drawn from the following discussion.

2. *The Royal Novella and the Book of Esther*

2.1. *An Earlier Frame*

It has been argued above that the frame which introduces the king (after section A) and 'enshrines' him (just before the dream interpretation) found in all four texts of Esther forms an inclusio presenting the same persona and literary intention: to show the legendary greatness of this potentate, and to show that his 'latter end' enjoyed more glory than his beginning. This inclusio or king-frame can now be investigated for possible generic prototypes.

There exists a form which persisted well into late antiquity that treats the exploits of a king or prince in a way that may relate to Esther. From more than twenty examples the following typicalities can be listed:

1. Texts open immediately with 'King PNN' and multiple divine and honorific titles. By modern standards the king seems to be over-glorified, even legendary.

2. King and counsellors interact:
   a. he speaks, posing a plan,
   b. his counsellors speak to him, or
   c. the king receives a revelation in a dream, or
   d. action begins in the king's and counsellors' presence with the arrival of a messenger.

3. He proposes a plan or reacts to the dream or message:
   a. he will build a temple, or
   b. establish a feast, or
   c. wage war, or
   d. accomplish a major feat or public work.

4. Counsellors encourage or discourage. Typically one expects them to encourage (so the majority of examples), then even though the mission is daring, posing the threat of failure, it is both confirmed and attempted by the greatest in the land. If conversely the counsellors discourage the king (as in a few cases), the king proceeds anyway and his invincible power or divine guidance is all the more starkly portrayed.

Up to this point the examples have not passed the narrative exposition stage.

5. The king or queen (e.g. Hatshepsut's expedition to Punt)[43] now proceeds with or without the blessing of the Council.

Here the body of narrative begins: it may or may not have a complication and a crisis/pivot point. Both are found, for example, in Rameses II's Battle of Kadesh,[44] where, in spite of good planning and military campaigning, superior forces isolate him from the protecting troops and

43. J.H. Breasted, *Ancient Records of Egypt* (5 vols.; Chicago: University of Chicago Press, 1906–1907; repr., New York: Russell & Russell, 1962–67); see 'The Eighteenth Dynasty: Thutmose III: Queen: The Punt Reliefs', in II, pp. 102-22

44. Breasted, *Ancient Records of Egypt*, III, pp. 123ff.; M. Lichtheim, *Ancient Egyptian Literature*. II. *The New Kingdom* (Berkeley: University of California Press, 1976), pp. 57ff.

he is about to be slain. Suddenly, acting like the god he is supposed to be (the use of semi-mythic language precisely at this point is noteworthy; the text compares him to a god and goddess), he slashes his way out of danger and on to victory.

6. The king or queen succeeds in the project (dénouement) and (usually) is honored/enshrined (conclusion).
7. The success may entail an edict regarding the continuance of a project, ritual honors or liturgies to be carried out in future generations. (See e.g. the Berlin leather roll concerning the building of the Temple of Atum in Heliopolis by Sesostris I [1971–1928 BCE], though the document dates from a later time, and *The Acts of Ahmoses for his Grandmother Teti-sheri*.)[45]

The question of the relationship between Esther and this form has not surfaced in the literature. Neither does one often, or ever in some cases, find questions concerning why these features occur in Esther, quite apart from the genre model being investigated here. The important point is that such questions are legitimate ones to ask.

The form just outlined, identified in 1938 by the Egyptologist A. Hermann[46] and called by him *Königsnovelle*, is not specifically structured within a frame. But because of the focus on the king and the success of his exploit (e.g. because of stress on a continuing legal obligation in some cases—such as continuing payments for, and performance of, the temple ritual or the festival established in the novella—or praise to the king/queen for the narrated accomplishment in most cases), these texts without fail begin and end with the king/queen/prince. That is to say, if the content and development of the body of these Royal Novella texts varies, the opening and close remain relatively similar and constant with regard to the presence of the ruler.

Thus if this form were available to the author of Esther, and if it were chosen, for reasons to be discussed, as a basic model for the Mordecai and Esther plot, the open and close would function as a frame or inclusio. Put another way, the shell document, stripped of its Egyptian content, would begin and end with the king. Beginning and end might encapsulate a bare minimum for recognition of the genre, but the king plus his counsellors would or could figure in other places along the way within the story. If the Royal Novella (hereafter RN) were available and

45. Breasted, *Ancient Records of Egypt*, II, pp. 14-16; A. Hermann, *Die Ägyptische Königsnovelle* (Glückstadt: Verlag J.J. Augustin, 1938), pp. 51-53.
46. Hermann, *Die Ägyptische Königsnovelle, passim*.

were used for some special authorial purpose in the Esther narrative, Mordecai and Esther would have to play out their roles within this frame. That means that if the RN generic model is used at all, one expects the king to appear in the opening and closure, and one may find him in some way or another connected with the *crisis* and/or *climax*. Thus, where the text narrates a complication (and it is not really a novella in the modern sense unless it does), the narrative *crisis* will also be a royal act, or will involve the royal persona.

Ramses II's Battle of Kadesh does offer a turning point—one judged by scholars to be partially romanticized, or entirely fanciful: the king delivers himself against impossible odds.[47] Delivers himself, yes, but one must remember the divine element is present throughout these short stories, or RNs, because the king or queen is identified with various gods through multiple titles and epithets from the very opening. In the Battle text just mentioned, the king's association with gods and goddesses figures prominently again at the crisis.

The king's deliverance may be hyperbolized, but no one doubts the facticity of the battle itself. Thus content-wise in these RNs (FOTL uses the term 'royal narrative'), one discovers a possible or probable historical core which is fused with the romanticizing pen of panegyric into dramatic royal propaganda. This fact, and the additional facts that a sanctuary and memorial festivals could be created or renewed within this form (see e.g. the stele of Thutmosis I from Abydos; and the Berlin leather manuscript of Sesostris I, recounting the building of Atum's Temple in Heliopolis) and that the inciting action may be a dream (!), all hold interest for the present investigation.

Genre-wise, the typicality of the king's greatness and the centrality of his role in this or that undertaking, plus the association of royal counsellors, coupled with the observations on content above, including the accompanying divine element, all bid one to explore possible connections with Esther.

Let it be clear that no claim will be made here that the author or redactors have slavishly copied or followed the RN genre. Rather the following discussion asks whether it could have served as a foundational framework or skeleton for Esther. In line with the definition of novella as a 'creative product of an artist's imagination' in which 'historical figures and events from history may be incorporated into the plot', though

---

47. Lichtheim, *Ancient Egyptian Literature*, II, p. 57.

'it must be stressed that the intent is not to report historical activity',[48] one must recognize a potentially different and in some ways unique literary product in each example of novella. Nevertheless, the presence of a frame narrative—or two frames in EG—must be dealt with in structure and in genre analysis.

This form—found probably 25 times in Egyptian, one additional time in Greek (Plutarch), and another time in Latin (through a repetition of Plutarch in Tacitus)—has been suggested as the underlying model for two or three passages in the biblical book of Kings.[49] If indeed the RN was the basic form/genre chosen by the Esther author (only as a *basic* or generative model for his creative work), it would go a long way in explaining the following questions:

1. why the story opens with a king who does not figure as the hero in any of the four Esther texts;

2. why the same opening presents the king more in the fashion of *Arabian Nights* than in sober historical terms (as noted above, RN, by consensus of the few who have worked therein, presents a historical but romanticized figure);[50]

3. why the counsellors appear almost immediately for the simple task of bringing the queen (a task and narrative step that could be skipped without hurting the plot; note that L does not list the seven names and the plot does not suffer, but nevertheless the author connects Ouastin's refusal with 'the will of the king by the hand of the eunuchs' [1.12aγ]);

4. why one does not hear the names of these counsellors again (unless Aman of o′ 1.10b becomes the antagonist), yet one hears several more times of the king and counsellors, and he asks counsel of Mordecai and Esther (this means, as the formalists would say, that the counsel is a function which can be filled by more than one character);

5. why the banqueting, and gathering/preparation of virgins and their (apparently protracted [Jos 11.200]) sexual contest, seems so extravagant (= romanticizing);

6. why the poor king cannot seem to make a move throughout the Esther story without counsel[51] (perhaps the author's ironic twist on the RN, which is supposed to be 'straight' glorification/propaganda?);

48. W.L. Humphreys, 'Novella', in Coats (ed.), *Saga, Legend, Tale, Novella, Fable*, pp. 86-87.

49. A. Hermann, *Die Ägyptische Königsnovelle*, p. 39; S. Hermann, 'Die Königsnovelle in Ägypten und in Israel', *Wissenschaftliche Zeitschrift der Karl-Marx Universität Leipzig* 3 (1953/4), pp. 51-62.

50. Lichtheim's phrase at this juncture of the narrative is 'entirely fanciful' (Lichtheim, *Ancient Egyptian Literature*, II, p. 58).

51. Cf. Clines, *Ezra, Nehemiah, Esther*, who also notices this motif (pp. 280,

7. why the pivot (with its fateful or divine intervention, depending on which text is referenced) focuses on the king instead of on the hero/ heroine;

8. why the king continues figuring more heavily than necessary for plot reasons in the dénouement (Mordecai, once promoted, and Esther, now vindicated, are quite sufficient to carry out what the king has granted);

9. why the story ends with a glorification of the king who has served principally as antihero throughout Esther; and possibly

10. why (in part) the divine name is absent from EH (in the light of the unchanging fact that the king or queen is identified with divine beings, or is associated with them throughout the examples of this genre).

2.2. *The Relation of the Royal Novella to Esther*

One must remember that the purpose of the RN is to glorify the king and 'enshrine' some particular accomplishment; thus a frame does not form a separate part of the Egyptian examples. Yet if the genre were to serve as a generating model for a story about some other hero/heroine, then the king, his counsellors and the problem or project would have to appear in the beginning and end, probably also in the middle, and perhaps in other places along the narrative line. The conclusion would present the king as in some way triumphant. Something of this order would be the mimimum for generic recognition. If the Esther author allowed the chief figure and his counsellors from the RN generative model to appear at the beginning and end of his new work, one would speak of a frame; if the author employed these figures at various places in the narrative, that would constitute more than a frame; one could speak of a skeleton, or a skeletal frame. In my opinion, the author adopted the RN in skeletal form, but the term 'frame' has been chosen for familiarity and convenience.

Several questions now need to be answered if the suggestion offered here is to help in any analysis of Esther. Why would an author want to choose this model for a story about Jewish heroes? It goes without saying that the king or queen in the ancient world was the most important person on earth for their people, and in various cultures was either god, a demigod, or at least the representative of god on earth. This importance emanated throughout every level of society and almost every facet of existence.

But that general background is not yet sufficient explanation for the case of Esther. What would be possibly sufficient, given that background,

314-15); see also his *The Esther Scroll*, pp. 47-48.

is a literary reason. Such a reason is not hard to find. Egypt, where the form probably originated, had produced poems, proverbs and wisdom texts, stories, laments, chronicles, biographies, incantations/magical texts and the short stories called royal novella, to name some of the most important categories.[52] The chronicles or annals are well known from the monuments and present the dry facts of names, dates and places. The biographies are less clinical, more personal, giving a sometimes sprawling overview of a major portion of some personage's life.

In contrast, the RN portrays a single incident, campaign or project carried out by the king, queen or prince—and with dramatic effect. No doubt the drama or tension involved pleased both the central figure, the king, and the listening audiences. The dramatic element serves propaganda purposes and is essential to storytelling. It seems that both government propaganda and storytelling go back as far as one can trace.

Most examples of the RN were inscribed or painted as inscriptions; one each has survived on leather (i.e. vellum: the founding of the temple of Atum by Sesostris I) and wood (the Carnarvon Tablet on the defeat of the Hyksos by Kamoses), while two are extant on papyrus (the prophecy of Neferti—purportedly to King Snefru of the 4th Dynasty, but told as *ex eventu* to Amenemhet I, first king of the 12th Dynasty—and the dream of Nektanebo).[53] These facts tell us something about the importance of the form to Egyptian royalty. Doubtless the effectiveness of literary dramatic effect for establishment propaganda would also recommend the form. However, one more important reason may exist.

Since the form in its cultural context always dealt with royalty, it would serve well as a vehicle to present one's hero/heroine in a high level or glorified position. If that aura of nobility, power, legitimacy or royalty would serve an author's purpose, namely to elevate his protagonist, what better instrument than a form already recognized as 'regal'?

Thus one is led to the next question: where would the RN be so recognized? Could this form have been known in Persia, assuming for a

52. Lichtheim, *Ancient Egyptian Literature*; Pritchard (ed.), *ANET*; E. Otto, *Die Biographischen Inschriften der Ägyptischen Spätzeit* (Probleme der Ägyptologie, 2; Leiden: Brill, 1954), esp. pp. 131ff. for translations of 'the most important inscriptions'.

53. See Lichtheim, *Ancient Egyptian Literature*, II, pp. 9-11. For a translation of the dream of Nectanebo, see Hermann, *Die Ägyptische Königsnovelle*, pp. 39-41; for the Greek text, see U. Wilckens, *Urkunden der Ptolemäerzeit. I. Papyri aus Unterägypten* (Berlin: de Gruyter, 1927), pp. 369-74.

moment the matrix (Knight) or historical situation (*sensu lato*) claimed in the text for Esther? The earliest extant example of the RN dates to sometime in the 13th century BCE.[54] The latest examples occur in the writings of the Greek, Plutarch, and the Roman, Tacitus.[55] So the life-span of the RN form would not be a major objection.

Three other factors make it possible that this form was known to Persia: Persia's conquest of Egypt in 525 BCE under Cambyses; the now-documented presence of Egyptian workers at Persepolis;[56] and the discovery of an Aramaic copy of the Behistun inscription in Egypt and the Arsames correspondence (letters originating in Mesopotamia, but found in Egypt!).[57]

The latter point of course does not establish a mutual trade in inscriptions and all forms of literature, but Persia and Egypt certainly did intercommunicate. Still, the fact that correspondence and a translation of a royal inscription (containing a list of conquests, royal commands, etc.) could be found at such a remove, plus the well known antiquity and glory of Egypt, combine to create the possibility that Egyptian literary forms, specifically the RN, might well have become familiar in Persia.

If the story originated later in Palestine under either Persian or Seleucid/Ptolemaic domination, or if the writing of it occured first in a Jewish community such as that of Alexandria (a real possibility for EG), the availability of such a model as the RN for a Jewish girl who married royalty, and her uncle who became near royalty, is easier to defend.

Assuming, then, for purposes of argument, that a skeleton RN inspired or served as the generating form for Esther, how could the RN's positive approach square with the ironic or 'put-down' treatment of the hapless king in Esther as it now exists? The difficulty could be explained in either of two ways. First, one could assume that a major goal of the narrative portion, even though generated from the RN, was

54. For a translation of the Sphinx Stela of Amenhotep II at Giza, see Lichtheim, *Ancient Egyptian Literature*, II, pp. 39-43.

55. For Plutarch's version of a late RN (Ptolomy Soter's dream in which an image of the god Pluto/Serapis requests that he bring the image to Egypt), see Plutarch, *Moralia* (LCL, V, pp. 361-62); for Tacitus' version of the same incident, see G.G. Ramsey, *The History of Tacitus* (London: John Murray, 1915), pp. 391-94.

56. J.M. Fennely, 'The Persepolis Ritual', *Bibilical Archaeologist* 43 (1980), pp. 135-62.

57. A.E. Cowley (ed.), *Aramaic Papyri of the Fifth Century B.C.* (Oxford: Clarendon Press, 1923; repr., Osnabruck: Otto Zeller, 1967); J. Fitzmyer, 'Aramaic Epistolography', *Semeia* 22 (1982), pp. 25-57.

to spoof and parody the king. In that case the content (though not the form) of the RN would be basically subverted; this would require bold creativity, but does not entail impossible liberties. Thus on this view the sober intention (principally in ch. 9) to establish a new feast—Purim—would almost necessitate another hand, a later level of redaction.

A second view would consider that the author's basically serious purpose does not prevent occasional ironic jabs at the over-bureaucratic captor government. After all, the buffoon-like portrayal of the king is offset by some benevolent (5.1ff.; 6.1ff.) and more or less 'neutral' vignettes of the king (e.g. 2.17-18; 8.7-8).

If one accepts that not all portrayals of Esther's king are pejorative, one thereby can accept the second view as a more balanced, more likely explanation. The following considerations also support that view. First, many commentators have missed the irony; the stinging jabs completely passed them by. Some of that missing can be attributed to Esther's canonical status and the (misguided but common) concomitant assumption that humor/irony has no place here. But some weight must also be given to the fact that serious purposes do exist in Esther, so the humor is not overpowering, the sarcasm is slight—at least for those who do not identify directly with the Esther narrative.

But in (albeit modern) Purim services, one discovers an entirely different perspective—a second support for the view offered here. The ironic humor engendered by the stupid king (in all texts) leads one to see that the narrative (as identified here without battle reports, etc.) deals with anti-Semitism in one of the few effective ways possible for a captive community: humorous parody.

Take for example 'the law of the Medes and Persians, which may not be altered' (only in Daniel and Esther): this implies a prejudice that is both irrational and irrevocable—surely a concern of Diaspora living, and all too frequently in Jewish life since. Notice also the bedroom–garden scene in 7.5-8: the villain might lose his pogrom and his post, but begging for mercy he is misjudged (as he misjudged Jews) to be sexually assaulting the queen—what a humorous absurdity! Surely this life-sustaining humor/power of Esther helps explain why it has survived, in spite of Jewish and Christian criticisms alike.

Thus it is argued here that a creative author used the RN as a generative model, but, going beyond the old content, created a skillful balance between serious intention (lives will be saved through divine intervention) and healthy humor. Further technical support for the influence of the RN can now be presented.

2.3. *The Royal Novella and Esther 10.1-3*

'Now King PN levied taxes [Greek: he wrote] on both the mainland and the isles...' Hebrew מס usually means forced or corvee labor, but here must mean something like 'forced payment'.[58] Moore says:

> Unfortunately, the author does not say why this tax was imposed, and many scholars have had difficulty seeing its relevance to the theme of Esther. It may, of course, be a piece of information which the author has taken from another source.[59]

Paton also opines that 9.20–10.3 derives from the annals, now lost, mentioned in 10.2. That may be, but the point here is the relevance or intention of the passage. Clines sees little relation to Esther in noting that it is 'distinctive from everything that precedes it in the book, so that again we are entitled to raise the possibility of a separate origin'.[60] After careful statement of vagaries and inconcinnities in this section, and a helpful comparison of conclusions to other heroic tales, Clines judges that

> 10.1-3 forms an inelegant and otiose conclusion to a book that already contained more than one quite satisfactory conclusion. It is certainly not by the author of chs. 1–8, but it is impossible to tell, in view of its brevity and disjointedness, whether it originally formed a piece with any of the matter of ch. 9 or was yet another redactional supplement.... It may be better to confess that no satisfying explanation for the presence of 10.1-3 suggests itself, apart perhaps from a desire to conclude the book with some grandiloquent phraseology that would match the self-esteem of a patriotic reader.[61]

The last-minute change in 10.1-3 to 'Media and Persia' does show tension with the book's standard 'Persia and Media', but may mean no more than that in the opening the reader needs to know that the king is Persian, and in the end the attempt is to be historical and annalistic, so the historical progression from Media to Persia is mentioned.

It is possible, if Daniel (possibly not in its final form) was much revered when this version of Esther began to circulate, that this closing

58. Clines, *Ezra, Nehemiah, Esther*, p. 332; D. Daube, 'The Last Chapter of Esther', *JQR* 37 (1947), p. 11; cf. מס in BDB, p. 587.

59. Moore, *Esther*, p. 98.

60. Clines, *The Esther Scroll*, p. 57.

61. Clines, *The Esther Scroll*, p. 59.

phrase imitated Daniel's invariable order. Even more likely, it is suggested here, the author/editor was influenced by canonical or near-canonical models and wished to place Esther squarely within the official history of Israel, and so called on phrases from Kings and Chronicles.

On this view one can argue that the epilog of 10.1-3 and parallel (showing development from the simple, choppy form in L to the smoother, fuller o′) more likely formed part of the authorial or redactional level of chs. 1–8.

Granting also that the tax seems a narrative weakness in that it lacks logical motivation, the suggestion offered here is that the RN form does give narrative or generic motivation if not logic, and that these verses score more than one point and serve either the 'original' author's intentions or those of a redactor. Granted, a tax or corvee has little to do with the prophetic dream, the narrative, or with Purim. But the tax means one thing: more money for the royal treasury. The portrait of the king paints an even greater empire than that of 1.1—it now extends to the isles. It portrays greater sprawling control and lavish wealth than at the beginning. Can anyone miss the dual intention of 'glorifying' the king and associating Mordecai with that glory?

Whatever one thinks of Cline's strictures here about 'ineffable vagueness' and 'not by the same author', the passage in three terse verses presents the king in his glory; then, by a smooth shift of subject (10.2), the putative documentation for this greatness, so that the reader is encouraged to believe (one can check for oneself!); and, by another shift (v. 3), Mordecai's association with the splendiferous, wellnigh universal rule of the king.

Can this passage possibly be a message to Gentile rulers that associating a loyal, talented and reliable Jew with themselves pays off? Even *if*, with Clines, one should reject Daube's ingenious suggestion that the levy was Mordecai's idea to recoup loss from the failure of Haman's plan,[62] the association of the two figures remains.

Also, multivalent possibilities for interpretation remain, but all in the direction of Mordecai's greatness or power, and perhaps all intentionally. Can it intend to show the near royal status of Mordecai (v. 3) and the exalted status of (Hellenistic) Benefactor which he became to his people? Can all this relate to a comforting and, at times, much needed deliverance story, and to the institution of (or justification for) a major feast not

---

62. Clines, *The Esther Scroll*, p. 57, refering to Daube, 'The Last Chapter of Esther'.

legislated in Torah? Would the RN concomitantly call for such a cap to the narrative and serve the author's purposes?

One must remember that RNs did deal with the restitution of worship and/or the establishment of memorial festivals (!). While this writer would not claim that all objections are covered by invoking the RN format, the above questions must even so be answered in the affirmative.

Yet one other intention in this passage could be explored within the area of comparative midrash, but the appropriateness of the RN genre model does not stand or fall on that midrashic intention; any further intentions must await a separate study.

Another question must remain open until earlier layers of the work as a whole can be discussed: when did the RN 'frame' and the narrative come together? The discussion may now move away from frames, whether generative or redactional, and proceed to examine some tensions between passages in ch. 9 and the narrative of chs. 1–8.

3. *Purim (Esther 9)*

3.1. *Esther 9.20-31/32 (o' and EH)*

According to Paton,[63] J.D. Michaelis (1783) first noted the peculiarities of 9.20–10.3, and concluded that these verses derived from a different source. Assuming the correctness of the preceding analysis regarding ch. 10 (*pace* Clines, the same author/redactor could have written the first verses of ch. 1 and 10.1-3), the focus will now be 9.20-32 in o' and EH. Paton presents a detailed argument on these thirteen verses (EH), noting tensions and contradictions with earlier chapters of Esther, and concludes that they were written by a different hand.

Moore, concentrating on EH, seems unsure: he first cites Bardtke's 'convincing' explanation that the contradictions are caused by compression/summarization; he then notes a division between 9.1-19 (a 'historical' basis for the first celebrations of Purim on the 14th and/or 15th of Adar) and vv. 20-32 ('which outline the three major steps whereby Purim, although a festival not sanctioned by the Pentateuch, ...became an important part of the Jewish religious calendar').[64] Sounding more certain now, Moore says the evidence for the independence of vv. 20-32 'is far from conclusive'. But he notes immediately:

63. L.B. Paton, *The Book of Esther* (ICC; Edinburgh: T. & T. Clark, 1908), p. 57; cf. also p. 78.

64. Moore, *Esther*, p. 96.

> To be sure, certain elements or traditions probably do represent subse-
> quent historical customs and developments which were read back into the
> author's original composition, for example... 'fasting and lamentations' in
> v. 31.[65]

In the informative note referred to at this point in his treatment, one
finds, among other things,[66] that the element of a memorial fast is missing from o', L, Jos and OL. This compels Moore to admit cautiously the
likelihood that the element of fasting and mourning is a 'later tradition
finally introduced into the MT at some later point'.[67]

The curious thing here is that fasting and lamentation have more
footing within the narrative plot (strictly, chs. 1–8) than does a two-day
festival. That two-day foundation is not laid until 9.1-19 which, like vv.
20-32, is report, not plot. Therefore, I agree with Moore that 9.31, with
its loosely fitting syntax, is a later MT plus. One must also point out that
even though EH has less words than any other Esther witness, it does
have this unique redactional plus and therefore shows signs of a growth
process not qualitatively unlike EG.

According to my microstructure, there are three parts within 9.20-
31/32: Mordecai's festal decree (vv. 20-22); a 'history of compromise'
(*cum* Moore) which can be taken as a type of compliance with the
decree (vv. 23-28); and the confirming legislation (vv. 29-31/32). The
troublesome passage, vv. 24-26, which sounds catechetic (Bardtke), is
dubbed a needless recapitulation of the events of chs. 3–8 by Moore.[68]
Moore leaves one uncertain here, saying that it differs sufficiently in
detail to be regarded as earlier, later, or at least independent, yet seems
to cite approvingly the 'convincing' explanation of Bardtke that the
summary nature of the passage 'is responsible for their contradictions,
not their being taken from a different source'.[69] It remains cloudy how
one is to combine these two views. If these recital- or catechetical-type
verses are not incorporated as a 'reason' for the second step in the
compromise (as presented in the microstructure), they then constitute an
independent unit. Against Bardtke, the tensions in vv. 24-26 vis-à-vis the
plot surely militate for a redactional addition of an already-formed, often-
recited capsule of the festival. By nature the compliance also must be

65. Moore, *Esther*, p. 97.
66. Moore, *Esther*, p. 96.
67. Moore, *Esther*, pp. 96-97.
68. Moore, *Esther*, p. 94.
69. Moore, *Esther*, p. 94.

later, since it reports what happened after the events and after Mordecai's letter. One suspects that vv. 29-32 have to be added in order to buttress a practice that lacks conformity or momentum. Otherwise, a new element is added to an older practice.

In o´ Mordecai has already instituted the feast in his letter of defense (8.3-10). Does he have to write the letter of vv. 20-22 because in an earlier layer the king wrote the letter of defense, as in L and (apparently) Jos? It must be noted that in Jos the king first tells Esther (!) to write whatever she wants to the Jews; presumably the matter of different addressees in the letter of defense means that Esther and the king wrote different letters.

If one answers the above question in the affirmative, namely that the king wrote the section E letter, that means Mordecai's short letter (9.20-22) is his first. It would be easy to see how, with the passage of time and the relative irrelevance of the king, Mordecai could be additionally credited with a larger role in writing section E, the letter of license.

So far in vv. 20-32 there is nothing that is so integral to the narrative plot nor that is absolutely necessary to establish a feast; the absolutely essential etiology and edict have already been reported in ch. 8 and the first half of ch. 9. Couple this with the detailed discussion of other glosses and tensions in Paton and Clines, which do not need to be repeated here, and one must say that these verses are only primary to the layer which is festal etiology. They are not necessary to close the narrative plot, as will be seen again below.

3.2. *Esther 9.1-19*

The first nineteen verses of ch. 9 display a double battle or victory report in EH and o´. Since the time and circumstance is different in each victory, they have been given equal footing in the structure. That means that ch. 9 (not that chapter divisions are followed, but that signals were properly followed by the chapter maker) has five parts. It has been argued that the last three parts belong in one or more later redaction layers of the growing book. The questions now arise: what are the first two parts of ch. 9, how do they function, and how do they relate to Esther?

If one asks after the relation of these (narrativized) battle reports to the form as it occurs, for example, in 1 and 2 Kings, they do not closely follow the Deuteronomistic, scriptural model.[70] These Esther examples

---

70. See Long, *1 Kings*, p. 244.

lack the crispness in general, and the first typical element, the gathering or confrontation of forces. The second element (the battle), the third (its results: victory or defeat) and the fourth (a characterizing or summary statement) can still be seen in vv. 1-19, if in a form that almost makes these Esther examples *sui generis*.

If one examines the relation of these two units to the foregoing narrative, one is struck by certain inconcinnities and tensions. At this point, the usual assumption among commentators (Paton and others), that vv. 1-19 do belong to the narrative of Esther, can be challenged.

Structurally one would not expect a story (the genre as yet only suggested, but a story nevertheless) to end with a chronicle-like battle report, even if it is partly narrativized. Thus it is debatable whether to label this *Doppelbericht* a narrative conclusion. It seems, however, to function as such at this level.

The structures which undergird this study show that the precise reversals of earlier 'narrative events' or plot advances have actually run their course: the first step of *complication*, Aman's promotion, has been offset/reversed by Mordecai's elevation of rank. That is to say that reversals 5-9 in MT, and 5-12 in o´ and L, have fulfilled the peripetic pattern (i.e. reversed each major element of plot complication). Each complicative knot has been untied, hence dénouement in the strict sense has been achieved.

This means that the dual battle reports do not further the tightly-knit reversal organization at all. Structurally they are appended to the core narrative. If we look for a reflex element earlier in the narrative with which to compare the two battles, there is no direct one. Rather, within the narrative it is the *threat* of annihilation. The reversal of the threat proper is the letter of license. So 9.1-19 transforms the potential death of section B beyond the necessary reversal of section E into actual slaughter.

Thus 9.1-19 appears suspicious on two structural counts, even though it would be easy to argue that it is emotionally satisfying—as plain vengeance, or as the fulfillment of a wisdom principle that what is planned to harm a righteous person actually happens to the evil planner.

Two questions which arose from a close look at the suggestion of the RN also occur to Clines on other grounds: why does the king offer something new to Esther and why would he step out of narrative character by acting without the advice of his council? Esther's request occasions the further narrative *non sequiter* of asking that the extra day of slaughter be 'according to this day's decree'. But if Jews were attacked on the 14th it would be an unauthorized, illegal *putsch* and the Jews could legally defend themselves. Both these unusual features indicate a later hand which did not read the decrees, or did not have them in his document, and did not read the king's character in a consistent way.

Narratively the doubt about the suitability of this material for a *conclusion* increases because Mordecai disappears, Esther's role is not brought to closure, the people have already experienced agony turned to joy in 8.17, and the king's relation to all this is questionable and does not come to closure either.

Narrative logic also slips here, as has recently been pointed out.[71] A major point of narrative suspense centers on the irrevocability of not just the decree of death but also its narrative counterpart, the letter of license. Just as the death decree is the narrative's major complication, so its 'reversal', the letter, is a necessary, balancing dénouement. Once Esther has sucessfully entered the king's presence and survived, once Mordecai has been unexpectedly honored instead of impaled, the implied reader will still be in suspense. What will happen to the people, the nation under sentence of slaughter? Will the chosen race perish under the sword of the sworn enemy Amalek/Bougaios/Gog? How will events ensue under the two irrevocable, but now unenforceable decrees?

Paton lucidly grasps this suspense, noting that 'lively times are to be anticipated'.[72] But if readers focus on the decretory crisis as the narrative has structured it, they will be puzzled, possibly surprised by 9.1-19. The result is not a fully nor partly successful defense which one would expect from the wording of section E. Neither is it a military stalemate *sans* battle and gore, which is another possible and reasonable dénouement after section E's letter. Narrative logic would require one of the above alternatives, or a statement from the author summarizing the net effect of the reversals.

Rather, one is surprised to learn that the events of 9.1-19 do not follow the stage set by the decree (section B) and the letter (section E). By a further shift in narrative logic the Jews turn license to defend into permission to attack. And whom do they attack? According to the two 'battle reports' of ch. 9, they attack those who do not try to stand against them!

---

71. Clines, *The Esther Scroll*, pp. 27ff., sees this as well.
72. Paton, *The Book of Esther*, pp. 282, 274.

So one finds the apparently deadlocking decree and letter overrunning the principle of reversal into new territory—almost into the land of Oz. No one in the empire attacks a Jew, and Jews suffer no casualty! The decree of Aman (section B) could indeed have been revoked, as far as ch. 9 goes. Once again a romantic or hyperbolic note appears—one which goes far to relieve the offence that some have felt regarding the slaughter, if one catches what is taken in this study to be the fictive, dramatizing and humorous elements of Esther.

While the battles of ch. 9 seem to come from another hand glossing in a glorious victory that was not necessarily called for by any narrative requirements (e.g. reversals), one must admit that these attacks could produce emotional satisfaction, the kind of satisfaction that would especially be a desideratum if the hearers were in a wronged or militarily defeated position. Can one deny that in times of threat—and even more so in defeat—such an addition to the core narrative of Esther would be sought by the downtrodden?

Admittedly the judgment of generations has caused this passage to stand, presumably because it does bring emotional satisfaction; the point being made here, however, is that it does not issue as logically from the narrative constraints as would limited skirmishes or truce and peace.

If the above is a closure or result not expected from nor explained by the narrative parameters, what of the end of ch. 8? Could these closing verses serve as narrative closure? In my opinion, the quick reversals which cluster right after the major structural turnabouts (section E versus section B) do reflect releases of the essential complications raised in the rising action of the story. Specifically in o´ and MT the reversals are 8-10: Mordecai's triumph (based on the earlier raise in rank, i.e. reversal 5), Sousa's joy (reflex in 3.15), and the people's joy (reflex in 4.3). These same reversals occupy 10-12 in L.

The main point with this cluster is that the 'arc of tension' is resolved in all areas expected of a tale or novella with one exception: a statement about Mordecai in relation to the king (provided by 10.1-3). As for the situation with the people and the two 'decrees', any of several eventualities might have ensued. The story could end with

> the threat of Jewish force counterbalancing the threat of anti-Jewish force, with the attempt at annihilation being stifled by the attempt at defense, with the first and second decrees attaining their only possible joint fulfilment by neither being executed, with obedience to the king's wishes being paid by disobedience to both his decrees. Yet any narrative statement of such non-events would be bound to be banal, and it is perhaps not

difficult to envisage an artful narrator leaving the 'history' of the 13th of Adar to the imagination of his readers.[73]

The quotation seems to cover two possibilities: a type of narrative stalemate, or an 'open' closure that relies on reader imagination. Either of those two would mean that little, or no more, was required after 8.15-17.

If the author wished to expand the three-verse conclusion, he could have included any of the following: a realistic statement recounting some fighting and losses among the Jews, who would nevertheless live to fight another day;[74] a more romanticized 'and those who dared attack the Jews were put to flight/death;' a more pacific final note, such as a truce, or an admission that the two decrees are unenforceable; or something like 'so the Jews prospered and peace reigned throughout the realm'.

Looking once again at 8.15-17, we see no tension, no suspense, no hope, no anticipation. The heroes are vindicated, or raised to a higher position than when the story opened. In terms of plot (as defined in the Introduction to this study), the characters and events have both determined and ordered a cause–effect sequence which has shaped the reader response, our emotional reactions. The closure is complete. Then how can one explain the battle material in 9.1-19?

3.3. *Generative sources of 9.1-19*

A generative source for these verses is difficult to ascertain. The gruesome battle reports and staggering casualty lists could be fictive, in line with the legendary and lavish ch. 1. The same reports could contain a historical kernel and/or be modeled after the classic writer's report of the killing of the Magi and its commemorative feast, *Magophonia*.

Alternatively, these verses could be a memory reflex of a real and victorious war (for independence, under the Maccabees?); at least that seems more likely than figures drawn from a successful 'defense' which is what the letter/decree calls for. Another possibility would be the editor's painful memory of a real Jewish military defeat and loss of life— a loss which could be ameliorated by the hyperbolized narrative of victory which is now vv. 1-19.

However it was generated, this present prosaic, report-like 'conclusion' is not necessitated logically nor stylistically by the vivid, suspenseful narrative. Thus it shows strong signs of being a redactional addition

---

73. Clines, *The Esther Scroll*, p. 29.
74. Clines, *The Esther Scroll*, p. 27.

But it is an addition judged to be emotionally satisfying by some editor and community.

However one judges those and other possible explanations for 9.1-19, the principal alternatives are either that another ending, now lost, accomplished the same end as 8.15-17 do now, or that 8.15-17, with its very satisfying conclusion (Gentiles being added to the faith [!] in o′, or Jews becoming circumcised [preserving race and faith] in L), 'originally' concluded the narrative. The second option is more likely to have been the case and, if it was, then a later editor would have added the RN frame in order to associate his characters with greater power. In my opinion, based on the smoothness of flow and lack of apparent joints in 1.1–8.17 + 10.1-3, the story began using the RN as a rough framework; therefore 8.15-17 was written as a plot closure, but at the same time as 10.1-3, which was intended as an epilog. This means that the frame prolog/epilog, and the first two chapters, were original to the Esther novella, not afterthoughts of an editor.

As another scholar[75] has pointed out (without benefit of a detailed microstructure), the rejoicing at 8.15-17 is the most elaborated one of that motif in the whole book, and gives no clue that further deliverance such as ch. 9 offers is, or should be, expected. As Clines puts it:

> The very shape of the paragraph 8.15-17, moving in its focus from Mordecai to the citizens of Susa, from them to the Jews throughout the empire, and from them to the citizens of the entire empire, creates an emphatically conclusive impression. It not only sounds like a concluding paragraph, but by the range of its contents actually draws together the principal threads of the plot.[76]

4. *The Rescue Novella (Esther 1–8)*

Sometimes one will find remarks to the effect that chs. 1 and 2 seem sluggish, delaying in nature, rather than narratively gripping. They do not seem to propel the reader toward the section called here *complication* (= rising action). Granted, the two chapters have the elements of another story—the king, his problem Queen Vashti (who disappears), and the problem of finding a new queen (by sexual raffle, as it turns out)—yet as the narrative now stands these two chapters do develop a picture of the Persian court, give some gentle tension/complication and

---

75. Clines, *The Esther Scroll*, pp. 27-29.
76. Clines, *The Esther Scroll*, p. 27.

arouse reader interest in the main characters. That is to say, they do not form a mere patchwork of smaller genres with giveaway vestiges of earlier sources, but a neatly crafted *exposition*. This background is essential in most ways to the rest of Esther.

4.1. *Genre*

What then can be said regarding a generic definition of Esther 1–8? The reader will have discovered by now that this study stands in partial agreement with Paton, Driver's 1913 *Introduction*, Berg's 1979 dissertation, Childs's *Introduction*, and others. According to these works, Esther is a *hieros logos* or 'festal legend'—better, perhaps, is the term 'feast etiology'.

But the structure analysis done here, and the fact that 'lots' do not occur in L at 3.7, show that the festal etiology exists exclusively at the final level of the text. Put another way, the festival concept and its connection with lots is definitely a later level of redaction. That is to say, the feast concept is a 'tack-on', not part of the story from the beginning.

It will be understood that the above statement is literary only, and says nothing about a possible historical connection of story and feast. Neither does the above say anything about the value of either layer, narrated story or feast account. That understood, the fact remains that the only hook or root for Purim in the early narrative is 3.7, which has long been considered a gloss.[77] It has been so judged on good grounds: a 'loose' fit in its context; lack of mention in other opportune places (Esther's appeal to the king, Mordecai's writings and/or the decrees, etc.). So then, one verse plus ch. 9 make the book into a festal story which functions as an etiology.

Of course 10.1-3, often taken as secondary with ch. 9, does not aid the festival cause. But this study has argued that it belongs with the story, at least in its written form. Written in report-like style, and without tension within itself, 10.1-3 nevertheless serves as part of the narrative, running parallel with, and expanding, the scene-setting 'prolog' of 1.1ff. If these three concluding verses were placed right after 8.17, they would sound like the end of a success or hero story.

True, a tale of a wise courtier could have been a previous kernel for

---

77. See Moore, *Esther*, p. 37; cf. also p. xlix; B.S. Childs, *Introduction to the Old Testament as Scripture* (Philadelphia: Fortress Press, 1979), pp. 599-600; conversely, note the arguments of Bardtke, *Das Buch Esther*, pp. 243-44, that 3.7 is not intrusive in the narrative flow.

Esther,[78] or one might prefer to suggest the more precise tale of court intrigue,[79] but this study cannot go further into source analysis. However, strong reasons have been shown to deny unity of authorship to 1.1–9.31/32, and probably even to 9.1-31/32. That limits the discussion now to chs. 1–8.

Clearly the rising–falling action, the 'arc of tension' in chs. 1–8, indicates a unified narrative. Artfully crafted reversals contained therein all have reflexes in an earlier part of the story, and one or more crises can be clearly seen. My judgment differs somewhat from that of Moore, who avers that the plot in EG peaks at a different juncture than in EH.

One can agree with Moore that Esther's entry scene (missing in EH) reaches a dramatic peak which is not surpassed by the next crisis (6.1ff., where the king unknowingly delivers Mordecai from Aman's hanging scheme). While the entry scene is truly a crisis, and possibly presents the highest drama, the plot (in terms of action and structure) still turns at 6.1ff. in all texts. Since the plot reversals do not begin with Esther's brush with death, the term 'crisis minor' was chosen, but that is not intended to diminish its undoubted drama.

The pivotal crisis of 6.1 itself does not lack drama; it simply seems less intense because it does not involve the personal feelings of either leading protagonist. Thus the Greek texts end up with Esther more involved in danger and dramatic action than does EH, and two or three peaks or crises (two in o´ and three in L). These differences in content and structure leave some room for subjectivity, or differing opinions among interpreters. Whether Esther's involvement with danger in this fleshed-out fashion was orginal to the story is difficult to say.

The net result—and more so with L's third crisis just before Esther reveals the skulduggery of Aman—is that in the Greek tradition Esther's activity and importance more nearly equals that of Mordecai. That factor may have played some role, but certainly not the major one, in the canonization of EH.

The options here for generic classification seem clear. All forms of Esther are either novel, novella or tale.

The physical factor of length, taken together with the limited number of digressions and subplots, rules out the novel. If chs. 1–8 had only

78. S. Niditch and R. Doran, 'The Success Story of the Wise Courtier: A Formal Approach', *JBL* 96 (1977), pp. 179-93; W.L. Humphreys, 'A Life-Style for Diaspora: A Study of the Tales of Esther and Daniel', *JBL* 92 (1973), pp. 221-23.

79. Collins, *Daniel*, pp. 42f.

three characters, only one crisis and no subplots (who will be picked as new queen; Mordecai versus Haman), it would be a tale.[80] Since it has a half-dozen characters and several subplots, and since it has time for digressions and flashbacks, and additionally, in the case of EG, for *ipssisima verba* prayers and decrees, yet has the arc of tension, it is clearly a *novella*.[81]

Meinhold[82] has offered the term *Diasporanovelle* for the genre of Esther. He can be credited with isolating likenesses among Esther and the Joseph narrative beyond previous work, with narrowing the possibilities in the area of setting and genre, and with focusing on crucial literary aspects of the two narratives. In particular, this study agrees that Esther is a novella. It also seems that Meinhold deserves more credit than has been forthcoming.[83]

Meinhold's term *Diasporanovelle* may serve as a macrogenre label, or as a handy collection title for works that may be profitably compared, but as a specific genre label it is problematic. It would be serviceable if setting and genre were combined, but that is an unusual procedure. One should not depart from literary canons unless the uniqueness of the material requires it. Thus one could avoid disparaging Meinhold's work and salvage his insights by changing his term to 'novella set in the Diaspora'.

The results of this investigation suggest that one can refine the Esther 1–8 novella classification: specifically, in terms of a subgenre, Esther's content, in all three texts (and Jos), requires the designation of 'rescue' or 'deliverance novella'.

---

80. See Coats's skillful treatment in *Saga, Legend, Tale, Novella, Fable*, ch. 5.

81. For the distinction between tale and novella, see A. Jolles, *Einfache Formen* (Tübingen: Max Niemeyer Verlag, 1950); K. Koch, *The Growth of the Biblical Tradition: The Form Critical Method* (New York: Charles Scribner's Sons, 2nd edn, 1969; the 3nd edn is *Was Ist Formgeschichte? Neue Wege der Bibelexegese* [Neukirchen–Vluyn: Neukirchener Verlag, 1977]); Humphrey's and Coats's articles in Coats (ed.), *Saga, Legend, Tale, Novella, Fable*.

82. A. Meinhold, 'Die Gattung der Josephgeschichte und des Estherbuches: Diasporanovelle I & II', *ZAW* 87 (1975), pp. 306-24 and 88 (1976), pp. 72-93.

83. Meinhold does not receive mention in either of Humphreys's two articles on novella and Esther, nor elsewhere in the same volume (Coats [ed.], *Saga, Legend, Tale, Novella, Fable*).

4.2. *Intention*

The intention of chs. 1–8, with their consistent style, artistry, rhetorical skill, integration from opening to conclusion and satisfying narrative closure, does not aim at festival legislation, but at personal and national encouragement. One sees this intention above all in the novella's content, which is rescue, salvation, deliverance from death.

Following Esther's numerous dyads, the intention must also be dual: the Esther rescue novella intends both to entertain (otherwise why the irony, why the hapless, even stupid king, why the caricature of Haman at home, why the bombast of the EG decrees?) and to encourage. More will be said of humor in the concluding chapter of this study; it must be observed here that failing to see the ironies and satirical thrusts of Esther leads to serious misunderstanding of the book, not to say unnecessary offence. Offence at what is mistakenly taken to be historical and intentional brutality is understandable, but not necessary in view of a humorous, vicarious, tongue-in-cheek portrayal.

Both entertainment and encouragement would find an anxious and needy audience among Diaspora Jews who are struggling to hold on to their identity while occupying a minority and, at times, a life-threatening position. For a detailed description of differences in authorial slant between o′ and L, see the next chapter of this study.

4.3. *Setting and Matrix*

Was Esther first written in the Diaspora or in the land where it reached canonical status? From the lack of references to temple, holy city, Zion, priests, prophets, or any Palestinian geographical sites, plus the clear locus in Susa, it seems unavoidable to assume that the geographical and chronological matrix was the Diaspora, somewhere between 400 and 250 BCE. Some general chronological development in the epithets of Haman/Aman can be detected, but that requires a special study. I think that the theocryptic names in Esther are best explained as deriving from a generative source outside Israel, along the lines of Lagarde's, Gunkel's, Levy's and Sanders's suggestions.[84]

---

84. For earlier hypotheses, see the handy summaries in Paton, *The Book of Esther*, pp. 77-94, and Moore, *Esther*, pp. lvii-lx. For Levy's erudite and penetrating study, see the reprint in Moore (ed.), *Studies in the Book of Esther*, pp. 160-84. Sanders brings another dimension to the understanding of the literary adaptation process: the humanizing of foreign deities in the service of a monotheizing process

The two social groups most likely to be involved in the creation and popularization of the Esther novella would be the bards and the Levites/priests. If the story originated as a secular one (more likely, in my opinion), then bards, troubadors or storytellers would constitute the social matrix. Little is known of this area of society in the Persian period. If some Levites were storytellers, as is probable, the story may have arisen in their circles, whether from secular or religious motives.

One can speculate that pious elders, or even a secular leadership, who simply wanted the Jewish community not to disappear, could well have told/read this story at times of civil community gathering—if there were such—or at religious assemblies, or even at a non-Israelite festival. Such a festival, whether Israelite or Gentile, would not necessarily have to have strong religious tones.

At some point in the Esther trajectory, if not at the inception of the story, the rescue novella became wedded to a festival. This as yet indeterminate feast either was from the beginning, or later became, the *Sitz im Leben*.

Such a story as chs. 1–8 offer could serve to keep some sense of community identity and unity, even more so by association with a feast. The feast could either commemorate an actual deliverance of Jews (a likelihood in my opinion) and/or it could represent a folk festival which caught on among exiles even though from non-Israelite origins (this is less likely as the only reason, but is common in Esther criticism). The possibility exists that both of these factors came together, and such a combination seems even more likely in the complicated world of late antiquity.

Leaving open the possibility of a secular origin for the novella, one can say that in any case a specific setting disclosed in EG (later layers, of course) is that of a worship service. Usage of EG in such a setting would certainly be fostered by a religious authority in a community of devotees.

4.4. *Redaction*

Perhaps there was an original Mordecai-versus-Haman court tale. Even more atomistically, there may have been a Mordecai source and a separate Esther source (so Cazelles, Bardtke—who speaks of three but can be understood to distinguish four—and, very tentatively, Clines). There is no effort here to disprove any source theory, be it a two-, three- or

(J.A. Sanders, *Canon and Community: A Guide to Canonical Criticism* [Philadelphia: Fortress Press, 1984], pp. 44-45, 56ff.).

four-source one, but separate Mordecai and Esther stories are here judged as less likely in view of the masterful development of suspense in the narrative. Two strands are not necessary to explain the story before us, in my view. More likely, but still hypothetical, is the existence of a tale of court intrigue which contained Mordecai and Esther as lead-ing characters from the outset. This possibility finds support from Humphreys, and Niditch and Doran.[85] Admitting the possibility of the existence of a court intrigue tale, an admission I am prepared to make, of course does not prove that it did exist prior to the novella under study. It would, however, be an easy developmental step from a court intrigue tale—one involving a favorite concubine, possibly related to Mordecai, who helps him thwart or best the antagonist—to the present rescue novella. The suggestion of a concubine connection arises due to the historical difficulty of having a Jewess as an unrecorded queen of Persia. At any rate, when the hypothetical and prior court intrigue tale would expand to cover a specific rescue/deliverance of the Jewish people, or (if there was no prototype) when the author originated the narrative, the RN frame would logically serve either the redactor's or the originator's purpose. A brief description of that purpose follows.

The intent of the author/redactor at this point in the evolution or origin of Esther is secondarily to entertain, but primarily to encourage and to give hope in an apparently hopeless situation. The author or editor knew well that the lives of kings and queens not only intrigue commoners but also serve as a focal point of power in society and hence in life. What better vehicle for the Esther novella than a genre already connected with royalty?

Thus it has been argued above that the RN best serves the purposes of achieving interest, gaining acceptance in a wide public, and producing awe of and assent to the hero(es). For these purposes no other form could be better in the secular arena, and few would be better in the religious arena (the exceptions could be theophany, dream vision, or some other prophetic category).

Once the novella and the festival inseparably intertwine, etiological redactions begin to occur, but the novella is left intact. Thus, so to speak,

---

85. Humphreys, 'Life-Style'; *idem*, 'The Motif of the Wise Courtier in the Book of Proverbs', in J.G. Gammie, W.A. Brueggemann, W.L. Humphreys and J.M. Ward (eds.), *Israelite Wisdom: Theological and Literary Essays in Honor of Samuel Terrien* (Missoula, MT: Scholars Press, 1978), pp. 177-190; Niditch and Doran, 'The Success Story of the Wise Courtier', pp. 179-93.

ch. 9 material occurs only in ch. 9, not throughout the novella.

If 10.1-3 (identified here as a skeletal remnant of an RN) were not previously a part of chs. 1–8, and were not 'stretched out' to allow the insertion of one or more parts of ch. 9, how could one explain a redactor's creating it, and adding it after the feast material? If 10.1-3 had not previously existed, one would expect an insertion (or better, an appendage) to treat festival matters, not narrative ones which refer back to the opening verses of ch. 1 and a secondary character, the king. The 10.1-3 passage must have been part of chs. 1–8 before the feast material was added.

Next in the order of redaction would come sections C and D, then B and E for further authentication, then finally the propheticization of the rescue novella feast etiology with the expansion of sections A and F. Refinements to this model can be found in the final chapter of this study.

5. A Proposed Text History

One must conclude that Esther is indeed a festal etiology, but underneath that macrogenre one must recognize that Esther is multigeneric in all its extant forms. An overview of Esther's polygeneric layers, multivalencies and growth timeline follows.

Once again starting with the end of EG—presumably the latest component of the text—one may ask what signals the texts give regarding successive redactions and functions.

(1) The final verses of both Greek texts evidence cultic/synagogal use, albeit in different structures and wordings. These verses and this function do not establish a genre, but neither can the verses be ignored nor subsumed under any generic label that could properly apply to the whole of Esther. Moreover, even if the suggestions of this study for the verses in question (namely *petiḥta*, homily and responsory or doxology) are rejected, the fact remains that these verses speak not of dream interpretation and not of festival matters. They speak of κύριος/יהוה (or θεός), who has intervened (signs) to save/rescue his people (mighty acts). In terms of theology, this is based broadly on a theology of creation and sustenance, and specifically is a concretization or actualization of a Yahwistic צדק (i.e. a cosmic order/justice) and a צדקה (a 'righteousness' or salvation) actualized among the people of God. Therefore the passage presents an actualization of an ongoing Torah story.

Thus EG shows evidence of memorializing a rescue/saving in subsequent generations, or it would not have survived. Whether this textual 'remembrance' (זכרון/ἀνάμνησις) was tied to a festival *ab initio* or became attached at a later *ad hoc* stage remains unclear, but with 'the day of Mordecai' (2 Macc. 15.36—not 'days', not *'Phrourai'* or 'Purim'), one must lean toward the later connection.

(2) The next layer back, the symbolic dream and interpretation with apocalyptic influence, which works prophetically, indicates an attempt at 'genericizing' or resignifying the story as a type of fulfilled message of salvation. It does not take the form of the oracle or announcement of salvation as identified by Gressmann, Westermann, Schoors, Melugin and others.[86] It seems those were long-established forms, whereas this type of enveloping a narrative core with apocalyptic-type dream and interpretation seems to be poorly attested and shortlived. In fact, one may judge—especially by the ultimate predominance of EH—that this attempt at propheticizing or apocalypticizing an earlier genre did not carry the day. Fortunately it carried enough to enter the stream of LXX transmission.

Nevertheless, a prophecy of physical rescue/salvation, plus reassurance of special election (a lesson drawn out in the homily) such as results from the dream–interpretation envelope, would speak to Diaspora needs. However weakly one feels the dream material attaches to EG, it survives and must be recognized as a legitimate literary and generic stage in the history of Esther transmission.

(3) Prior yet to the apocalypticized prophecy stage was the *Festlegende* or, as preferred here, the 'festal etiology'. Chapter 9 betrays the appearance of unity, as argued above, but apart from the shorter glosses shown above to be late, the question remains whether the two major blocks of vv. 1-19 and 20-31/32 were inserted at the same time, or separately. The frequent repetitions of motifs ('rest', 'rest', 'did not rest'), dates, 'the Jews', observing the days, and so on, seem to indicate discreet traditions which arose in separate areas to explain differences in practice. One tradition developed the battle etiologies, another the writing role of Mordecai. However, it is difficult to rule out the probability that these two blocks were brought together and inserted between the narrative and the epilog at the time a document was needed to solidify and generalize community practices.

---

86. J.H. Hayes, *Old Testament Form Criticism* (San Antonio, TX: Trinity University Press, 1974), pp. 141-77.

(4) One surmises that the *time period* for this standardization of feast practice would have taken place somewhere within the approximate century of Jewish independence (164–68 BCE). It would have paralleled the process still evident in 2 Macc. 1.7-9, where Palestinian Jews write to Alexandrian Jews (a mention of an earlier letter in 143 BCE, and the mention of 'now [we] see that you keep the Feast of Booths in the month of Chislev, in the 188th year [124 BCE]'). The document goes on (in the letter to Aristobulus 1.10–2.18) to suggest standardizing the Feast of the Fire [Hanukkah] between Jerusalem and Alexandrian communities.

Although the book of 2 Maccabees came to completion sometime after 110 BCE,[87] and mentions only the 'day of Mordecai', one can postulate a similar process for Purim going on within the last decades of the second century and on into early decades of the first. This is especially true if one notes the two most probable dates for the colophon of o', namely 114 and 77 BCE. If communities were trying to harmonize and standardize at this time of self-rule, a logical probability, it would be important to have Dositheus and his son Ptolomy come to Alexandria and present a copy of EG, which, it is claimed in the colophon, had been translated by Lysimachus, a member of the Jerusalem community (o' F 11).

(5) The Rescue Novella, the narrative of chs. 1–8 + 10.1-3, as supported and outlined above, with its arc of tension and closure, has been the lowest level of redactional investigation undertaken here, although the possibility of a pre-existing tale has been granted. As narrative, the novella offers the most flexible and most multivalent form of all the layers listed above. Small wonder that it has survived, and that it has been resignified more than once.

(6) In my opinion, the usual criteria for detecting separate literary sources (doublets, tensions, success in disengaging more or less self-contained strands, etc.) do not strongly argue for the two-source theory of Cazelles nor the three-source proposal of Bardtke.[88] And, as argued above, the theory that accounts for L as a rewriting of o' must be abandoned.

87. J.A. Goldstein, *II Maccabees* (AB, 41A; Garden City, NY: Doubleday, 1983), pp. 71-83.

88. Bardtke, *Das Buch Esther*, pp. 248-52.

Curiously enough, Tov[89] has elsewhere pointed to a scholarly consensus regarding the history of the Greek text of the Song of Deborah which also seems to explain the interrelation between o´ and L. Of course, the article in question speaks not of two text traditions contained in many MSS, but of MS A versus MS B; nevertheless, two separate text traditions seem to be represented by these two major MSS. Tov explains as follows:

> One may…speak of a common opinion, namely that the A text is closer to the original translation than the B text, and that the B text probably incorporates an early revision of the original translation. This view has recently been supported by the investigation of D. Barthelemy, who included the B text in the *kaige*–Theodotion group, a view which is probably correct but has yet to be proven in detail.[90]

The most important point for comparison with L and o´ is in the statement immediately following the above quotation. Here it is explained that, even if A basically reflects the original translation of Judges, it does not represent the Old Greek itself 'because it contains various doublets as well as interpolations from the B text and from the Hexapla'. That is to say, both the MSS evidence separate traditions, yet also a mixing between the two.

This model opens the possibility that L, whether OG or not, can be earlier than o´, yet contain interpolations from o´; that is, a mixing of texts took place at a later time. In my opinion a model such as this does more justice to the complex interrelationship of L and o´.

It will be helpful at this point to present some results of this study in graphic form. The first schematic shows a proposed oral/textual history which collects and organizes the hypotheses of several scholars regarding sources (which have not been examined nor necessarily accepted here), and displays a broad trajectory discovered in this study (i.e., my view of a possible prehistory behind a proto-Semitic archetype).

Allowing the hypothetical possibility of other, or yet prior, forms of Esther (yet without arguing that such forms actually existed), one notes that the first two levels here (in brackets) may have been either or both oral and written.

---

89. E. Tov, 'The Textual History of the Song of Deborah in the A Text of the LXX', *VT* 28 (1978), pp. 224-32.

90. Tov, 'The Textual History of the Song of Deborah', p. 224.

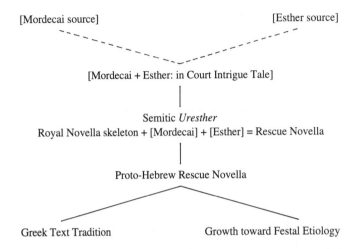

From here forward, as one focuses on MT, o′ and L, the picture becomes more complex. If one remembers that sections A, C, D and F (the latter especially in the case of L) reveal a Semitic groundform, while B and E come from Greek originals, then one must consider, not the necessity, but the probability, of two or more separate redactions of EG with regard to the non-canonical sections.

Now follows a second, more detailed graphic to explain—and draw tentative conclusions from—the evidence uncovered in this study. This summarizing chart intends to be suggestive and heuristic.

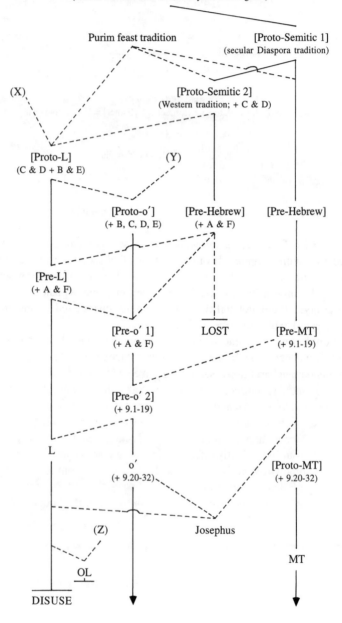

In the chart just presented, bracketed capital letters indicate non-textual forces (the feast of Purim) and/or a generative oral or narrative 'pool' which, in my opinion, is necessary in order to explain the wide variations in tradition elements. Brackets surround hypothetical sources; dotted lines indicate either influence or direct translation. (Note that 'proto-Semitic' in the case of Esther may have been eastern Aramaic.)

The Semitic *Uresther*, if indeed it derived largely from non-Israelite sources as Gunkel and others suggest, would at first be depolytheized and domesticated by importing Israelite characters.[91] The hypothesis here is that religious disinterest plus occasional use in arousing Jewish ethnic support and/or secular community identity would explain the preservation of a profane text in the East.

Returning Jews would bring this secular story to Palestine, where more pious and increasingly anti-Gentile forces would tend to sacralize the story (witness the putting away of Gentile wives in Ezra, and the continuing anti-Samaritan struggles). Of course it is possible that a secular story would enter the religious remnant within the Diaspora, so that a version with references to the divine name (and perhaps other sacral elements) could have existed before the Return. Thus two forms of the story (secular and religious) could have arisen outside of Palestine.

It is posited here that the first growth of the secular story toward 'sanctification'—whether inside or outside of Palestine—would be the insertion of prayers (sections C and D, which latter both balances the narrative in Esther's direction and offers another opportunity for Yahweh's intervention). Sections B and E, though composed in Greek, can be seen as indirect testimony for Yahweh's Torah (attacked in B; vindicated by Persian authority in E!). Moreover, section E—at the final level of the text—directly testifies to Yahweh's guidance of Persia, again by the Persian monarch himself! These sections would be added at their present (but individually different) intrusive places sometime after 250 BCE. Somewhere early in the third century, and continuing into the second, Hellenistic historiography established the pattern of documenting/substantiating its writing by the addition of official documents and

---

91. For Sanders's suggested four-step canonical process model for the adaptation of foreign elements into Israel, and eventually into the canon, see his *Canon and Community*, pp. 56ff.

correspondence—in Esther, form critically, a royal edict and a royal letter.[92]

Finally, sections A and F would be the last non-canonical additions, following the tendency to attribute prophethood to bygone heroes and the desire to monotheize, as one now sees in the dream and interpretation, where terrible trial and deliverance alike are attributed to one God—ὁ θεός. During this growth process the two major units of EH ch. 9 would enter the textual stream.

---

92. Bickermann attributes the beginning of this movement to Timaeus (c. 250 BCE); see E.J. Bickermann, 'Notes on the Greek Book of Esther', in Moore (ed.), *Studies in the Book of Esther*, p. 506.

Chapter 5

SUMMARY AND CONCLUSIONS

The following summary and concluding statements may now be made, with the understanding that the first section, 'The Background of the Texts', was not the focus of in-depth study.

1. *The Background of the Texts*

In the course of this study, no evidence was found to connect the L text with Lucian of Antioch or with a late date. Evidence was cited to suggest how L became mislabelled as Lucianic and therefore late.

In support of Seyberlich,[1] evidence was found while comparing o′ and L structures that, in the cases where L and o′ differ and are therefore are distinguishable, Jos did use either L itself or a tradition known only to L. This is not to deny that Jos also knew o′ and perhaps other traditions not known to us. Thus the traditions L uses, or the origins of L itself, date to no later than the first century CE. It is argued later, on the bases of a probable text prehistory and L's rougher narrative structure, that a proto-L derives from the late third century BCE.

L gives evidence of being a literate rendering of one or more Semitic *Vorlagen*, but R.A. Martin's method for detecting translation Greek through 17 syntactic features has yet to be applied to L in a rigorous way. L's *Vorlage* differed in significant ways from MT.

2. *Redaction and Transmission*

2.1. *Structure, Earliest Redactions and Genre*
Based on the micro-analyses (Chapters 2 and 3 of this study), the final

---

1 R.-M. Seyberlich, 'Esther in der Septuaginta und bei Flavius Josephus', in H.-J. Diesner, R. Günther, J. Mathwich and G. Schrot (eds.), *Neue Beiträge zur Geschichte der Alten Welt*. I. *Alter Orient und Griechenland* (Berlin: Akademie-Verlag, 1964), pp. 363-66.

macrostructures show that structurally the two EG texts are similar. Both Greek texts have six parts and nine subunits (A–I); however, of these subunits, G and H in o′ versus G and H in L show considerable differences in both structure and content. Even greater differences begin to stand out between the two EG texts just below the macrostructure level. MT has four parts and six subunits, with all its parts and subunits corresponding roughly with the nine subunits of EG. In spite of this correspondence, EH and the two EG texts exhibit distinct genre identities.

Narrative considerations in conjunction with the structure and the definition of plot used here (the set of rules which both determine and organize the characters and events so that an affective response is produced) all combine to show that typicalities of more than one type exist within Esther (EG and EH). The books of Esther, Jos included, do contain a narrative in the usual literary sense: a written representation of action(s) involving characters who pass through tension and release. In the case of Esther the tension moves through an arc which at its simplest could be compressed into *exposition, complication* and *dénouement*. However, recent work in narratology plus the Esther texts themselves suggest a six-part refinement: *exposition, complication, plan and further complication, crisis, dénouement* and *conclusion*. This study concludes that narrative tension extends from 1.1 through 8.17 and parallels (in all texts including Jos).[2]

The passage 8.15-17 wraps up the major narrative threads of Esther in one of several possible plot-concluding ways, providing both affective response and satisfactory closure for the reader. Under this view one finds here a conclusion which may have been the story's only ending at an earlier level of the text. By its placement immediately after the letter/decree of defense, it resolves the seemingly insoluble crisis created by a decree of death which 'cannot be altered'; it simply allows the contradictory letter/decree to freeze the action of the plot. The Jews' enemy is removed and his 'legal' document of death has, by an opposing document, been stalemated.

Since neither decree can now be implemented (as 8.15-17 seems to imply), the Jews are rescued, Mordecai is royally honored, the Jews find 'light and gladness', and many (non-observant) Jews become Torah-minded through circumcision (L), or even many Gentiles (former foes) become friends ('support the Jews', EH?) or even become Jewish proselytes through circumcision (EH?, o′).

2. With Clines, *The Esther Scroll*, ch. 3.

Another indication that vv. 15-17 constitute a *conclusion* is that the final *reversals*, by definition an event that has an earlier antipode or contrapositive in the story, are completed in these three verses. One also notes that rejoicing, such as is described in vv. 15-17, is premature and unlikely if the two decrees are to be put to the test of battle. Therefore vv. 15-17 present an early *conclusion*, albeit one which was interpreted in different ways by discrete believing communities, but one which is a narratively satisfying conclusion nonetheless.

Therefore one must conclude that 1.1–8.17 stands in some tension with 9.1-31/32, where non-narrative materials were identified, events take place that have no antipode in the foregoing narrative (therefore the well balanced peripetic structure is stretched), vocabulary and style change noticeably, and the focus shifts from plot and character to history and festival. However, ch. 9 is skilfully attached to the narrative proper, so that it now continues to resolve the tension created by the 'decree of death' versus the 'decree of defense', but in a way unlike 8.15-17: in 9.1-19 because of, or in spite of, the decrees, battles take place. And the battles are strange indeed. Apparently there is no armed resistance, and there are no Jewish casualties. Thus what could have been a peaceful stalemate (8.15-17), or an all-out war which was another possibility if both decrees were implemented, turns into a lopsided massacre—only one decree is operative! Questions of morality, holy war and barbarous times aside, one sees that the one-sided battles/victories do produce affective reader response. Still, as will be summarized next, under close scrutiny ch. 9 appears as an afterthought.

Form-critically the two units which comprise 9.1-31 (o´; L's minus text has some parallels) or 9.1-32 (EH) consist of various types of subunits: battle reports, brief dialogs (without the usual narrative setting), etiologies, and reports, some of which function as commands. At the final level of the text, the first of these units (9.1-19 and parallel, containing dual appendices) must be classified as a (second and third) *conclusion*. One concludes that this material was appended to the narrative portion of Esther, and that the purpose of the dual battles and dual etiologies is to explain communal differences regarding the dating of the two-day feast. The following unit, the appendix of 9.20ff., differs yet again from 9.1-19. This block presents a history behind the establishment of Purim, some parts of which function as legislation for its celebration. Perhaps further study will show that this section also functions as another (subclass of?) etiology. While the *raison d'etre* for Purim

certainly resides in the narrative portion, and while 9.20ff. relies on 9.1-
19 in part, the bulk of 9.20ff. derives from a source not available to us; it
is largely new material which implies some historical distance from the
feast date differences and Mordecai's two-day compromise, and even
more distance from the Esther narrative.

Did ch. 9 become attached to the narrative of chs. 1–8 at one time, or
in two separate redactions? The slight clues that can be drawn from
differences in style and vocabulary between 9.1-19 and 20-31/32 point
toward 9.20ff. as being added to 9.1-19 at a later stage in Esther's
literary history, but these clues alone are insufficient to establish this as a
fact. In the verses which are parallel to 9.20ff., L exhibits a laconic text
which is difficult to explain as an intentional scaling down of o´; it is
better to see L here as an earlier tradition, written when the problems
addressed by o´ and EH had not yet arisen. The contrast between L's
minus and o´'s fuller development can be taken as further evidence
pointing to the addition of 9.20ff. at a later stage than that at which 9.1-
19 was appended to chs. 1–8. Still, one cannot speak of certainty, only
probability, on this point; I conclude that ch. 9 probably came into existence through a two-step redactional process.

However, in light of the above evidence regarding differences in form
and content (and the additional fact that style and vocabulary are more
marked between both units of ch. 9 on the one hand, and chs. 1–8 on
the other), one can say with more certainty that the ch. 9 material, with
its victory reports, feast etiologies (functioning as secondary conclusions), and appendix (presenting Purim history and legislation), was not
originally a part of Esther.

The now isolated and identified macrounit of 1.1–8.17 is classified
through its structure, the interconnection of its units, and its content, as
a rescue novella with reversal-type, or peripetic, structure (following
Aristotle[3] and agreeing in part with Humphreys[4]). Such reversal/peripety
would be diagrammed as a large capital V—with the low point or *crisis*
at the bottom of the V, and the characters rising to, or beyond, their
former and deserved well-being at the end—rather than as a pyramid

---

3. Aristotle, *The Poetics*, 10.1-4; 11.1-4 (LCL, pp. 38-41). Aristotle connects
'discovery' (ἀναγνώρισμος) with 'reversal' (περιπέτεια), but allows that the two
may not occur simultaneously, as they do not in Esther.

4. W.L. Humphreys, 'Novella', and 'The Story of Esther and Mordecai: An
Early Jewish Novella', in Coats (ed.), *Saga, Legend, Tale, Novella, Fable*, pp. 82-
113.

(*pace* Freytag). While it must be admitted that the pyramid apex accurately describes the rising tension and its falling release, the nadir of the V describes the plot in terms of the deteriorating physical and emotional states of the leading characters. This V-shaped pattern finds its closest relative outside Israel in the somewhat later Hellenistic romances. A prior tale[5] (as opposed to novella) of court intrigue underlying the 1.1–8.17 novella layer is a possible but not necessary way of explaining the narrative evidence.

The two redactional (secondary) layers of ch. 9 establish all of MT (at the final text level), and EG (minus sections A and F), as *Festlegenden*— or, as preferred here, festival etiologies—and as multi-generic. In EG, at a later layer, a final seven-part command to observe *Phrourai* or Purim also supports this generic classification. In all three texts studied, an earlier rescue novella has been pressed into the service of an etiology for the festival of Purim—a celebration which *may* not have been originally connected with the Mordecai and Esther story. In support of this conclusion, it is interesting to note that Jos, though including the battles (from 9.1-19), a report of Mordecai's letter (from 9.20ff.), and the concomitant feast of *Phruraioi* (a double plural?), adds his own frame to Esther which stresses not the feast ordinance or its etiology, but the novella's rescue aspect (through God's intervention).

I conclude that this tensive combination of dual generic entities and consequent twofold intention—one presumably authorial, one redactional—helps to explain the wide variation of genre definitions which have been proposed for EH. A single generic title/classification may in the end be used, but it should be chosen only after due regard has been paid to the twofold combination as outlined above.

2.2. *A Generative Model behind EG and EH: An Early Frame and Footing for Textual History*

Before the discussion proceeds to the further redactions of EG, another point of structure which involves all three texts (as well as Jos) must be mentioned. The understanding of this point both throws light on some unusual elements of the novella and gives a foothold for tracing the redaction history of EG. In the course of investigating EH it was discovered that 10.1-3 is not an appendix (*pace* Paton), nor does the author simply 'end his story in the same way he began it' (*pace* Moore.) Not

---

5.   For the generic typicalities of tale, see G.W. Coats, 'Tale', and 'A Threat to the Host', in Coats (ed.), *Saga, Legend, Tale, Novella, Fable*, pp. 63-81.

only do 1.1-4 and 10.1-3 closely interrelate in content and literary intent, not only do they act as a special frame, they also represent the head and feet of a narrative skeleton which is still discernible throughout the Esther novella.

Attention paid to this skeleton, which portrays the king in terms of his immense power and his ever-present counsellors, leads to the discovery of an earlier generic and generative model which was adapted by the Esther author in order to give his novella the widest possible circulation and to give his heroes the most royal appearance possible. That generic form/model is the Egyptian royal novella or *Königsnovelle*, the first known example of which dates to c. 1200 BCE, and the last of which surfaces in Plutarch (Greek) and Tacitus (Latin).

This form treats a major event or accomplishment in a given king's reign; it involves the royal wise-men/counsellors (cf. Haman, Mordecai, several groups of pages and wise men) and in some cases it opens with a dream (cf. EG). In some examples it leads to the renewal or creation of a cult or a festival (cf. Purim). In all cases it appears to serve the purposes of establishment propaganda, namely good public relations (note that Mordecai becomes grand vizier, or even the king's successor, in 10.1-3).

This study argues that a royal novella, perhaps already in a Persian version, served as a generative model for the author of the Semitic Esther novella, the *Uresther*. (Of the many exemplars of the royal novella genre which must have existed, some 25 non-biblical ones are extant; several passages in Kings have been suggested to be modeled after this genre).[6] Stripped of its original plot in order to serve as receptacle, or created anew to serve as a structural (and 'marketing') device, this recognizable and politically effective form then received its present plot which we now know as the Esther novella.

Thus a book bearing an Israelite queen's name, Esther, begins and ends with a Gentile king. More: the king figures prominently in the *complication*, uniquely in the *crisis*, and importantly several times in the *dénouement*. But notice that the content of this remodeled form of Esther dictates that it be classified, not as a royal, but as a rescue novella.

Thus the identification of a non-Israelite literary form explains why the Jewish rescue novella begins and ends with a foreign king who, though important, is not the central character,[7] and with whom the reader never

6.   See Long, *1 Kings*, pp. 57ff.

7.   The book of Daniel treats Nebuchadnezzer in some detail, but Daniel and his prophecies are central; the book of Ruth begins and ends with Israelites although

identifies. It also explains why the king seemingly cannot move without counsel throughout the narrative, and why the pivot point involves the king before it does either hero: these elements are typicalities constitutive of the royal novella.

This model could easily have been available in areas other than Egypt (specifically in Susa, under late Persian or early Greek/Seleucid rule, where the story has its setting). What remains of the royal novella form—a receptacle or skeleton—causes the central *crisis/pivot* to highlight the king and counsellors, and more importantly, causes 1.1ff. and 10.1ff. to stand now as a frame, both like and unlike a modern prolog and epilog. Based on this apparent frame, further conclusions can now be drawn about EG.

2.3. *A Later Frame and Final Redactions of EG*
The discussion will now proceed outward, beyond the 'king frame', in order to establish the overall shape of EG; sections B, C, D and E can await treatment under the history of text transmission, below. EG exhibits three other secondary, or later, redactional layers: the dream and its interpretation, a report of worship ceremonies, and a final command to observe *Phrourai*.

It is concluded that the dream and its interpretation were attached by a redactor after chs. 1–8 + 10 had been composed, and after the secondary ch. 9 had been interpolated, because redactionally it is easier to explain the 'dream frame' as later and additional to the 'king (royal novella) frame' than the other way around. Thus Mordecai's dream/interpretation becomes an outside, primary frame (so that 1.1ff. + 10.1ff., the 'king frame', becomes a frame within a frame—a secondary one). However, in terms of a timeline, the 'king frame', as part and parcel of the rescue novella, was both prior and primary.

Under this configuration, the rescue novella and the festal etiology become the fulfillment of a prophetic dream. The author colors this symbolic dream (as distinct from a message dream) with apocalyptic symbols, motifs and words.

As to function, the later 'dream frame' operates to cast the entire novella and feast legislation as a type of prophetic revelation, and to raise Mordecai to the rank of prophet. As to intention, this study concludes that the primary goal in such a propheticization is to legitimize a festival that was not part of the five books of Torah, probably at a time when

Ruth herself is a Moabitess (Gentile); this means Esther is canonically unique.

communal identity needed to be solidified, and/or communal variations needed to be harmonized. The possibility of a secondary purpose, that of midrashic 're-biography' of the Benjamin–Saul–Mordecai line, must await a separate study.

A time period which would favor such propheticization of Mordecai and the various practices of Purim, and would call for such fortifying injunctions as occur in the final verse of both EG books, is the near-century 165–68 BCE, when the Jewish state achieved independence and the rival temples in Egypt and diverse practices in the Diaspora needed to be harmonized with the revivified Judean home as much as possible.

Both o´ and L append a penultimate pericope (each with individual content) which has been identified in this study as a report of a worship service with opening *petiḥta* (opening scripture quotation), homily and responsory/doxology (o´/L, respectively) from the congregation(s). This uncommon testimony to (synagogal?) services does not totally recast the genre of EG, but does testify to the use of both Greek texts in actual worship.[8] Given the message of the kernal homily, it is possible to understand the homily as reflecting a usage either inside or outside of the Purim festival, or both. The appended homilies (different in each text) point not only to their usage in the community, but to their usage in different communities, and to a move toward eventual canonization.

No doubt the final, text-closing command to observe Purim was attached as it became important to minimize cultic differences between Jerusalem and the Diaspora communities, and to maximize unanimity in worship and national identity. In my view, this command shows the true function of the reported acts and letters in 9.20ff., which is that of legislation; however, 9.20ff. is somewhat indirect and its intended normative character could possibly be missed. Hence the additional final injunctions. Brief as it is, the terse imperative style, the unmistakable intent and the closing position all impact the function, and hence the genre, of the text.

Generically, at this stage, the whole work becomes a (multigeneric) propheticized festal etiology. I conclude that EG is at least one step more complex than EH. Another possible way to distinguish the two texts

---

8. This is both similar to and different from the conclusion reached in Wilcoxen's study of the relationship between the feast of Passover and Joshua 1–6: J.A. Wilcoxen, 'Narrative Structure and Cult Legend: A Study of Joshua 1–6', in J.C. Rylaarsdam (ed.), *Transitions in Biblical Scholarship* (Chicago: University of Chicago Press, 1968), pp. 43-70.

would be to label EH as 'bi-generic', and EG as 'multi-' or 'poly-generic'. Again, as with EH, EG may receive a single classification—'*Phrourai* festal etiology', for example—but only as long as each text tradition's multi-generic, *sui-generis* quality is somehow recognized and given its due.

Regarding EH, it has been asked why Judith, seemingly more orthodox, did not become canon, while Esther, with its unorthodox elements, its lack of the divine name, and its much-debated status, did finally 'defile the hands', i.e. become part of the holy books. It is suggested here that the question be looked at the other way around. This shortest text was the one which achieved canonical status in the period of formative Judaism precisely because, as shorter, less specific and more allusive, and with its (somewhat domesticated) unorthodox elements and joyous festival, it is the most multivalent of the four traditions of L, o′, Jos, and EH.

No answer is offered here for Judith's near miss. But as multivalent and secular-sounding, EH can appeal both to the religious and the materialist mind; the 'neutrality' of EH has the power to speak to more than one human/communal need. Therefore it stood a chance of being preserved by more than one element of the population, and its dynamic could span more than one generation. Thus canonization was almost inevitable.

But it must be said that the two books of EG analyzed in this study, with their similarities and contrasts, their narrative and theological richness, and with their reports of worship (not to mention the colophon, which is rare for biblical books), open up vistas to the understanding that one would lose if one were to limit oneself to EH, or if one had only a critical apparatus in mind, and went at these EG texts simply for culling out *lectio varia*. Both texts were deemed to be authoritative by some communities, or we would not have them today. We would be much the poorer for lack of either o′ or L.

2.4. *A History of Text Transmission (Including Sections B, C, D and E)*

This study suggests that several generative impulses can be detected behind the origin and successive redactions of Esther. Proposals concerning any originating impulses must be made tentatively on the basis of form-critical work herein, without benefit of original study in ancient Near Eastern religions or in source criticism. However, fresh analysis in the area of redaction may be claimed. First, brief proposals (which arise from this study, but go well beyond its confines) regarding generative factors are summarized. Secondly, in a heuristic way, this study applies some of Sanders's insights regarding the canonical process[9] (especially those explaining the adaptation of materials from outside Israel toward eventual canonization) to the redaction history of Esther.

With Gunkel[10] and others, it can be said that one generative impulse behind the Esther novella was probably a story (or stories) of a struggle between Marduk and Ishtar; whether the Elamite deities Humman/Humban and perhaps his consort Mashti entered through the Marduk/Ishtar story, or through separate sources, is not clear.

With Levy,[11] it can be said that there would also be a non-literary force helping to shape an original Esther narrative: the Persian year-end (apparently ten-day) festival called *Farvardigan*. Until more is known of this important celebration (whose name is preserved in *Phrourai* and variants), one would not wish to rule out some Babylonian influence with regard to the setting of fates or lots for the new year. Certain structural evidence uncovered here (the rescue novella) can be interpreted as pointing in the direction of a separate existence of a literary Esther for at least some time before being permanently joined to any festival. But this evidence of itself is far from compelling: the literary and the festal/social elements could have been combined *ab initio*. That question must remain open until more is known about the Persian background of Esther. Certainly the combination of the two helped ensure Esther's literary survival.

In addition to the above creative forces, my opinion is that *some* historical event within a foreign court, involving male or female Jewish influence (however small, but with beneficial results for the exiled 'chosen people'), would probably also underlie the creation of literary Esther. I recognize that both the Joseph narrative and the Exodus story may have influenced Esther, but an actual event helps to explain why the story does not fantasize a complete overthrow of Gentile rule, and why the story gained such wide acceptance, in spite of some of its features which did not meet the ideals of Jewish orthodoxy.

---

9. Sanders, *Canon and Community*, pp. 56ff.

10. H. Gunkel, *Schöpfung und Chaos in Urzeit und Endzeit* (Göttingen: Vandenhoeck & Ruprecht, 1896), pp. 309ff.

11. J. Levy, 'The Feast of the 14th Day of Adar', *HUCA* 14 (1939), pp. 127-51; reprinted in Moore (ed.), *Studies in the Book of Esther*, pp. 160-84.

There can be no doubt that the formation of scripture involved the reuse of earlier authoritative traditions. Thus Sanders describes the core of this reuse with the three terms *selection, repetition* and *resignifi-cation* (that is, contemporizing interpretation).[12] However, for occasions when the canonical process begins with materials from outside Israel, as is the case with Esther, the same scholar suggests that the adaptation process will generally pass through four steps. Those steps seem to throw light on the creation of Esther, and on the history of Esther's growth and textual transmission, as follows: coupling the aforementioned polytheistic religious content with the royal novella form (or hull), the author of Esther first depolytheizes (Sanders's first step) and Israelitizes (the second step) his 'new' story; this creative combination of form, content and adaptational steps results in a 'first edition' which is a secular, humanizing and humorous one (see section 3.2 below, 'Content and Style Analysis'). The term 'secular' here is not intended *contra* ancient and modern commentators who discern an implied faith or covert theology in EH; rather it means secular-sounding, or without explicit theology, as EH currently appears, in contrast to the overt mention of God and his saving deeds as in EG.

It is quite possible that the story, without containing any overt religious elements, would be popular in the Diaspora—a minority community which according to Second Isaiah must have contained skeptical elements and groups which had assimilated to the dominant culture/religion. In spite of skepticism and assimilation, a story which helps foster national roots and identity, even without piety, and pokes gentle fun at the overlords, could clearly catch on.

Alternatively, the 'first edition' may have been created with religious elements, divine names, and so on, at its inception. That being the case, one could accept Torrey's[13] explanation, *viz.* that the originally religious story was desacralized sometime before 200 CE in order to avoid contamination of God's name through its use in the now revelrous Purim feast. Thus, according to Torrey, one *begins* with a pious Esther (as evidenced in the two EGs and Jos) and *ends* with the current, rather secular-sounding EH (again this is not to deny theological overtones and values which are present in biblical Esther).

12. Sanders, *Canon and Community*, p. 33, see his 'Hermeneutics', in *IDBSup*, pp. 402-407, esp. p. 404.

13. C. Torrey, 'The Older Book of Esther', *HTR* 37 (1944), pp. 1-40; reprinted in Moore (ed.), *Studies in the Book of Esther*, pp. 448-87.

Contra Torrey, the view offered here begins *and* ends with a less- or non-religious original, because it is more difficult to find reasons, and a suitable time period (at least up to the first century CE), for a religious story's secularization than it is to explain the reverse—a secular one's 'sacralization'—and the furor which a desacralization would cause would likely leave a trace, of which there is now none. Two other reasons—fostering national identity and poking fun at the overlords—have already been adduced above. Throughout the Persian and Hellenistic periods Diaspora Jewry was likely to have contained significant populations which were more interested in national identity than in traditional piety.

If this is so, there would be reason to depolytheize and Israelitize a foreign story, and to spread it in a secular form (that is, without the third step, Yahwizing). Thus the suggestion offered here *begins* with a secular-sounding original (due to depolytheization) which, in Hebrew or Aramaic, subsequently bifurcates: one *Vorlage* and its offspring remain secular—most likely in circles mainly interested in nationalism; another *Vorlage*, through adaptation of the secular one, or through independent creation, becomes overtly religious in thrust through the mention of Yahweh. On this view, the first *Vorlage*, even though it undergoes redactions, never becomes religious, at least in the circle that preserves EH. The second Semitic edition, however, with explicit mention of Israel's God, serves as a *Vorlage* for proto-L, and later for proto-o', both of which undergo varying development in two separate Greek-speaking communities.

Neither view is without difficulties, but on the understanding of a secular *Urtext* which survived either directly or in a derivative form, it is possible to see how EH could become part of the canon, without leaving Mishnaic or other traces of arguments over desacralization. This is especially true if EH was perceived to be buttressed in a wider, intertextual or socio-literary matrix by the EGs' expressly theological text traditions. Torrey's explanation of *why* such a 'neutral' text as EH was chosen instead of a semitic form of the EGs' theological one would still retain validity.

At any rate, most older and current explanations of Esther, whether EG or EH, seem to assume that originally, and for long after, or ever after, there was only one edition of Esther—all else was translation. It was this single ancestor (called Model 1 for convenience) that somehow must be made to explain both EGs. The graph at the end of Chapter 4 of this study also shows a single *Uresther*, so a unique original is not denied here. What is suggested is that more than one edition of this story could have sprung up almost simultaneously, or very early in Period I, the time of *Urtexte* no longer available to us. In my view, this configuration (Model 2), or some variant of it, comports best with the multiplex social situation of the first centuries BCE, and with the now undoubted Semitic *Vorlage(n)* behind sections A, C, D and F. Put another way, not all the MSS stemma need to branch from one trunk.

What is insisted on here is that, however one decides regarding models (including presumed translations), the integrity of each text tradition be respected in terms of study—certainly holisitic in approach—before the usual text-critical work is begun. That such study can prove to be a necessary pre-stage in text criticism is supported by the summaries and conclusions that follow.

It is possible that these postulated *Vorlagen* both originated in the Diaspora (Model 2A), or that the sacralized one did not come into existence until the story arrived in the more concentrated religious circles of Jerusalem/Palestine (Model 2B). Under either view, the depolytheized, Israelitized and largely secular rescue novella would next undergo step three: Yahwization. This third step of the adaptation or canonical process still falls within Period I of the history of the transmission of the text. Yahwization, but in Greek dress—ὁ θεός, ὁ κύριος, δεσπότης, κτλ.— involves the redactional addition of sections C and D (containing Mordecai's and Esther's prayers, and an intervention of Yahweh on Esther's behalf), plus the explicit mention of a divine name (L and o' differently) in the *crisis*, an intervention on behalf of Mordecai.

At this point, another redaction (outside of the adaptional four steps) takes place, probably in two stages, as suggested above. Since Yahweh is involved, holy war imagery can be called upon and the battles can take place (apparently) without casualties; the unit 9.1-19 and parallel enters the tradition. Soon after, the materials which directly establish the Purim or *Phrourai* feast (9.20ff.) would be added so that the principal function of this text level is to legislate (*ex post facto?*) and explain the feast. Hence the text becomes a festal etiology.

The fourth step, monotheizing, may account in part for the redactional addition of the two letter/decrees, sections B and E. Both of these units appear to be original Greek compositions, but intrusive in their present respective places. The intrusiveness by itself indicates a later stage of the growth process and fits well with the rough timetable of the four steps, for B and E may be seen as defending Yahweh's Torah through the attack on Jewish laws in B and through the acquital of people, law and custom in E. Moreover, E overtly monotheizes by testifying to Yahweh's guidance of Persia, and, putatively, in the words of the Persian monarch himself! It is not suggested, however, that monotheization is the only reason for the addition of sections B and E in their individually different narrative junctures. Another reason is the growing practice in Hellenistic historiography, after 250 BCE,[14] of documenting and substantiating what was said via purported verbatim accounts.

Next, sections A and F become attached as an outer frame, following the tendency in the centuries immediately prior to the Common Era to attribute prophethood to bygone heroes, and the desire to monotheize. The latter can be seen in the dream and interpretation where terrible trial and providential deliverance alike are allowed by, or attributed to, the one God.

Finally, as the texts became used in the cult, a report of worship was added, probably as a guide to the proper interpretation, or as an indication of the orthodox constraints which should be observed. And, so that no misunderstanding could occur, the final message was appended: observe the feast.

2.5. *Final Comments on Redaction*

As a conclusion to the redaction study, four points must be remembered.

First, if the concept of a proto-L may be accepted (that is, an L with no sections not found in MT, and with an earlier end at 7.41 or 7.52), then the hypothetical proto-L text may be clearly postulated as earlier than either o′ or MT. The way is now open to consider both L and o′ as independent witnesses, and to do further text-critical work—work which among other things might establish that mixing did take place between L and o′ at later stages of growth.

Secondly, both Greek and Hebrew Esther grew by redaction; in this sense the term 'Additions' is correct, but one never sees the term applied to the ninth chapter of EH. This means that the label 'Additions' stands in serious need of correction. After all, the reverse phenomenon, the much shorter LXX Jeremiah, is rightly not referred to as 'Subtractions', or as a 'subtractive text', nor (also rightly) is its longer Hebrew counterpart called 'Additions'.

14. Under the influence of Timaeus; see E.J. Bickermann, 'Notes on the Greek Book of Esther', in Moore (ed.), *Studies in the Book of Esther*, p. 506.

Thirdly, the term 'non-canonical', as applied to the seven-part command, the homily, and the rest of the sections, needs to be understood properly. From a twentieth-century point of view, where EH is canonical, one can easily forget that o´, L and EH went through one or more stages of becoming scripture, even canon, to some living community. One may think the terms 'Additions' and 'non-canonical' are too well ensconced in Esther studies to disappear, but if the text history offered here (and the canonical process implied with it) is lost sight of, these terms will continue distorting both historical fact and modern appreciation of a genuine heritage. One hopes that our modern views will give greater weight to the ancient views of the living communities who treasured these texts and preserved them for us.

Fourthly, each Greek text, including Jos (which could not be thoroughly treated here), deserves to have its integrity both respected and studied. It may be hoped that the OL of Esther with its unique readings (witness the elsewhere unattested prayer of the community in ch. 3) and what remains of the Ethiopic text would also be approached in this fashion, since they are presumed to be translated from a 'Septuagint' *Vorlage*.

3. *Setting, Style and Intention*

3.1. *Matrix/Setting*

If one accepts the broad outlines of the redaction and text transmission history proposed above, an 'original' matrix can be detected in the conflux of Mesopotamian and Diaspora oral and literary traditions. More specifically, the earliest level of Esther investigated here, the rescue novella, would arise in an exiled Jewish community which enjoyed at least a minimum of homogeneity, either as part of patriarchal 'stock in trade', used to help maintain identity, or as part of the storyteller's stock, used to entertain (for the novella certainly contains good development of tension and no little humor and satire), or as a Jewish interpretation of a foreign festival that was perceived by community leaders as needing some justification and domestication. Since none of these three possibilities is mutually exclusive of the other two, some combination is possible.

If the suggestion is correct that an explicitly religious version of Esther arose after the secular one, whether in Mesopotamia or in Palestine, then a matrix involving usage in the cultus can be posited toward the end of the redactional process. It has already been theorized above that a historical situation or matrix for the addition of the two ch. 9 units can be found in the Hasmonean period, when divergent cultic and cultural practices were under pressure to conform in order to forge a stronger national unity. This idea should not be interpreted to mean that a festival connection did not take place until after 165 BCE. Such a connection could have taken place much earlier.

3.2. *Content and Style Analysis*

There are narrative features in L which in their simplicity, directness, smoothness and storytelling appeal indicate a more 'primitive' or earlier form of the material than o´. This applies almost equally to the narrative—that is, the rescue story—and to the legal section.

However, admittedly there are a few cases where examples from o´ may be interpreted as indicating an earlier, less developed form of the story: for example, o´´'s transition in section A from dream proper to its first fulfillment, which is more abrupt than L's; L's use of a verb to remove the asyndeton of 1.6-8, which o´ leaves dangling as does EH; L's lesser irony and greater rationalization in the implications of Ouastin's refusal, versus o´´'s heightened irony; o´´'s plus in 2.19-23, which as a whole can certainly be read as a later development than L, and which contains two clauses which seem more orthodox than L (fearing God, obeying Mordecai, not changing her lifestyle). Orthodoxy is not lateness, but L has a majority of such cases, so o´´'s apparent exceptions must be duly noted, and left open in anticipation of a detailed text-critical study. It is hoped that such a study would now be conducted in light of the conclusions of this investigation.

A few other examples of o´´'s apparent priority can be seen in the microstructure and notes. These apparent cases are not numerous in their totality; they become fewer still when the examples from the sections and from o´´'s pluses are segregated and treated separately. (No study was done here to determine relative priority among the sections, with the exception of unavoidable, but preliminary, observations that both length and complexity point toward L as preserving an earlier form of both B and E.) In sum, o´´'s apparently early readings are too few, relative to the number of examples in L, to argue for the general priority of o´´'s novella over that of L.

The question of further refinements of priority in the sections and possible textual mixing, especially in ch. 9, must remain open, awaiting a special study. Speaking of the two texts as a whole, the following generality can be proffered: either o''s apparently early elements can be explained on grounds other than historical priority—such as narrative or plot considerations, a poor/rougher *Vorlage* (one must remember that we are not limited to L copying o' nor vice versa), and the desire to preserve more than one authoritative reading (thus leading to repetition or combination, scribal preference or error, etc.)—or one can argue that textual mixing took place, with L as prior.

Both o' and L show clear signs of being based on varying Semitic *Vorlagen*. And although the core narratives are alike, certain tendencies of style can be differentiated in each text. Conclusions about differences in style and content now follow.

Samples of o''s reportorial, historical/objective style begin in o' A 9 // L A 6, where o' reports the dream in the third person, but L has 'we cried', and the reporting style continues throughout to 'all his people' (o' 10.3, less personal; cf. L 'by all Jews', more personal). It must be admitted that these are nuances, tendencies and smaller differences, but they do count as data, both individually and collectively. At the end of the narrative, for example, o' has the Hellenistic flavor of *aristeia* in the words διηγεῖτο τὴν ἀγωγήν ('conducted his life', more philosophic), but L has the more biblical ἡγεῖτο αὐτῶν ('he ruled over them', socio-politically a preoccupation with the 'chosen people' and foreign oppression, and perhaps with 'biographic rehabilitation' of the Saulide clan, which must yet be investigated).

The o' text is more detailed; L is more succinct. The lengths of the two texts support that judgment in general, o' having 5,837 words against L's 4,761. Specifically, the same judgment finds support in this less obvious fact, now made clear in the microstructures: while o' shows only a few entire pericopae as pluses to L, within passages shared by both texts, o' shows many pluses (details not found in L).

Since a good number of variants between the two texts are numbered in Chapters 2 and 3 of this study, only a few examples of o''s greater detail need be stated or restated here. The o' text offers more elements in:

1. the description of the eunuchs (A 12);
2. the time frame of Artaxerxes' reign (1.1);
3. description of the court of Artaxerxes (1.5-6);
4. naming of chosen eunuchs to bring in Astin (1.10);
5. naming of counsellors who advise the king (1.14);
6. naming Muchaeus as speaker to king (1.16);

7. specifying repercussions of Astin's refusal (1.18);
8. detailing the proposed outcome of the decree (1.21-22);
9. being more detailed in legal aspects (manner of decree publication, king plus court officials agree 'according to the law of the Persians and the Medes', court record of Mordecai's loyal actions, court recorders' draft edict of death, king seals with his ring, etc.);
10. chronicling the background of Esther, her lineage, Mordecai's purpose in raising her (2.7);
11. detailing Gentile rites of women's purification (2.12-13);
12. expanding details of Esther's coronation (2.15-16);
13. adding a banquet in honor of Esther (2.18);
14. detailing how the death decree is to be published (3.12-13);
15. giving specifics as to how Esther hears the news of the death edict and sends a message to Mordecai (4.4-5);
16. describing the wealth and prestige of Aman (4.11);
17. other minute descriptions throughout the narrative, e.g. the king's dress when confronting Aman (6.8);
18. listing of ten son's names, versus five (or six) in L (9.6-7);
19. listing precise figures of those slain by Jews (9.26-27).

In all of these examples, and multiple others not listed here, o´ is more detailed than L—either in a word, a phrase, or a whole thought.

It does not appear, however, that L is simply condensing o´. There are times when it would be appropriate for L, if L were rewriting o´, to include some of o´'s detail (such as the writing of commendation in the court records for Mordecai's loyalty), since it would help the plot to seem more credible or to flow more smoothly.

The pluses in o´ seem to function to historicize the novella. The details of o´ which are not necessary for the plot or the overall structure, nonetheless serve good storytelling. Such decorative items would be more likely to exist, however, in a writing culture. Detail, while extant in an oral society, is most often necessary detail, not mere minutiae. From a Semitic or early Hebrew narrative standpoint, detail is given when credibility is at stake, or to substantiate an otherwise unbelievable statement, and less so for creating mental pictures in the way of Homer or later novelists.

Further, the detail which characterizes o´ seems removed from the author himself.[15] That is, while o´ often strives to give detail, it appears that this detail is less important to him personally. Contrast this objectivity with the fewer times that L exceeds o´ in detail: o´ spells out

15. Let the pronouns be understood as generic and inclusive, not as gender specific.

minutiae of the court, the legal aspects of the court, the dress of the king, the names of court persons, and so on, but has nothing to say of Aman's reaction when the king encounters his evil plot. Here is where a reader who identifies with the story wants detail and pathos! While one must be careful not to impose modern demands on ancient narrative, audience identification with characters and affective response were known prior to Aristotle's time. In that sense the reader 'deserves' to know what is going on in Aman's mind—this is an important part of the dénouement in terms of pathos and audience response—but o′ gives only a hint, an outward sign, of Aman's psyche (Aman's prostration at Esther's feet or lap, a fact contained in all texts). L provides critical insights which at least many readers must have desired and treasured (see further below).

Thus, in summary, o′ tends to be personally detached from the story—at least more so than L. It is in my view a good story, perhaps historically conceived, perhaps part of the community's treasure, but it is history in which the writer of o′ participates less than the writer of L. The writer's community is at some remove from the communities represented in the narrative—he may therefore write out of distance and dispassion.

Not so with L. L knows how Esther feels, thinks and acts; how Mordecai mourns, prays, agonizes. More yet, L exposes the reader to the inner feelings of Aman at the critical moment—at one of the narrative climaxes. (In the Introduction to this study, crisis, on which the plot turns, was differentiated from climax, which gives the reader emotional release.) Thus L lets the reader see how justice is done when Aman feels caught in his own trap; and how the community of which he seems to be a part exults in righteous rejoicing at the turn of fortune. Such personal identification is likewise evidenced by the use of the first person at A 6 in L as opposed to the third person in o′.

To summarize: in every way the author of L sees himself as part of the story. L must himself be a Jew, writing to Jews. This seems the best conclusion in view of the lack of incidental, storytelling detail on the one hand, and the filling in of the personal, an inner look into the characters, on the other. Such filling in shows a hope for the success of the Jewish nation, and a disdain for Gentiles as a whole, or at least for Gentile overlords. o′ has the first drinkfest 'not according to law/custom' while L has it 'according to law/custom'. In light of other examples of slant in the two texts, the likely interpretation is this: for o′ such drunkenness was neither customary nor good; for L it was common among Gentiles, even considered 'lawful'!

The above does not deny all affective reader reaction to o´; the content of o´ will produce emotional response. But similar content in L, fused to the greater psychological character development and evident personal slant, produces that response, so to speak, in living color.

Another rhetorical element deserves more attention than it can be given here, but it must not be omitted. Satire, irony and humor are evident in all forms of Esther, with Jos as probably the most sober of the four (since he incorporates Esther into his history, and specifically emphasizes God's saving watchfulness over his people). Of the remaining three texts studied here, o´ pokes the most fun at the incredibly frivolous Persian court, the bumbling monarch[16], the ludicrous situation of Persian might brought to bear in order to help husbands keep their wives in line, and so on.[17] However, it must be recognized that all Esther texts partake of parody and humor. If one accepts the presence of irony in Esther, it is not a distant step to agree with Greenstein in seeing a 'tongue-in-cheek' approach in the Esther scroll. This approach would go far in removing, or at least ameliorating, the offense so many have taken to various items in Esther, especially the one-sided killing in ch. 9.[18]

3.3. *Intention*

I conclude that the pluses, minuses and lexical differences in L and o´ indicate diverging authorial intentions. If one invokes audience criticism,

---

16. 'He [the king, as portrayed in both EH and EG] is stupid, like all good kings'—J. Sanders in personal communication. The same scholar's unpublished notes on Esther, dating to the late '60s, highlight humorous points in the narrative, especially Haman's casting himself on Esther to plead for his life, and being perceived (in a life threatening moment, no less!) as sexually assaulting the queen.

17. The most justice to these ironic and humorous elements has been done by Clines, *Ezra, Nehemiah, Esther*, and E.L. Greenstein, 'A Jewish Reading of Esther', in J. Neusner, B. Levine and E. Frerichs (eds.), *Judaic Perspectives on Ancient Israel*, (Philadelphia: Fortress Press, 1987), pp. 225-43. The latter author highlights certain fictitious and humorous elements in the narrative, using phrases such as 'tongue in cheek', 'comedic hyperbole', etc. Not to be overlooked is the long-standing connection of Esther with 'festive celebration [which] has always determined the seriousness—or rather lack of seriousness—with which it has been taken' (p. 226).

18. See Greenstein, 'A Jewish Reading of Esther', p. 225; cf. D. Marcus, 'Viewing the Epilog of the Book of Judges as Satire' (SBL paper, Chicago, 1988).

the same point could be restated as follows: L and o´ shape a common core of tradition in the direction of quite disparate communities: o´ to a Hellenized Diaspora audience; L to a more orthodox, less Hellenized community, perhaps in Palestine itself. As Sanders puts it:

> There is no early biblical manuscript of which I am aware, no matter how 'accurate' we may conjecture it to be, or faithful to its *Vorlage*, that does not have some trace in it of its having been adapted to the needs of the community from which we…receive it. Such observations are relative and pertain not to method in text criticism, but to the concepts on which method is based. All versions are to some extent relevant to the communities for which they were translated: it was because the Bible was believed relevant that it was translated… Even biblical Hebrew texts are to some extent, greater or less, adapted to the needs of the communities for which they were copied.[19]

Selected demonstrations of the distinct intentions shown by L and o´, taken from the microstructures and the notes that summarize each structural unit, now follow.

L shows its Jewishness or lack of Hellenization in these ways:

1. first person in A 6;
2. in Mordecai's dream, o´ has the nation fearing κακά ('defeat', A 8aβ), but L makes no mention of such fear (the people cry to, and trust, God);
3. the court guards are given Greek names (o´ has Semitic names, but would not a Jewish reader question other Jews being guards in the Persian court?);
4. L gives more specifics of boundaries of the king's rule (1.1), something important to the Diaspora;
5. L makes repeated reference to the covenant with Abraham, the inheritance of the Lord (= Israel), and the promise God made to the fathers (C 16-17, 20, 57)—a central aspect of canon within the community, adaptable for life, under Persian, Greek or Roman oppression;
6. o´ details the purification rights of the Persian court, while L omits this description, because it does not want to cast the Gentiles in a good light (they do not parallel the sanctified nation of Israel—especially with her laws of purity and holiness); Aman in o´ is 'haughty' but in L he is 'uncircumcised' (C 15 and parallel); o´ has Esther cut her hair, something L could not have a proper Jewish woman do; o´ C 26 has 'menstruous cloth', while L uses a euphemism ('cloth of a separated woman') and refers to a Levitical law of cleanliness;
7. in o´ the body of Aman is hung for public display and left overnight, but L does not have this, because such a defilement is contrary to Torah,

19. Sanders, 'Text and Canon', p. 13.

8. o′ has Mordecai raising his niece for the purpose of marriage, not found in L, because once again this would be contrary to Torah legislation (cf. Lev. 18.12-13);

9. in o′ Esther hides her Jewishness, but not in L, where the reader is asked to be proud of being Jewish (for Esther to hide her community relationship is to defeat the author's ethnic–constitutive or 'homiletical' intention);

10. o′'s secrecy over Esther's nationality serves the plot and creates reader interest, while L's interest centers not on secrecy and plot but on the didactic message (be proud of Jewishness; God causes the Jewish nation to succeed in spite of its enemies);

11. in o′ Mordecai is detailed as a 'Jew from Jerusalem living in Sousa', while in L this is lacking, because L's community knows this (everyone must know Mordecai and Esther; L writes the story to encourage identification with them, not merely to introduce them to the community).

As noted above, one senses that the author of o′ stays neutral to the story, while L takes it personally. Thus one may posit a 'homiletical', or at least an ethnic, communal, constitutive intention for L vis-à-vis a didactic, history-oriented, documentary authorial intention for o′. In this light, o′ may be simply another necessary part of a large work—perhaps that of extending the LXX, or a documenting of festivals, or just a work of translation.

L, on the other hand, translates the story of Esther into Greek so that segments of the Jewish population (in the homeland or in the Diaspora) could not only read it, but appreciate it as their story, their history, their life. This author wants, in every way, to bring the reader to a point of admiration, not only for Mordecai and Esther, but also for the Jews as a nation, and their God as the All-Controller of their history, indeed of the world's history. Both o′ and the feast of *Phourdia*,[20] founded upon the rescue story, are good for the Jewish people and sanctioned by God himself. But quantitatively, o′'s plus concerning the history of festival compromise (9.20ff.) and his extra development of the two battles (9.1ff.), contrasted with L's minus, result in a greater emphasis in o′ on feast observance and a greater emphasis in L on God's divine deliverance.

---

20. Φουρδια, which probably residually preserves *Farvardigan*, is the reading of MS 19, while 19's corrector shows Φουρμαια, and MS 319 gives the Aramaic-appearing Φαραια.

4. *Textual Integrity*

The differences in vocabulary, style, content and even in structure between o´ and L, which show up quickly and at times dramatically when a detailed analysis is conducted, demonstrate that some differences cannot be explained by recourse to textual variants/emendation; that o´ and L reflect differing Semitic *Vorlagen*; and that behind or beyond those discreet parent texts varying bits of community tradition were available to the two respective editors/translators of o´ and L.

In general terms these diverse bits, or motifs, elements, speeches and prayers (notice, among other unique readings not cited here from the OL, the community prayer at the end of ch. 3),[21] may be said to derive from a 'narrative pool', for lack of a better term. In form-critical terms one would now speak of a matrix (which in fact includes various matrices, such as history, culture, social institution, literary or intertextual relations, even *Zeitgeist*), to try to do justice to the complex environment and discreet communities from which documents such as the books of Esther must have arisen. However one phrases it, the point here is not terminology, but that neither o´ nor L derive directly from one another; and that each text deserves, before a hermeneutic of suspicion can justifiably be applied, a hermeneutic of respect for its integrity.

It is gratifying to find that a premier model of scholarship (complete with initial contributions, responses and re-responses, plus a report of a final oral discussion), examining the relation of the short LXX and long MT witnesses to 1 Samuel 16–17, shows that the conclusions reached here regarding Esther are partly paralleled and supported. While the four authors end their joint effort maintaining individual points of view, they also came to some important general agreements, several of which J. Lust summarizes as follows:

> The participants agreed that for several biblical books more than one text must have existed. To a certain extent the final character of such a text depended on its functioning and its acceptance by a religious community. This led to…the appraisal of the MT and the LXX as two different canonical forms of the text…it should be clear that both versions, the MT and LXX, are valuable ones and stand in their own right. The one should not be

---

21. P. Sabatier (ed.), *Bibliorum Sacrorum Latine Versiones Antiquae* (Rheims, 1739–1743; repr., Paris, 1751), pp. 804-805.

corrected by the other. This rule should be applied to all cases in which the differences between the MT and LXX [and L, I would add] are not to be explained as accidental errors.[22]

The cumulative impact of the above points forces one to the conclusions that L is not a rewrite of o′, although one may agree with Tov[23] on three other major points, not to mention numerous correct details. These major points now follow.

First, the six sections (which Tov rightly labels 'the so-called apocryphal additions') along with the 'canonical sections in L...should be regarded as one *organic unit*'.[24] While this unity is valid—indeed, must be insisted upon—at the final level of the text, it must not blind us to redactional layers, or to redaction's close relative, the history of text transmission. (The need for histories of redaction and text transmission looms especially urgent in light of Tov's use of contradictions between L and MT in order to show that L is secondary to MT; see the third point below). Neither should organic unity opaque to our eyes critical differences of origin behind individual sections, such as the Greek *Vorlage(n)* that undergirds sections B and E, or the probably discrete Semitic *Vorlagen* that lie behind o′'s and L's differing section F and parallel. Of course some considerations referred to in the above discussion on textual integrity fall outside the discipline of text criticism proper, but they inform the concepts on which text-critical method is based.[25] Much text-critical work remains to be done among o′ and L, no matter how one judges the suggestion made here. But if that work is done with an eye to o′'s and L's individual unities (i.e. if the task is approached through respect for textual integrity), accuracy in both text criticism of manuscripts and reconstruction of *Urtexte* can be improved.

Secondly, in agreement with Tov as far as his statement goes, the Hebrew *Vorlage* behind L's pluses to MT differed from MT. But this study goes beyond L's pluses to conclude that a Semitic *Vorlage* differing from MT underlies the whole of L, except for sections B and E.

Thirdly, Tov's last section on Esther attempts a characterization of L based on the organic unity of the so-called canonical and non-canonical

22. D. Barthelemy, D. Gooding, J. Lust, and E. Tov, *The Story of David and Goliath: Textual and Literary Criticism. Papers of a Joint Research Venture* (OBO, 73; Fribourg: Editions Universitaires Fribourg Suisse, 1986), p. 156.

23. Tov, 'The "Lucianic" Text' (see my discussion in Chapter 4).

24. Tov, 'The "Lucianic" Text', p. 11.

25. Sanders, 'Text and Canon', p. 13.

parts. While some characterizations carry conviction, the judgment that L is secondary to MT (because the six sections contradict canonical EH) must be challenged. Since the sections have already been taken by Tov as organically unified with the rest of L (apparently *ab initio*), L is (wholly) secondary. But, as noted above, analyzing the text's final level, necessary and admirable as it is, should not cause one to ignore redactional tensions which lead to the discovery of prior layers (e.g., L's A 17 seems to contradict 6.4d!). This study has argued that redactional layers can be detected, and that L's form of the novella and ch. 9 material is the earliest among the four Esther texts. Therefore the characterization of L as secondary at all levels cannot be maintained. Notice this admission:

> It seems impossible to conciliate the literal and the free elements in L. Moreover, the LXX [o′] reflects renderings of both types throughout the canon. Accordingly, their juxtaposition in the L text of Esther is not surprising.[26]

But elsewhere Tov has helped us to see that the LXX is not the same text throughout the Greek canon, and one is dealing here with Esther; EG's relation to other LXX books would first have to be established. So that point carries little weight. And precisely because it is 'impossible to conciliate literal and free elements in L', and an integral look at L and o′ reveals diverse authorial intentions and communal concerns, I have concluded that L did not rewrite Esther from o′.

Respecting Tov's cautions regarding the terms version, recension and text type,[27] one may also conclude that L is not a 'Septuagint type' text or version, nor is it a revision of o′. Rather, L embodies its own discreet tradition deriving from a living community.

As Sanders has recently reminded us:

> What needs to be stressed…is the need to have respect for each witness in its own integrity. Text criticism as formerly practiced made pillaging of ancient and medieval manuscripts a righteous act done in the service of an imagined original. They were plucked without regard to what their mission for some ancient or medieval community had been. The focus often seemed to be on how much some scribes goofed, on the one hand, but how well other scribes willy-nilly preserved nuggets of 'original' readings.[28]

26. Sanders, 'Text and Canon', p. 15.
27. Tov, 'A Modern Textual Outlook', pp. 11-27, *passim*.
28. Sanders, 'The Hermeneutics of Text Criticism and Translation', p. 4.

Therefore L must be analyzed *in its integrity* before comparative text-critical work is done between it and either o′ or EH. Put another way, without prejudice to any text, L, o′ and EH constitute independent textual witnesses—in effect they are separate books of Esther.

In comparing the three texts, EH the two EGs (keeping Jos in purview as a fourth tradition), one must conclude that L contains the earliest known form of the core tradition: the rescue novella. Under this view L may gain both greater value and scholarly attention.

5. *Final Conclusion*

The traces of discrete authorial aims and clues concerning adaptation to distinct communal needs, now exposed in L, o′ and EH, show once again the need for a hermeneutic of respect in text criticism. That is to say, the textual integrity of each witness should be researched and respected as a prelude to both textual and higher criticism.

In an elucidative study of the Hebrew and Greek texts of 1 Samuel 1, S. Walters[29] concludes that the two texts are 'discrete narratives, each with its own interest and design'; he cautions against modifying either text under the pattern of the other, lest 'the result be a hybrid text with no distinctive character at all'.[30] Walters says that the Hebrew and Greek texts of 1 Samuel 1 are (reasonably) integral and independent, in line with my conclusions regarding Esther traditions. Asking the reader to link the three (or four) Esthers to the following quotation, where Hannah of MT and Anna of OG become representatives of their independent text traditions, I conclude:

> Hannah and Anna. Are they the same woman, or different women? The two personal names—one contained within the other, the same yet different, related yet discrete—the two personal names epitomize the relationship between the MT and the OG. Hanna and Anna exist in different stories, in distinct social circumstances, breathing different theological air, and they pass before us in the narrator's art to play different roles.
> Let us allow them both to go on living.[31]

One hopes that the books of Esther will also go on living.

---

29. S.D. Walters, 'The Translator and the Text: Which Text Do We Translate?' (SBL paper, Boston, 1987); see his 'Hanna and Anna: The Greek and Hebrew Texts of 1 Samuel 1', *JBL* 107 (1988), pp. 385-412.

30. Walters, 'Hanna and Anna', p. 408.

31. Walters, 'The Translator and the Text', p. 10.

BIBLIOGRAPHY

Abrams, M.H., *A Glossary of Literary Terms* (New York: Holt, Rinehart and Winston, 4th edn, 1981).

Allen, R.B., 'Beyond Parallelism: The "New" Poetics' (Plenary Address, Northwest Regional Meeting of the Evangelical Theological Society, Portland, 1986).

Alter, R., *The Art of Biblical Narrative* (New York: Basic Books, 1981).

Anderson, B.W., 'The Book of Esther', in G.A. Buttrick (ed.), *The Interpreter's Bible* (New York: Abingdon Press, 1954), III, pp. 823-74.

Auerbach, E., *Mimesis: The Representation of Reality in Western Literature* (Princeton, NJ: Princeton University Press, 1974).

Bagnall, R.S., and P. Derow, *Greek Historical Documents: The Hellenistic Period* (SBLSBS, 16; Chico, CA: Scholar's Press, 1981).

Baldwin, J.G., *Esther* (TOTC; Downers Grove, IL: Inter-Varsity Press, 1984).

Bardtke, H., *Das Buch Esther* (KAT, 27/5; Gütersloh: Gerd Mohn, 1963).

—'Zusätze zu Esther', in W.G. Kümmel (ed.), *Jüdische Schriften aus hellenistisch-römischer Zeit*. I. *Historische und legendarische Erzählungen* (Gütersloh: Gerd Mohn, 1973).

Barthelemy, D., D. Gooding, J. Lust and E. Tov, *The Story of David and Goliath: Textual and Literary Criticism. Papers of a Joint Research Venture* (OBO, 73; Fribourg: Editions Universitaires Fribourg Suisse, 1986).

Barthelemy, D., A.R. Hulst, N. Lohfink, W.D. Hardy, H.P. Rueger and J.A. Sanders (eds.), *Preliminary and Interim Report on the Hebrew Old Testament Text Project* (5 vols.; Stuttgart: United Bible Societies, 1976–1980).

Bartlett, J.R., *The First and Second Books of Maccabees* (CBCNEB; Cambridge: Cambridge University Press, 1973).

Barucq, A., and S.D.B. Judith, *Esther* (Paris: Cerf, 1959).

Beckwith, R., *The Old Testament Canon of the New Testament Church and its Background in Early Judaism* (Grand Rapids: Eerdmans, 1985).

Berg, S.B. 'After the Exile: God and History in the Books of Chronicles and Esther', in J.L. Crenshaw and S. Sandmel (eds.), *The Divine Helmsman* (New York: Ktav, 1980), pp. 107-27.

—*The Book of Esther: Motifs, Themes and Structure* (SBLDS, 44; Chico, CA: Scholars Press, 1979).

Bergey, R.L, 'The Book of Esther—Its Place in the Linguistic Milieu of Post-Exilic Biblical Hebrew Prose: A Study in Late Biblical Hebrew' (PhD diss., Dropsie College, Philadelphia, 1983).

—'Late Linguistic Features in Esther', *JQR* 75 (1984), pp. 66-78.

—'Post-Exilic Hebrew Linguistic Developments in Esther: A Diachronic Approach', *JETS* 31 (1988), pp. 161-68.

Best, O.F., *Handbuch literarischer Fachbegriffe* (Frankfurt: Fischer Taschenbuch Verlag, 1982).

Bettan, I., *The Five Scrolls* (Cincinnati: Union of Hebrew Congregations, 1950).

Bickerman, E.J., 'The Edict of Cyrus in Ezra 1', *JBL* 65 (1846), pp. 249-75.

—*Four Strange Books of the Bible* (New York: Schocken Books, 1967).

—*From Ezra to the Last of the Maccabees* (New York: Schocken Books, 1962).

—'Notes on the Greek Book of Esther', in *idem* (ed.), *Studies in Jewish and Christian History* (Leiden: Brill, 1976).

Bloch, R., 'Midrash: Methodological Note for the Study of Rabbinic Literature', in W. Green (ed.), *Approaches to Ancient Judaism: Theory and Practice* (Missoula, MT: Scholars Press, 1978), pp. 51-75.

Booth, W.C., *The Rhetoric of Fiction* (Chicago: University of Chicago Press, 2nd edn, 1983).

Botterweck, G.J., 'Die Gattung des Buches Esther im Spektrum neuerer Publikationen', *BibLeb* 5 (1964), pp. 274-92.

Brandt, W.J., *The Rhetoric of Argumentation* (Indianapolis: Bobbs–Merrill, 1970).

Breasted, J.H., *Ancient Records of Egypt* (5 vols.; Chicago: University of Chicago Press, 1906–1907; reprint New York: Russell & Russell, 1962–67).

Brooke, A.E., N. McLean and H.S.J. Thackeray (eds.), *The Old Testament in Greek* (Cambridge: Cambridge University Press, 1940).

Brown, C.S. (ed.), *The Reader's Companion to World Literature* (New York: Holt, Rinehart and Winston, 1971).

Brownlee, W.H., 'Le Livre grec d'Esther et la royaute divine', *RB* 73 (1966), pp. 161-85.

Bruce, F.F., 'Prophetic Interpretation in the Septuagint' (BIOSCS, 12; Manchester: University of Manchester, 1979), pp. 17-26.

Brueggemann, W., 'Kingship and Chaos: A Study in Tenth Century Theology', *CBQ* 33 (1971), pp. 317-32.

Budge, E.A.W., *The Rosetta Stone in the British Museum* (London: Religious Tract Society, 1929).

Cairo Codex of the Bible (2 vols.; Jerusalem: Makor, 1971).

Callaway, M., *Sing, O Barren One: A Study in Comparative Midrash* (SBLDS, 91; Atlanta: Scholars Press, 1986).

Chatman, S., *Story and Discourse: Narrative Structure in Fiction and Film* (Ithaca, NY: Cornell University Press, 1978).

Childs, B.S., 'Midrash and the Old Testament', in J. Reumann, (ed.), *Understanding the Sacred Text: Essays in Honor of Morton S. Enslin on the Hebrew Bible and Christian Beginnings* (Valley Forge, PA: Judson Press, 1972), pp. 45-59 .

—*Introduction to The Old Testament as Scripture* (Philadelphia: Fortress Press, 1979).

Clines, D.J.A., *The Esther Scroll: The Story of the Story* (JSOTSup, 30; Sheffield: JSOT Press, 1984).

—*Ezra, Nehemiah, Esther* (NCBC; Grand Rapids: Eerdmans, 1984).

Coats, G.W., *From Canaan to Egypt: Structural and Theological Context for the Joseph Story* (CBQMS, 4; Washington, DC: Catholic Biblical Association of America, 1976).

—*Genesis, with an Introduction to Narrative Literature* (FOTL, 1; Grand Rapids: Eerdmans, 1983).

—'Moses and Amalek: Aetiology and Legend in Exodus XVII 8-17', in G.W. Anderson (ed.), *Congress Volume, Edinburgh* (VTSup, 28; Leiden: Brill, 1975).

—*Saga, Legend, Tale, Novella, Fable: Narrative Forms in Old Testament Literature* (JSOTSup, 35; Sheffield: JSOT Press, 1985).

Cohen, S.J.D., *Josephus in Galilee and Rome: His Vita and Development as a Historian* (Leiden: Brill, 1979).

Collins, J.J., *Daniel, with an Introduction to Apocalyptic Literature* (FOTL, 20; Grand Rapids: Eerdmans, 1984).

Constantelos, D., R.A. Kraft, S.E. Johnson, A.P. Wikgren and B.M. Metzger, '3 and 4 Maccabees', in H.G. May and B.M. Metzger (eds.), *The New Oxford Annotated Bible with the Apocrypha, Expanded Edition, Revised Standard Version* (Oxford: Oxford University Press, 1977), pp. 294-329 (Apocrypha).

Cook, H.J., 'The A Text of the Greek Versions of the Book of Esther', *ZAW* 81 (1969), pp. 367-76.

Cook, J.M., *The Persian Empire* (New York: Schocken Books, 1983).

Cowley, A.E., *Aramaic Papyri of the Fifth Centry BC* (Oxford: Clarendon Press, 1923; repr., Osnabruck: Otto Zeller, 1967).

Culler, J., 'Defining Narrative Units', in R. Fowler (ed.), *Style and Structure in Literature* (Oxford: Basil Blackwell, 1975), pp. 123-42.

Culley, R.C., *Studies in the Structure of Hebrew Narrative* (Philadelphia: Fortresss Press, 1976).

Dancy, J.C., *The Shorter Books of the Apocrypha* (CBCNEB; Cambridge: Cambridge University Press, 1972).

Daube, D., 'The Last Chapter of Esther', *JQR* 37 (1947), pp. 139-47.

David, M., *Das Targum Scheni* (Berlin: Verlag M. Poppelauer, 1898).

Davies, W.D., *Jewish and Pauline Studies* (Philadelphia: Fortress Press, 1984).

Dinter, P., 'The Range of Meanings of Midrash' (SBL paper, 1977).

Dittenberger, G., *Sylloge Inscriptionum Graecarum*, I (Leipzig: Hirzelium, 3rd edn, 1915; repr., Hildesheim: Georg Olms, 1960).

Dommershausen, W., *Die Estherrolle: Stil und Zieleiner alttestamentlichen Schrift* (SBM, 6; Stuttgart: Verlag Katholisches Bibelwerk, 1968).

—*Ester* (Stuttgart: Echter Verlag, 1980).

Doty, W.G., 'The Concept of Genre in Literary Analysis', in L.C. McGaughy (ed.), *SBL 1972 Proceedings*, II, pp. 413-57.

Dover, K.J., *Greek Word Order* (Cambridge: Cambridge University Press, 1962).

Driver, G.R., *Aramaic Documents of the Fifth Century B.C.* (Oxford: Clarendon Press, 1957).

Dubarle, A.M., *Judith: Formes et sens des diverses traditions* (2 vols.; AnBib, 24; Rome: Pontifical Biblical Institute, 1966).

Egan, K., 'What Is a Plot?', *NLH* 9 (1978), pp. 455-73.

Emmet, C.W., '3 Maccabees', in *APOT*, I, pp. 155-73 .

Enslin, M.S. (ed.), *The Book of Judith: Greek Text with an English Translation, Commentary and Critical Notes* (Leiden: Brill, 1972).

Erman, A., *The Ancient Egyptions: A Sourcebook of their Writings* (New York: Harper & Row, 1966).

Evans, C.D., W.W. Hallo and J.B. White (eds.), *Scripture in Context: Essays on the Comparative Method* (Pittsburgh: Pickwick Press, 1980).

Fennely, J.M., 'The Persepolis Ritual', *BA* 43 (1980), pp. 135-62.

Fitzmyer, J.A., and D.J. Harrington, *A Manual of Palestinian Aramaic Texts* (Rome: Pontifical Biblical Institute, 1978).

Fitzmyer, J.A., *The Aramaic Inscriptions of Sefire* (BibOr, 19; Rome: Pontifical Biblical Institute, 1967).

—*The Dead Sea Scrolls: Major Publications and Tools for Study, with an Adden-dum* (SBLSBS, 8; Missoula, MT: Scholars Press, 1977).

Foakes-Jackson, F.J., *Josephus and the Jews* (Grand Rapids: Baker, 1977).

Fox, M.V., 'Frame-Narrative and Composition in the Book of Qohelet', *HUCA* 48 (1977), pp. 83-106.

—'The Structure of Esther', in A. Rofe and Y. Zakovitch (eds.), *Isaac Leo Seelig-mann Volume* (Jerusalem: E. Rubinstein, 1982), III, pp. 291-304 (non-Hebrew section).

Friedman, N., 'Point of View in Fiction: The Development of a Critical Concept'. *PMLA* 70 (1955), pp. 1160-84.

—*Form and Meaning in Fiction* (Athens, GA: University of Georgia Press, 1975).

Fuerst, W.J, *The Books of Ruth, Esther, Ecclesiastes, The Song of Songs, Lament-ations* (CBCNEB; Cambridge: Cambridge University Press, 1975).

Gerleman, G., *Esther* (BKAT, 21; Neukirchen–Vluyn: Neukirchener Verlag, 1973).

Gershevitch, I. (ed.), *The Cambridge History of Iran. II. The Median and Achaeme-nian Periods* (Cambridge: Cambridge University Press, 1985).

Gerstenberger, E.S., *Psalms, Part 1, with an Introduction to Cultic Poetry* (FOTL, 14; Grand Rapids: Eerdmans, 1988).

Ginzberg, L., 'Critical Notes', *JBL* 79 (1960), pp. 167-69.

Görg, M., *Gott-König-Reden in Israel und Ägypten* (Stuttgart: Verlag W. Kohl-hammer, 1975).

Gooding, D.W., 'An Appeal for a Stricter Terminology in the Textual Criticism of the Old Testament', *JSS* 21 (1976), pp. 15-25.

—*Relics of Ancient Exegesis: A Study of the Miscellanies in 3 Reigns 2* (SOTSMS, 4; Cambridge: Cambridge University Press, 1976).

Goodman, P., *The Purim Anthology* (Philadelphia: Jewish Publication Society of America, 1949).

Gordis, R., 'Studies in the Esther Narrative', *JBL* 95 (1976), pp. 43-58.

Goshen-Gottstein, M.H. (ed.), *The Aleppo Codex* (Jerusalem: Magnes Press, 1976).

Greenstein, E.L., 'A Jewish Reading of Esther', in J. Neusner, B.A. Levine and E.S. Frerichs (eds.), *Judaic Perspectives on Ancient Israel* (Philadelphia: Fortress Press, 1987), pp. 225-43.

Gregg, J.A.F., 'The Additions to Esther', in *APOT*, I, pp. 665-84.

Grossfeld, B., *The Targum to the Five Megilloth* (New York: Hermon Press, 1973).

Gunkel, H.E., *Jahve und Baal* (Religionsgeschichtlichen Volksbücher, 2nd series, 8; Tübingen: Mohr, 1906).

—'Eine hebräische Meistererzählung', *IMWKT* 14 (1920), pp. 73-90, 155-68.

Hallo, W.W., 'Biblical History in its Near Eastern Setting: The Contextual Approach', in C.D. Evans, W.W. Hallo and J.B. White (eds.), *Scripture in Context: Essays on the Comparative Method* (PTMS, 34; Pittsburgh: Pickwick Press, 1980), pp. 1-26.

—'The First Purim', *BA* 46 (1983), pp. 19-29.

Hallo, W.W., J.C. Moyer and L.G. Perdue (eds.), *Scripture in Context*, II (Winona Lake, IN: Eisenbrauns, 1983).

Hanhart, R. (ed.), *Esther* (Göttingen: Vandenhoeck & Ruprecht, 1966).

Hanson, P.D., *The Dawn of Apocalyptic: The Historical and Sociological Roots of Jewish Apocalyptic Eschatology* (Philadelphia: Fortress Press, 1983).

—'Jewish Apocalyptic Against its Near Eastern Environment', *RB* 78 (1971), pp. 31-58.

Harvey, D., 'Esther, Book of', in G.A. Buttrick (ed.), *The Interpreter's Dictionary of the Bible* (Nashville: Abingdon Press, 1962), II, pp. 149-51.

Haupt, P., 'Critical Notes on Esther', *AJSL* 24 (1907–1908), pp. 97-186; reprinted in Moore (ed.), *Studies in the Book of Esther*, pp. 1-90.

Hermann, A., *Die ägyptische Königsnovelle* (Glückstadt: Verlag J.J. Augustin, 1938).

Herrmann, S., 'Die Königsnovelle in Ägypten und in Israel', *Wissenschaftliche Zeitschrift der Karl-Marx Universität Leipzig* 3 (1953/4), pp. 51-62.

—'2 Samuel VII in the Light of The Egyptian Königsnovelle—Reconsidered', in S. Israelit-Groll (ed.), *Pharaonic Egypt* (Jerusalem: Magnes Press, 1985), pp. 119-28.

Holman, C.H., and W. Harmon, *A Handbook to Literature* (New York: Macmillan, 5th edn, 1986).

Hrushkovski, B., 'Hebrew Prosody', *EncJud*, XIII, pp. 1196-240.

Humphreys, W.L., 'Esther, Book of', in K. Crim (ed.), *The Interpreter's Dictionary of the Bible, Supplementary Volume* (Nashville: Abingdon Press, 1976), pp. 279-81.

—'A Lifestyle for Diaspora: A Study of the Tales of Esther and Daniel', *JBL* 92 (1973), pp. 211-23.

—'The Motif of the Wise Courtier in the Book of Proverbs', in J.G. Gammie, W.A. Brueggemann, W.L. Humphreys and J.M. Ward (eds.), *Israelite Wisdom: Theological and Literary Essays in Honor of Samuel Terrien* (Missoula, MT: Scholars Press, 1978), pp. 177-90.

—'Novella', in G.W. Coats (ed.), *Saga, Legend, Tale, Novella, Fable*, pp. 82-96.

—'The Story of Esther and Mordecai: An Early Jewish Novella', in G.W. Coats (ed.), *Saga, Legend, Tale, Novella, Fable*, pp. 97-113.

Ishida, T., *The Royal Dynasties in Ancient Israel: A Study on the Formation and Development of Royal-Dynastic Ideology* (BZAW, 142; Berlin: de Gruyter, 1977).

Jewett, R., 'The Form and Function of The Homiletic Benediction', *ATR* 51 (1969), pp. 18-34.

Jolles, A., *Einfache Formen* (Tübingen: Max Niemeyer Verlag, 1950).

Jones, B.W., 'The So-Called Appendix to the Book of Esther', *Sem* 6 (1978), pp. 36-43.

—'Two Misconceptions About the Book of Esther', *CBQ* 39 (1977), pp. 171-81.

Kaiser, O., *Einleitung in das Alte Testament* (Gütersloh: Gerd Mohn, 5th edn, 1984).

Kermode, F., *The Sense of an Ending: Studies in the Theory of Fiction* (Oxford: Oxford University Press, 1968).

Kim, C.-H., *The Familiar Letter of Recommendation* (Missoula, MT: Scholars Press, 1972).

—'The Papyrus Invitation', *JBL* 94 (1975), pp. 391-402.

Knierim, R., 'Cosmos and History in Israel's Theology', *HBT* 3 (1981), pp. 59-123.

—'Criticism of Literary Features, Form, Tradition and Redaction', in D. Knight and G. Tucker (eds.), *The Hebrew Bible and Its Modern Interpreters* (Chico, CA: Scholars Press, 1985), pp. 123-65 .

—'Old Testament Form Criticism Reconsidered', *Int* 27 (1973), pp. 435-68.

Kuhl, C., 'Die Wiederaufnahme—ein literarkritisches Prinzip?', *ZAW* 64 (1952), pp. 1-11.

Lagarde, P. de, *Librorum Veteris Testamenti Canonicorum Pars Prior Graece* (Göttingen: Arnold Hoyer, 1883).

—*Hagiographa Chaldaice* (Osnabruck: Otto Zeller, 1967).

Lawrence, A.W., *The History of Herodotus: A Life of Herodotus and the Behistun Inscription* (Bloomsbury: Nonesuch Press, 1935).

LeDeaut, R., 'Apropos a Definition of Midrash', *Int* 25 (1971), pp. 259-82.

Levenson, J.D., 'The Scroll of Esther in Ecumenical Perspective', *JES* 13 (1976), pp. 440-51.

Levine, E., *The Targum to the Five Megillot: Codex Vatican Urbinati I* (Jerusalem: Makor, 1977).

Lichtheim, M., *Ancient Egyptian Literature*. I. *The Old and Middle Kingdoms* (Berkeley: University of California Press, 1973).

—*Ancient Egyptian Literature*. II. *The New Kingdom* (Berkeley: University of California Press, 1976).

Loader, J.A., 'Esther as a Novel with Different Levels of Meaning', *ZAW* 90 (1978), pp. 417-21.

Long, B.O., *1 Kings, with an Introduction to Historical Literature* (FOTL, 9; Grand Rapids: Eerdmans, 1984).

—*Images of Man and God: Old Testament Short Stories in Literary Focus* (Bible and Literature, 1; Sheffield: Almond Press, 1981).

—*The Problem of Etiological Narrative in the Old Testament* (Berlin: Verlag Alfred Töpelmann, 1968).

Luckenbill, D.D., *Ancient Records of Assyria and Babylonia*. I. *Historical Records of Assyria* (Chicago: University of Chicago Press, 1926).

Mack, B.L., *Wisdom and the Hebrew Epic* (Chicago: University of Chicago Press, 1985).

Mahaffy, J.P., *The Empire of the Ptolemies* (London: Macmillan, 1895).

Mann, J., and I. Sonne, *The Bible as Read and Preached in the Old Synagogue*, II (Cincinnati: Hebrew Union College, 1966).

Mann, J., *The Bible as Read and Preached in the Old Synagogue*, I (New York: Ktav, 1971).

Marcus, R., 'Dositheus, Priest and Levite', *JBL* 64 (1945), pp. 269-71.

—'Jewish and Greek Elements in the Septuagint', in S. Lieberman *et al.* (eds.), *L. Ginzberg Jubilee Volume* (New York: Academy for Jewish Research, 1945), pp. 227-45 (English section).

Martin, R.A., *Syntactical Evidence of Semitic Sources in Greek Documents* (SBLSCS, 3; Missoula, MT: University of Montana, 1974).

—'Syntax Criticism of the LXX Additions to the Book of Esther', *JBL* 94 (1975), pp. 65-72.

Mason, R.A., 'The Purpose of the Editorial Framework of the Book of Haggai', *VT* 27 (1977), pp. 413-21.

McFague, S., *Speaking in Parables* (Philadelphia: Fortress Press, 1978).

—*Metaphorical Theology* (Philadelphia: Fortress Press, 1982).

McFall, L., *The Enigma of the Hebrew Verbal System* (HTI, 2; Sheffield: Almond Press, 1982).

Meinhold, A., 'Die Gattung der Josephgeschichte und des Estherbuches: Diaspora-novelle I & II', *ZAW* 87 (1975), pp. 306-24; 88 (1976), pp. 72-93.

Millard, A.R., 'The Persian Names in Esther and the Reliability of the Hebrew Text', *JBL* 96 (1977), pp. 481-88.

Miller, C.H., 'Esther's Levels of Meaning', *ZAW* 92 (1980), pp. 145-48.

Miller, M., 'Reflections on Scripture and Midrash' (Institute for Antiquity and Christianity paper, Claremont, 1978).

Milne, P.J., 'Folktales and Fairy Tales: An Evaluation of Two Proppian Analyses of Biblical Narratives', *JSOT* 34 (1986), pp. 35-60.

Moore, C.A., *Daniel, Esther and Jeremiah: The Additions* (AB, 44; Garden City, NY: Doubleday, 1977).

—'Eight Questions Most Frequently Asked about the Book of Esther', *BR* 3 (1987), pp. 18-31.

—*Esther* (AB, 7B; Garden City, NY: Doubleday, 1971).

—'Esther Revisited: An Examination of Esther Studies over the Past Decade', in A. Kort and S. Morschauser (eds.), *Biblical and Related Studies Presented to Samuel Iwry* (Winona Lake, IN: Eisenbrauns, 1985), pp. 163-72.

—'Esther Revisited Again: A Further Examination of Certain Esther Studies of the Past Ten Years', *HAR* 7 (1983), pp. 169-86.

—'The Greek Text of Esther' (PhD diss., Johns Hopkins University, 1965).

—'On the Origins of the LXX Additions to the Book of Esther', *JBL* 92 (1973), pp. 382-93.

—Review of G. Gerleman, *Esther* (BKAT, 21/1-2), *JBL* 94 (1975), pp. 293-96.

—*Studies in the Book of Esther* (New York: Ktav, 1982).

Motzo, B., *Saggi di Storia e Letteratura Giudeo-Ellenistica* (Florence: Felice Le Monnier, 1924).

Murphy, R.E., *Wisdom Literature: Job, Proverbs, Ruth, Canticles, Ecclesiastes, Esther* (FOTL, 13; Grand Rapids: Eerdmans, 1981).

Neusner, J., *What Is Midrash?* (Guides to Biblical Scholarship; Philadelphia: Fortress Press, 1987).

Niditch, S., and R. Doran, 'The Success Story of the Wise Courtier: A Formal Approach', *JBL* 96 (1977), pp. 179-93.

Niditch, S., *The Symbolic Vision in Biblical Tradition* (Chico, CA: Scholars Press, 1983).

Oates, J.F., R.S. Bagnall and W.H. Willis, *Checklist of Editions of Greek Papyri and Ostraca* (Chico, CA: Scholars Press, 2nd edn, 1978).

Oesterley, W.O.E., and T. Robinson, *An Introduction to the Books of the Old Testament* (London: SPCK, 1949).

Oikonomou, E.B., *The Book of Esther* (Athens, 2nd edn, 1971).

Olmstead, A.T., *History of the Persian Empire* (Chicago: University of Chicago Press, 1948).

Olrik, A., 'Epic Laws of Folk Narrative', in A. Dundes (ed.), *The Study of Folklore* (Englewood Cliffs, NJ: Prentice–Hall, 1965), pp. 129-41.

Ong, W.J., *Orality and Literacy: The Technologizing of the Word* (London: Methuen, 1982).

Oppenheim, L., *The Interpretation of Dreams in the Ancient Near East, with a Translation of an Assyrian Dream-Book* (The American Philosophical Society, New Series, 46/3; Philadelphia: American Philosophical Society, 1956).

Orlinsky, H.M., *Biblical Culture and Bible Translation* (New York: Ktav, 1974).

Otto, E., *Die Biographischen Inschriften der Ägyptischen Spätzeit* (Probleme der Ägyptologie, 2; Leiden: Brill, 1954).

Pardee, D., and S.D. Sperling (eds.), *Handbook of Ancient Letters* (SBLSBS, 15; Chico, CA: Scholars Press, 1982).

Paton, L.B., *The Book of Esther* (ICC; Edinburgh: T. & T. Clark, 1908).

Patte, D., *Early Jewish Hermeneutic in Palestine* (SBLDS, 22; Missoula, MT: Scholars Press, 1975).

Petersen, D.L., 'A Thrice-Told Tale: Genre, Theme, and Motif', *BR* 18 (1973), pp. 30-43.

Petersen, N.R., 'When Is the End not the End? Literary Reflections on the Ending of Mark's Narrative', *Int* 34 (1980), pp. 151-66.

Porten, G., 'Defining Midrash', in J. Neusner (ed.), *The Study of Ancient Judaism. I. Mishnah, Midrash, Siddur* (New York: Ktav, 1981), pp. 55-92.

Rahlfs, A. (ed.), *Septuaginta* (2 vols.; Stuttgart: Württembergische Bibelanstalt, 9th edn, 1971).

Rajak, T., *Josephus the Historian and his Society* (London: Gerald Duckworth, 1983).

Ramsey, G.G. (ed.), *The Histories of Tacitus* (London: John Murray, 1915).

Rawlinson, G., 'The Book of Esther', in F.C. Cook (ed.), *The Holy Bible with Commentary* (New York: Charles Scribner's Sons, 1886), III, pp. 473-74.

Re'emi, S.P., *Israel Among the Nations: A Commentary on the Books of Nahum, Obadiah and Esther* (Grand Rapids: Eerdmans, 1985).

Rogers, R.W., *Cuneiform Parallels to the Old Testament* (New York: Abingdon Press, 1926).

Rost, L., *Einleitung in die alttestamentlichen Apokryphen und Pseudepigraphen einschliesslich der grossen Qumran-Handschriften* (Heidelberg: Quelle & Meyer, 2nd edn, 1979).

Rotenberg, M., 'The "Midrash" and Biographic Rehabilitation', *JSSR* 25 (1986), pp. 41-55.

Rudolph, W., *Esra und Nehemia* (HAT, 20; Tübingen: Mohr, 1949).

—'Textkritisches zum Estherbuch', *VT* 4 (1954), pp. 89-90.

Sabatier, P. (ed.), *Bibliorum Sacrorum Latine Versiones Antiquae* (Rheims, 1739–43; repr., Paris, 1751).

Sanders, E.P., *Paul and Palestinian Judaism* (Philadelphia: Fortress Press, 1977).

Sanders, J.A., *Canon and Community: A Guide to Canonical Criticism* (Philadelphia: Fortress Press, 1984).

—'The Hermeneutics of Text Criticism and Translation' (SBL paper, Boston, 1987).

—*From Sacred Story to Sacred Text* (Philadelphia: Fortress Press, 1987).

—'Initial Statement' (SBL paper, Boston, 1987).

—'Isaiah in Luke', *Int* 36 (1982), pp. 144-55.

—'The Vitality of the Old Testament: Three Theses', *USQR* 21 (1966), pp. 161-84.

Saunders, E.W., 'Esther (Apocryphal)', in *IDB*, II, pp. 151-52.

Savage, M., 'Literary Criticism and Biblical Studies: A Rhetorical Analysis of the Joseph Narrative', in C.D. Evans, W.W. Hallo and J.B.White (eds.), *Scripture in Context: Essays on the Comparative Method* (Pittsburgh: Pickwick, 1980), pp. 79-100.

Schedl, C., 'Das Buch Esther und das Mysterium Israel', *Kairos* 5 (1963), pp. 3-18.

Scholes, R. (ed.), *Approaches to the Novel* (San Francisco: Chandlers, 1966).

Scholes, R., and R. Kellogg, *The Nature of Narrative* (Oxford: Oxford University Press, 1966).

Seeligmann, I.L., 'Hebräische Erzählung und biblische Geschichtsschreibung', *TZ* 18 (1962), pp. 305-25.

Seyberlich, R.-M., 'Esther in der Septuaginta und bei Flavius Josephus', in H.-J. Diesner, R. Günther, J. Mathwich and G. Schrot (eds.), *Neue Beiträge zur Geschichte der Alten Welt*. I. *Alter Orient und Griechenland* (Berlin: Akademie-Verlag, 1964), pp. 363-66.

Shea, W.H., 'Esther and History, I', *Ministry* (1962), pp. 26-27.

Sheppard, G.T., 'Canonization: Hearing the Voice of the Same God through Historically Dissimilar Traditions', *Int* 36 (1982), pp. 21-33.

—'The Epilogue to Qoheleth as Theological Commentary', *CBQ* 39 (1977), pp. 182-89.

—*Wisdom as a Hermeneutical Construct* (BZAW, 151; Berlin: de Gruyter, 1980).

Shipley, J.T. (ed.), *Dictionary of World Literature* (Paterson, NJ: Littlefield, Adam, 1962).

Skehan, P.W., 'Why Leave Out Judith?', *CBQ* 24 (1962), pp. 147-54.

Spina, F.A., 'Canonical Criticism: Childs Versus Sanders', in W. McCown and J.E. Massey (eds.), *Interpreting God's Word for Today* (Anderson, IN: Warner Press, 1982), pp. 165-94.

Stephens, F.J., 'The Ancient Significance of Sisith', *JBL* 50 (1931), pp. 59-70.

Stevick, P., *The Theory of the Novel* (New York: Free Press, 1967).

Stone, M.E., 'Armenian Canon Lists: I. The Council of Partaw (768 CE)', *HTR* 66 (1973), pp. 479-86.

Styles, F.A., 'Why Esther?' (STM diss., Union Theological Seminary, 1966).

Sweeney, M.A., *Isaiah 1–4 and the Post-Exilic Understanding of the Isaianic Tradition* (BZAW, 171; Berlin: de Gruyter, 1988).

Swete, H.B., *Introduction to the Old Testament in Greek* (Cambridge: Cambridge University Press, 1902).

—*The Old Testament in Greek* (3 vols.; Cambridge: Cambridge University Press, 1901).

Thackeray, H.S.J., *Josephus: The Man and the Historian* (New York: Ktav, 1967).

—*The Septuagint and Jewish Worship* (Oxford: Oxford University Press, 1921).

Tigay, J.H., 'On Some Aspects of Prayer in the Bible', *AJSRev* 1 (1976), pp. 363-69.

Torrey, C.C., *The Apocryphal Literature: A Brief Introduction* (New Haven: Yale University Press, 1948).

Tov, E., 'Did the Septuagint Translators Always Understand their Hebrew Text?', in A. Pietersma and C. Cox (eds.), *De Septuaginta* (Mississauga, Ontario: Benben, 1984), pp. 53-70.

—'The Impact of the LXX Translation of the Pentateuch on the Translation of the Other Books', in P Casetti, O. Keel and A. Schenker (eds.), *Melanges Dominique Barthelemy* (Fribourg: Editions Universitaires Fribourg Suisse, 1981), pp. 577-92.

—'The "Lucianic" Text of the Canonical and Apocryphal Sections of Esther: A Rewritten Biblical Book', *Textus* 10 (1982), pp. 1-25.

—*The Text Critical Use of the Septuagint in Biblical Research* (JBS, 3; Jerusalem: Simor, 1981).

—'The Textual History of the Song of Deborah in the A Text of the LXX', *VT* 28 (1978), pp. 224-32.

Ulrich, E.C., *The Qumran Text of Samuel and Josephus* (HSM, 19; Missoula, MT: Scholars Press, 1978).

Usher, J., *De Graeca Septuaginta interpretum versione syntagma: cum libri Estherae editione Origenica, et vetera Graeca altera, ex Arundelliana bibliotheca nunc primum in lucem producta* (London: J. Crook, 1655).

Van Seters, J., *Abraham in History and Tradition* (New Haven: Yale University Press, 1975).

Van Uchelen, N.A., 'A Chokmatic Theme in the Book of Esther: A Study in the Structure of the Story', in M. Boertien, A.G. van Daalen, F.J. Hoogewoud and E.H. Plantenga (eds.), *Verkenningen in Een Stroomgebied* (Amsterdam: University of Amsterdam, 1974), pp. 132-40.

Vermes, G., 'Bible and Midrash: Early Old Testament Exegesis', in P.R. Ackroyd and C.F. Evans (eds.), *The Cambridge History of the Bible*, I (Cambridge: Cambridge University Press, 1970), pp. 199-231.

Via, D.O., Jr., 'Religion and Story: Of Time and Reality', *JR* 56 (1976), pp. 392-99.

Walters, S.D., 'Hanna and Anna: The Greek and Hebrew Texts of 1 Samuel 1', *JBL* 107 (1988), pp. 385-412.

—'The Translator and the Text: Which Text Do We Translate?' (SBL paper, Boston, 1987).

Weil, G.E., *Massorah Gedolah iuxta Codicem Leningradensem B 19a*, I (Rome: Pontifical Biblical Institute, 1971).

Weis, R., *A Handbook of Old Testament Exegesis* (Claremont, CA: Claremont Graduate School, 2nd edn, 1983).

Welles, C.B., *Royal Correspondence in the Hellenistic Period: A Study in Greek Epigraphy* (New Haven: Yale University Press, 1934).

Westermann, C., *Forschung am Alten Testament* (Munich: Kaiser, 1964).

—*The Promises to the Fathers: Studies on the Patriarchal Narratives* (Philadelphia: Fortress Press, 1980).

White, J.L., *Light from Ancient Letters* (Foundations and Facets: New Testament; Philadelphia: Fortress Press, 1986).

—'Epistolary Formulas and Cliches in Greek Papyrus Letters', in P.J. Achtemeier (ed.), *SBL Seminar Papers*, II (Missoula, MT: University of Montana, 1978), pp. 289-319.

Whitehead, J.D. (comp.), 'Handbook of Early Aramaic Letters' (SBL paper, 1975).

Wikgren, A., *Hellenistic Greek Texts* (Chicago: University of Chicago Press, 1947).

Wilcoxen, J.A., 'Narrative Structure and Cult Legend: A Study of Joshua 1–6', in J.C. Rylaarsdam (ed.), *Transitions in Biblical Scholarship* (Chicago: University of Chicago Press, 1968), pp. 43-70.

Wittig, S., 'A Theory of Multiple Meanings', *Semeia* 9 (1977), pp. 75-103.

Würthwein, E., *The Text of the Old Testament* (Grand Rapids: Eerdmans, 1979).

Würthwein, E., K. Galling and O. Plöger, *Die Fünf Megilloth* (HAT, 18; Tübingen: Mohr, 1969).

Zaba, Z., *Les Maximes de Ptahhotep* (Prague: Editions de l'Academie Tchecoslovaque des Sciences, 1956).

Zuber, B., *Das Tempussystem des biblischen Hebräisch: Eine Untersuchung am Text* (BZAW, 164; Berlin: de Gruyter, 1986).

OTHER ANCIENT REFERENCES

INDEX OF AUTHORS